CW00924075

WISDOM
RISING

ALSO BY LAMA TSULTRIM ALLIONE

Women of Wisdom

Feeding Your Demons:
Ancient Wisdom for Resolving Inner Conflict

WISDOM RISING

*Journey into the Mandala
of the Empowered Feminine*

LAMA TSULTRIM ALLIONE

ENLIVEN BOOKS

—

ATRIA

New York   London   Toronto   Sydney   New Delhi

ENLIVEN™
ATRIA

Enliven Books
An Imprint of Simon & Schuster, Inc.
1230 Avenue of the Americas
New York, NY 10020

First Enliven Books hardcover edition May 2018

This publication contains the opinions and ideas of its author. It is intended to provide helpful and informative material on the subjects addressed in the publication. It is sold with the understanding that the author and publisher are not engaged in rendering medical, health, or any other kind of personal professional services in the book. The reader should consult his or her medical, health, or other competent professional before adopting any of the suggestions in this book or drawing inferences from it.

The author and publisher specifically disclaim all responsibility for any liability, loss, or risk, personal or otherwise, which is incurred as a consequence, directly or indirectly, of the use and application of any of the contents of this book.

ENLIVEN BOOKS / **ATRIA** BOOKS and colophon are trademarks of Simon & Schuster, Inc.

For information about special discounts for bulk purchases, please contact Simon & Schuster Special Sales at 1-866-506-1949 or business@simonandschuster.com.

The Simon & Schuster Speakers Bureau can bring authors to your live event. For more information or to book an event, contact the Simon & Schuster Speakers Bureau at 1-866-248-3049 or visit our website at www.simonspeakers.com.

Interior design by Suet Yee Chong

Manufactured in the United States of America

10 9 8 7 6 5 4 3 2

Library of Congress Cataloging-in-Publication Data
Names: Allione, Lama Tsultrim, author.
Title: Wisdom rising : journey into the mandala of the empowered feminine / Lama Tsultrim Allione.
Description: First Enliven Books hardcover edition. | New York : Enliven Books, 2018. | Includes bibliographical references.
Identifiers: LCCN 2017055791 (print) | LCCN 2018011737 (ebook) | ISBN 9781501115059 (eBook) | ISBN 9781501115035 (hardcover) | ISBN 9781501115042 (pbk.)
Subjects: LCSH: Mandala (Buddhism) | Tantric Buddhism. | Tantras. | Spiritual Life—Buddhism.
Classification: LCC BQ5125.M3 (ebook) | LCC BQ5125.M3 A45 2018 (print) | DDC 294.3/437—dc23
LC record available at https://lccn.loc.gov/2017055791

ISBN 978-1-5011-1503-5
ISBN 978-1-5011-1505-9 (ebook)

I dedicate this book to all my teachers,
starting with
my beloved parents,
Ruth Dewing Ewing and James Dennis Ewing,
who guided me from birth
and then set me free to find my own path,
which led me to the extraordinary
Tibetan lamas,
who introduced me to the dakinis
and the mandala principle.

Being a dynamic principle, the dakini is energy itself;
a positive contact with her brings about a sense of freshness
and magic. She becomes a guide and a consort who activates
intuitive understanding and profound awareness, but this
energy can turn suddenly and pull the rug out from under you,
if you become too attached and fixated. This can be painful.
When the energy becomes blocked and we feel pain caused by
our fixation, this is the wrathful dakini. Her anger pushes us
to let go of this clinging and enter her mysterious home.

—LAMA TSULTRIM ALLIONE, *WOMEN OF WISDOM*

Contents

PART 4
WISDOM RISING: PRACTICES

Author's Note

Dear Reader,

As the subtitle describes, this book is a *journey* into the mandala of the empowered feminine. Because my wish is that you will have the most successful journey possible, take a few minutes to read the Introduction. In it I share some key concepts and information that will be helpful knowledge as you travel through this book.

How you begin a journey can make a world of difference, and my hope is for you to get the most out of this experience.

Thank you for taking this journey,

Lama Tsultrim Allione

INTRODUCTION

If there is one thing we know from history, it is that patriarchal models of the spiritual have not been kind to women. Consciously or unconsciously, the constructs that begin with spirit as the highest and descend to matter as the lowest have traditionally relegated women and nature to the bottom of the scale.

—SHERRY RUTH ANDERSON AND PATRICIA HOPKINS,

THE FEMININE FACE OF GOD

The question that women most frequently ask me is how to integrate their spiritual lives with their everyday lives. The fact that we have to ask that question indicates the extent to which we are alienated from spirituality with a feminine presence, because a reference point in all religious traditions with a prominent feminine presence is an integration of spirit and matter, spirit and the body, which leads to spirituality being inseparable from daily life and to the divine as immanent rather than transcendent.

Merriam-Webster's Collegiate Dictionary defines *patriarchy* as "social organization marked by the supremacy of the father in the clan or family, the legal dependence of wives and children, and the reckoning of descent and inheritance in the male line; broadly: control by men of a disproportionately large share of power." A vast majority of our world is governed by patriarchy, and patriarchal structures govern all major religions. Invariably, patriarchal religions separate spirit or the godhead from the feminine, nature, and matter; in fact, the word *matter* is derived from the Latin *mater*, defined as "origin, source, mother."

Both nature and the earth have been associated with the feminine, as in Mother Earth, Mother Nature, and references such as a "virgin" forest, as a place not yet penetrated or disturbed by man. Historically, when the feminine was disempowered or denigrated within patriarchal religions, there has been a parallel disrespect for nature—a failure to see the earth as something sacred that should be respected—and, equally, a view that nature and women are obstacles on the exalted, disembodied spiritual quest for the ascendent divine. Within this context, the natural world was perceived as being controlled by demonic powers and women were seen as the gateway of sin and an obstacle to union with the divine.

As the philosopher Elizabeth Dodson Gray says, "[T]o get away from the ordinary, the natural, the unsacred—away from women, fleshly bodies, decaying nature, away from all that is rooted in mortality and dying. 'Up, up and away' is the cry of this religious consciousness as it seeks to ascend to the elevated realm of pure spirit and utter transcendence where nothing gets soiled, or rots, or dies."[1]

Thus, in these religions, we see story lines, beliefs, and rules that control women and their bodies. There are sexual taboos, with the frequent addition of celibacy and chastity for priests or monks, so male clerics avoid physical contact with women and may consider them a dangerous threat to their relationship with the divine. Women are also forbidden equal and empowered roles, especially leadership positions. Women are certainly present in all religions. However, these religions have idealized the masculine and largely disempowered women, who remain under the control of men. Likewise, nature is seen as something to dominate, to use, to abuse as desired, to subdue and to have dominion over.

It is not my purpose to do an extensive analysis of theology, nor to write extensively about ecofeminism in this book. There are several good books on these subjects.[2] My scope is to explain the situation in which we find ourselves, in terms of spirituality and religion and the denigration of the sacred feminine, and how this framework is fundamentally influencing our current world situation.

Seeing then the connection between patriarchal attitudes toward women and the earth, is it any coincidence that President Donald Trump's withdrawal from the Paris climate agreement, the slashing of national monuments by some two million acres, and the opening of coastal waters to drilling parallels his misogynistic, disrespectful, rape-culture behavior toward women? It is this kind of lethal disregard that has led to our current ecological crisis and rampant abuse of women. We can see the correspondence between the violence against women and the violence against the earth in the following statistics. First, here are some statistics about climate change reported in the *Guardian* in 2017:

* Global surface temperatures are already rising about twenty times faster than earth's fastest natural rate of climate change, which occurs during the transitions in and out of ice ages. And unless we take serious action to cut human carbon pollution, that rate will rise to perhaps fifty times faster than earth's fastest natural climate change.[3]
* The IPCC (Intergovernmental Panel of Climate Control) projects that by century's end, 40 percent or more of global species could go extinct.[4]
* Since 2008, each year an average of 21.5 million people have been forcibly displaced due to rapid-onset climate change–related hazards, according to the Intergovernmental Panel on Climate Change (IPCC). They expect the frequency and intensity of these events to increase. The organization says that climate change also acts as a "threat multiplier" in areas of ongoing conflict. "Climate change sows seeds

for conflict, but it also makes displacement much worse when it happens."[5] The slow onset of climate change, due to environmental degradation and its impact, is also causing a mass exodus of people who are seeking safety and viable livelihoods.

* In April 2017, it was revealed that two-thirds of Australia's Great Barrier Reef has been severely damaged by coral bleaching. This occurs when algae living within the coral tissue are expelled, usually as a result of water temperatures being too high.[6]

As I write these statistics now, a Category 4 hurricane with winds of 130 miles per hour and torrential rain recently inundated southeast Texas, causing catastrophic floods and destruction; several days later, one of the strongest hurricanes ever recorded worldwide, a Category 5 storm, caused devastation in the Caribbean and Florida, followed by another. There have been three destructive earthquakes in Mexico this week; one was the worst earthquake to affect the country in this century. There were twenty-seven forest fires burning simultaneously in the western United States in 2017. As of December 22, 2017, 9.8 million acres of land have burned in 2017—4.3 million acres more than in 2016. There now are earthquakes in places that have never known them, and winds at a velocity that we have never seen before; the global temperature is increasing every year, even faster than was predicted by the scientists who warned us of global warming.

For millennia our patriarchal religions and political systems have ignored the warnings of climate change, continuing to abuse and dishonor nature, bringing all of humanity to the brink of disaster. Naomi Klein says in *This Changes Everything*: "Climate change has never received the crisis treatment from our leaders, despite the fact that it carries the risk of destroying lives on a vastly greater scale than collapsed banks or collapsed buildings."[7]

Looking at the statistics on women's abuse, the World Health Organization (WHO) reports:[8]

* Violence against women, particularly intimate partner violence and sexual violence, is a major public health problem worldwide.
* Global estimates indicate that about one in three women worldwide (35 percent) have experienced either physical and/or sexual intimate partner violence or non-partner sexual violence in their lifetime.
* Most of this violence is intimate partner violence. Worldwide, almost one-third (30 percent) of women who have been in a relationship report that they have experienced some form of physical and/or sexual violence by their intimate partner in their lifetime.
* Globally, as many as 38 percent of murders of women are committed by a male intimate partner.

In recent years allegations of sexual harassment emerged against media personalities like Bill Cosby, Bill O'Reilly, and Roger Ailes. These revelations picked up steam when they were followed by women speaking out against the media mogul Harvey Weinstein. All of this began a flood of allegations about him and other high-profile men in the media. The extent of the problem was further revealed when the hashtag creator Tarana Burke and the actress Alyssa Milano took to Twitter and urged any women who had been sexually harassed or assaulted to write two words on Twitter at #MeToo. The social media reaction was explosive, creating a movement, not a moment. Short stories or a few words accompanying #MeToo made it clear that this issue is widespread and definitely not limited to the entertainment industry. *Time* magazine named the social movement #MeToo, "The Silence Breakers," as Person of the Year in December 2017, pointing it out as the fastest-

moving social change in decades. The movement #MeToo was followed by #TimeIsUp, and it seems like new revelations of sexual
abuse emerge in the media daily.

It is as though a closet was opened that had been stuffed to the
gills with suffering and anger, and it all began to spill out. Women
who had been silenced or felt powerless or afraid to say anything
began to speak out and tell their stories. On October 17, 2017, the
Washington Post reported: "A solid majority of Americans now say
that sexual harassment in the workplace is a 'serious problem' in the
United States. Nearly two-thirds of Americans say men who sexually
harass female co-workers usually get away with it. . . . One-third of
women say that they had experienced sexual advances from a male
co-worker or a man who had influence over their job, and one-third
of this group of women say their male co-workers' behavior consti-
tuted sexual abuse."[9]

The extent of violation of women and violence to the earth per-
petrated by men does not mean that all men are perpetrators. It is
important to acknowledge that there are many forward-thinking
males around the world who recognize these same problems and are
working in collaboration with women to change them. While I am
focusing on the need for the empowerment of women in this book,
and the devastating results of the lack of women's equality and their
abuse, ultimately we need a partnership society. In the end, we need
to develop the model of mutually empowered partnership with men
rather than domination of either gender, societies that promote *power
with* rather than *power over* each other.

The loss of feminine qualities is an urgent psychological and ecological issue in modern society. It is a painful loss in our emotional
lives and a disastrous loss for the safety of life on earth. In woman,
it affects her central identity; and in man, it affects his ability to feel
and value. The loss of the feminine in man causes him to feel moody
and lonely. In woman, it causes her to lose faith in herself. We are
slowly awakening to the crisis of the earth and the effect of the loss

of the sacred feminine, but few people understand that the causes of the crisis have spiritual values at their roots—values of the sacred as immanent, imbued in all of life, and all life as interdependent.

"The loss of feminine qualities is an urgent psychological and ecological issue in modern society. It is a painful loss in our emotional lives and a disastrous loss for the safety of life on earth."

What can we do to restore and heal the balance? In order to find balance, we need to equalize human rights and the economic situation of women and men; and we must move away from religions that model male dominance and into spiritual models of partnership and respect for our precious planet. It is by empowering the sacred feminine and by listening to the earth as she tries to communicate with us that we will ultimately heal.

When my husband Dave and I moved to the land in southwest Colorado that would become Tara Mandala in the spring of 1994, I felt we needed to make contact with the original inhabitants of the land and ask for their support and help. Synchronistically, earlier that spring at a gathering in Texas, before we moved to Colorado, I sat next to Grandmother Bertha Grove, a respected elder in the Ute tribe who would be our closest neighbors in Colorado. She was in her seventies at the time: a diminutive woman with gray hair, high cheekbones, and thick glasses. It was always hard to tell where she was looking. During the gathering, we talked a little and exchanged addresses.

When we arrived in Colorado, I immediately contacted her and then visited her small white house in Ignacio, about a half-hour drive through rolling hills, meadows, and majestic rock formations. Behind her house, I could see the round dome of a sweat lodge. She welcomed me at the door and I entered her living room, which was clean and open, with Native American blankets on two couches. We passed through the living room into the kitchen, which was painted white, with a white gas stove and refrigerator. There were herbs in neatly labeled jars on the shelves. She offered me water to drink and we sat at her kitchen table. I made my request right away.

"It is by empowering the sacred feminine and by listening to the earth as she tries to communicate with us that we will ultimately heal."

"Grandmother, we just moved onto seven hundred acres of land east of here with the intention of creating a retreat center. Will you come and help us build a sweat lodge and do ceremonies to ask for guidance on how to enter the land in a good way?"

She agreed. She and her husband Vincent came a few weeks later, driving a small brown camper in which they stayed. At the time, we had no buildings and everyone was camping. We built our lodge in a small, flat meadow near our outdoor kitchen, which was located under a large box elder tree. The sweat lodge, or stone people's lodge, is a dome-shaped structure made of red willow branches that are bent into a kind of upside-down basket; in front of the door, which faces east, is the fire where the stones are heated. As the lodge was constructed, it was covered with blankets and tarps until it was sealed.

Upon completion of our lodge, we entered the darkness to begin the ceremony; there the fire keeper delivered the red-hot rocks into a pit in the center. The entry flap was lowered, and the prayers began as the heat increased from the steam when water was poured onto the rocks. Vincent was the water pourer and led the songs in the Ute language, songs of purification, healing, and rejuvenation. During the ceremony, we were invited to make prayers out loud that could be for specific reasons or for specific people. I prayed for guidance from the spirits of the Tara Mandala land.

When we came out of the lodge and were sitting in the grass recovering from the intensity, Grandmother Bertha sat next to me and said, "What you want to do here is already here. . . . I can see it. I can see the temple and all the other buildings, they are hovering over the land. You just have to bring it out of the ethers onto the earth." This turned out to be much harder than it sounded, and over the years when I became discouraged, I would remember her words until we finally completed Tara Mandala.

I also studied herbal medicine with Grandmother Bertha. One day when we were out collecting herbs in the upper meadow, she said, "When you want to take any herb, first ask permission, and then pull out a hair from your head and leave it as an offering. There always has to be an exchange with Mother Earth. . . . That little pain you feel in your head when you pull out a hair, the earth also feels when you take a plant, and this is a good reminder."

Then she moved over to a small plant with yellow flowers and said, "See this yellow gumweed? It's for lungs and good for coughs—squeeze the yellow flower at the base and you can feel the stickiness." She picked one and held it up for me to feel. "That's healing medicine in the plant. But when you pick it, never take the strongest plant, because the strongest one will bring back a more powerful next generation. If you take the medium-size ones, they still have power, and you're not depleting the whole group."

In this small exchange, I learned so much about how to have right relationship to plants and to all our resources. Grandma Bertha always referred to the earth as Mother Earth, saying, "We should honor Her." Whether it's with our own mothers, the Mother Earth, or anyone or anything else, we are always in an interdependent relationship with everything.

We, both men and women, need to work toward a united and creative partnership between genders and Mother Earth—an integration of spirit and matter. We must learn to leave something when we take something. We must learn to leave the best and the strongest, so it is present for future generations, and not to take the best for ourselves. As Chief Crazy Horse said, "Treat the earth well: it was not given to you by your parents, it was loaned to you by your children. We do not inherit the earth from our ancestors, we borrow it from our children."

THE FIERCE FEMININE DAKINI

Before the female Buddha Tara came into being, she was a princess named Wisdom Moon, who was very devoted to the Buddha's teachings and had a deep meditation practice. She was close to reaching enlightenment, and had developed the intention to attain enlightenment for the benefit of all beings.

Her teacher, a monk, approached her, saying, "What a pity it is that you are in the body of a woman, because of course there is no possibility you can attain enlightenment in a woman's body, so you will have to come back as a man before you can become enlightened."

The princess answered back brilliantly, demonstrating her understanding of absolute truth, saying, "Here there is no man; there is no woman, no self, no person, and no consciousness. Labeling 'male' or 'female' is hollow. Oh, how worldly fools delude themselves."

She went on to make the following vow: "Those who wish to attain supreme enlightenment in a man's body are many, but those who wish to serve the aims of beings in a woman's body are few indeed; therefore may I, until this world is emptied out, work for the benefit of sentient beings in a woman's body."

From that time onward, the princess dedicated herself to realizing complete enlightenment; once she accomplished that goal, she came to be known as Tara, the Liberator. I like to say that Tara is the first feminist, and I joke that in her form as Green Tara, she is the spiritual leader of the Green Party: guardian of the forest, fast-acting, and compassionate. Tara is depicted with one foot in the world and one foot in meditation—a place where many of us find ourselves.

"Those who wish to attain supreme enlightenment in a man's body are many, but those who wish to serve the aims of beings in a woman's body are few indeed; therefore may I, until this world is emptied out, work for the benefit of sentient beings in a woman's body."

Like Tara, I firmly believe that at the absolute level we are beyond gender, and any notions of gender are limited and not our true nature. At a relative level, men and women are different, and that difference is precious. I am not in favor of women becoming more like men in order to be acceptable and successful. We don't need more men, or more women who act like men—although I certainly support women following the paths or professions they are drawn to, and certainly they should be treated equally. When I discuss the masculine and feminine in this book, it does not matter whether you identify as male, female, or nonbinary, or what your sexual orientation may be: the masculine and feminine energies are alive within each of us and in our world. That said, there are rules and laws and cultural messages worldwide that specifically affect and disempower women. My wish is that we don't lose touch with that unique magic of the primal feminine, the unique power we can bring to bear on the challenges of these times.

Feminine models of strength have been largely lost, repressed, or hidden from view, particularly images that are not acceptable or are not safe in a patriarchal society. Those images of the sibyl, the wise woman, the wild woman—women who are embodiments of specific powers of transformation, magical, spiritual, and psychic—become "wicked witches." Estimates of the number of women executed as witches from the fifteenth to the eighteenth centuries, primarily by being burned alive, as it was considered a more painful death, range between 60,000 and 100,000. Those were times of puritanism and sexual repression, and the women burned as witches were often independent or rebellious women who lived alone and practiced herbalism, or women who disobeyed their husbands or refused to have sex with them.

Images of the devoted, peaceful mother have always been safe. Such images have always been acceptable in all cultures, even patriarchal ones; but there's another level of reflection of the primal feminine experience that has not been present and that both men and women long for. And this is an experience that comes from the intuitive sacred feminine, a place where language may be paradoxical and prophetic, where the emphasis is on the symbolic meaning, not the words; a place where women sit in circles naked wearing mud, bones, and feathers, women who turn into divine goddesses and old hags— who turn into the fierce *dakinis*.

The Sanskrit word *dakini* in Tibetan becomes *khandro*, which means "sky dancer," literally "she who moves through space." The dakini is the most important manifestation of the feminine in Tibetan Buddhist teaching. She can appear as a human being or as a deity, often portrayed as fierce, surrounded by flames, naked, dancing, with fangs and a lolling tongue, and wearing bone ornaments. She holds a staff in the crook of her left elbow, representing her inner consort, her internal male partner. In her raised right hand, she holds a hooked knife, representing her relentless cutting away of dualistic fixation. She is compassionate and, at the same time, relentlessly tears away the ego. She holds a skull cup in her left hand at heart level, representing impermanence and the transformation of desire. She is an intense and fearsome image to behold.

"The Sanskrit word dakini *in Tibetan becomes* khandro, *which means 'sky dancer,' literally 'she who moves through space.' The dakini is the most important manifestation of the feminine in Tibetan Buddhist teaching."*

The dakini is a messenger of spaciousness and a force of truth, presiding over the funeral of self-deception. Wherever we cling, she cuts; whatever we think we can hide, even from ourselves, she reveals. The dakini traditionally appears during transitions: moments between worlds, between life and death, in visions between sleep and waking, in cemeteries and charnel grounds.

Observing my two daughters' four labors, which produced four marvelous grandchildren, two for each daughter, and remembering my own three labors, I think of the dakini in the time called "transition" during childbirth, when the cervix must open the last few centimeters for the baby's descent into the birth canal. Transition is generally the most painful and most challenging period during labor, and during this time the woman must touch her wildness, take charge, and enter her deepest primal power. She often becomes fierce and must access the powerful dakini within, in order to move through transition, the tunnel of darkness, and bring her baby into the light. No one else can do it for her.

I remember during my first labor, witnessing the potency of the dakini unleashed and in her full power. It was only months after coming back from India with my husband, and less than a year since I'd disrobed from being a Buddhist nun. Living on Vashon Island in Puget Sound off the coast of Seattle, I chose to have a natural birth at home. We were living in a small berry-picker's cottage, which had housed migrant workers harvesting currants on the island. Our heat and cooking came from a small woodstove.

When the day came, I went into labor in the morning, and right away it was intense. By evening, I had been in hard labor for eight hours when the doctor arrived from Seattle. My labor wasn't progressing, and he thought the baby's head was in the wrong position. Suddenly I thought: *I have to get this baby out! It's up to me, no one else can do this. What do I need to do?*

I tuned in to my body, got off the bed and onto the floor on my hands and knees, and told the doctor to leave me. I began weaving and shaking back and forth, up and down. My husband tried to approach to tell me to be calm and breathe quietly, but I told everyone to get out of the way. I wasn't nice or calm; I was fierce and clear. I was like a primal animal: sweating, shaking, and moaning, swaying back and forth wildly.

The labor began to move forward. I got wilder as I entered transition, my body shaking while still on all fours. And before long, I held my newborn daughter in my arms. Had I done what I was told, I would not have turned her position; it was all the wild movement on all fours that helped to shift her. Had I not taken it on, becoming fierce and clear and guiding myself from within, I might have had to be airlifted to a hospital in Seattle for a cesarean section.

TUNING IN TO THE POWER
OF A "NASTY WOMAN"

Fierce compassion is not limited to women; in fact, the Dalai Lama is a good example of it.

I was once at a lunch with the Dalai Lama and five other Western Buddhist teachers at Spirit Rock Meditation Center in Marin County, California. We were sitting in a charming room with white carpets and many windows. The food was a delightful, fragrant, vegetarian Indian meal. There were lovely flower arrangements on the table and gentle, graceful students serving the meal. We were discussing sexual misconduct among Western Buddhist teachers. A woman Buddhist from California brought up someone who was using his students for his own sexual needs.

One woman said, "We are working with him with compassion, trying to get him to understand his motives for exploiting female students and to help him change his actions."

The Dalai Lama slammed his fist on the table, saying loudly, "Compassion is fine, but it has to stop! And those doing it should be exposed!"

All the serving plates on the table jumped, the water glasses tipped precariously, and I almost choked on the bite of saffron rice in my mouth. Suddenly I saw him as a fierce manifestation of compassion and realized that this clarity did not mean that the Dalai Lama had moved away from compassion. Rather, he was bringing compassion and manifesting it as decisive fierceness. His magnetism was glowing like a fire. I will always remember that day, because it was such a good teaching on compassion and precision. Compassion is not a wishy-washy "anything goes" approach. Compassion can say a fierce *no!* Compassion is not being stupid and indulging someone and what they want. Trungpa Rinpoche called that "idiot compassion,"[10] like giving a drug addict drugs.

The way I am using the word *fierce* in this book is in the sense of how a mother animal defends her young—a laser beam of fierceness, of pure energy that when harnessed and directed is powerful and unstoppable. It is fierceness without hatred or aggression. Sometimes a wrathful manifestation is more effective than a peaceful approach. It is by understanding the dakini's fierceness as a productive

and creative source of raw energy that we see the dakinis in action—
wielding the power to subdue, protect, and transform.

We must find the sources to access this fierce dakini power and
bring it to bear on what matters to us in our lives, be it emotional,
spiritual, intellectual, or political. Meeting our strong feminine energy, we will develop as women, and not as women trying to be like
men or asexual beings. We are different, and until that difference
is known, owned, and maximized, our true feminine potency and
capacity to bring this world into balance will not be realized. The
powerful, fierce feminine is very much a part of the psyche, but it is
repressed; and when it is not acknowledged because it is threatening,
it can become subversive and vengeful. But when it is acknowledged
and honored, it's an incredible source of power.

*"We are different, and until that difference
is known, owned, and maximized, our true
feminine potency and capacity to bring this
world into balance will not be realized."*

Until recently, being a feminist carried something of a stigma. I
encountered this myself and was criticized by my Buddhist teacher
for being "too feminist," when actually I was only trying to bring
balance to Buddhism and talk about the empowered feminine, sexual
abuse, and patriarchal aspects of Buddhism. Later, he changed his
view and was very supportive, but it was a challenging time when
feminist was a dirty word. Some women have been quick to distance
themselves from that title, afraid of being labeled "an angry feminist"
and being unattractive to men. But if you ask those same women who

say they are not feminists if they believe in equal pay for equal work, reproductive freedom, and protection from male violence? Most will say, "Yes, of course." So actually, they are feminists but afraid of being seen as anti-male.

Now this is changing. Feminism is coming back as a label to be proud of, for both men and women. Both Barack Obama and Justin Trudeau call themselves feminists. Trudeau said he was "proud" to stand as an advocate for "He for She,"[11] a UN movement of men standing up for women. Feminism's comeback is especially true as the movement is becoming more inclusive and intersectional, taking into account the unique experiences of women of color, transgender women, and low-income women.

Remember the "such a nasty woman" insult Donald Trump used to denigrate Hillary Clinton during the 2016 presidential elections? It didn't work. Women took it and turned it into a slogan of empowerment: *Never underestimate the power of a nasty woman*. We transformed this intended offense into something women wanted to own. We stopped asking for permission to be forceful, outspoken, and decisive. We chose to bond together within our power, standing up to obnoxious patriarchy.

Trump's insult became a movement. *Never underestimate the power of a nasty woman* went viral; women tapped the fierce part of themselves and bonded in the Women's March on January 21, 2017, the day after Trump's inauguration. Women together with many supportive people of other gender identifications marched to protect women's rights, human rights, and the rights of the earth. They had a sense of humor, wearing pink knitted hats with cat ears carrying the slogan PUSSY POWER. The marchers were nonviolent and joyful, but not to be deterred; never before had there been such a huge global protest.

Worldwide participation in the Women's March of 2017 has been estimated at five million.[12] At least 673 marches were reported worldwide, on all seven continents.[13] In Washington, DC, the protests were the largest demonstrations since the anti–Vietnam War protests in the 1960s and 1970s. It was the busiest day on record in the city's Metro. There were no arrests; all remained peaceful and nonaggressive, with the marchers carrying an array of provocative placards reading NASTY WOMEN RULE, SAVE THE PLANET, IF YOU TAKE AWAY MY BIRTH CONTROL I'LL JUST MAKE MORE FEMINISTS, FIGHT BACK, BITCHES GET STUFF DONE, MISOGYNY KILLS, WE ARE THE GRANDDAUGHTERS OF THE WITCHES YOU DIDN'T BURN. A ninety-year-old woman held a sign saying NINETY, NASTY, AND NOT GIVING UP.

Men of a variety of races and cultural backgrounds walked in solidarity with women during the march and held signs saying I ALSO FEEL STRONGLY ABOUT THIS, MEN OF QUALITY DO NOT FEAR EQUALITY, REAL MEN ARE FEMINISTS, THIS FEMINIST HAS BALLS, TEACH BOYS THEY ARE NOT ENTITLED TO WOMEN'S BODIES, REAL MEN GET CONSENT. There was a young man with a placard saying ALL MEN CAN STOP OBJECTIFYING WOMEN. A middle-aged man carried a little boy, the two of them holding signs that read I AM COMMITTED TO RAISING MY SON TO RESIST MISOGYNY AND EMBRACE FEMINISM. There was a man with gray hair and his college-age son. The father's sign said ALL MEN SHOULD BE FEMINISTS; the younger man held one declaring WOMEN'S RIGHTS ARE HUMAN RIGHTS. A young, grinning, multiracial couple, both wearing pink pussy power hats with little ears, held a sign together that said PATRIARCHY IS FOR DICKS. Another young man carried one saying END TOXIC MASCULINITY, END RAPE CULTURE.

There was tremendous energy and cohesion expressed in the Women's March, but afterward I noticed that the energy seemed to dissipate somewhat, although the conversation is still very much alive. I have also talked to some women who were feeling discouraged, unsure, and frustrated. Perhaps we don't know what next steps could be effective? What I saw was a need for an inner resource of empowerment and inspiration with which to build from the momentum the march generated.

We need to have a method to build on that energy, an inner practice to sustain and take it beyond protest and into full embodiment. We need to tap into the potent, untamed, yet wise energy of the dakinis. We will learn to do this by journeying in the Mandala of the Five Dakinis in this book, taking that sacred feminine—which has been relegated to the unconscious, to the negative, to the "shadow," the "hag," the "witch," the "bitch," and, yes, the "nasty woman"—and bringing her energy forward and applying her positive potential in our lives.

In April 2016, I taught the Mandala of the Five Dakinis during a Wisdom Rising retreat at a yoga center in western Massachusetts. I returned the following year after the election of President Trump to teach the same workshop for 150 women. Toward the end of the retreat, a blond woman of about forty raised her hand and asked to speak.

She said, "I have to say something. This practice changed my life. I did the Mandala of the Five Dakinis every day after last year's retreat. For years I have been complaining about the political situation. Now I feel so empowered that I've taken charge of my life, and I'm running for Congress!" The women in the room roared with encouragement, and those near her slapped her on the back. I loved that her inner strength was translating into action.

Another woman said she wanted to speak too: "I am an activist, but I had been feeling so depleted and burnt-out, hopeless, and drained by the current political climate. I was here last year, and I practiced the Mandala of the Five Dakinis all year and it has been amazing. It restores my inner strength and renews my energy no matter what happens outside."

A third woman with short-cropped brown hair raised her hand and said, "In my life I have experienced very little happiness. I was severely abused as a child and have dealt with depression, addictions, and suicidal ideation my whole life. I have hated being a woman. But here in this retreat for the first time, I could honestly say for the first time ever, I have felt joy in my female body and empowered to be part of the change."

As for these women, the dakinis have a gift to present to you too. They offer a feminine model that is fierce, wise, spiritual, and embodied. They give us the energy of the undomesticated feminine; they are not meek or submissive. They are luminous, subtle spiritual energy, the gatekeepers and the guardians of the unconditioned wisdom and sacred earth. By practicing and entering the Mandala of the Five Dakinis, we stimulate this archetype within us and trigger the transformative energy of the feminine.

We will see that the female body, manifesting as the dakini, is a potential vehicle for enlightenment. The Mandala of the Five Dakinis has deep, profound roots that are timeless and inclusive. It is a practice that can help you meet the challenges of everyday life—when you feel scattered and pulled in many directions at once, when you need centering, when you have a decision to make, when you feel hopeless or stuck; by entering the mandala and meeting the dakinis within, you will access deep clarity and power.

ABOUT THE BOOK

I have had the wonderful good fortune to study with some of the great lamas of Tibet who escaped from the Chinese invasion to India and Nepal. Before the invasion, the country of Tibet, surrounded on all sides by high mountains, acted as a kind of laboratory for spiritual development in the center of Asia, and was for many years protected from outside influences. Within this special environment, a depth of wisdom and meditation developed, as well as an enlightened process of fostering compassion within the society.

Ever since meeting the Tibetan tradition in 1967, I have been committed to bridging East and West. I felt as though I had stumbled across a chest of jewels, which I wanted to share with others in a way that they could experience the beauty and preciousness of these gems. The jewels I most wish to share in this book include the core mandala and dakini principles, introducing the five buddha families and wisdom dakinis, and demonstrating how all that is synthesized in the practice of the Mandala of the Five Dakinis.

I am well aware that in a book like this I cannot possibly transmit all the power and depth of the Tibetan tradition and the mandala as it was originally transmitted to me. And yet in these unprecedented, challenging times, we must find ways to make the profound wisdom that emerged from the isolated land of Tibet accessible. So whether you are Buddhist or not, woman or man, my hope is to share these principles and make them effective and applicable in your daily life, and so help to heal the rifts in our world. If we can change our spiritual paradigm, our society and culture will change.

This book offers the personal work that will help women (and anyone else interested) respond with greater wisdom and effectiveness to the distress, challenges, and chaos of our global reality. It is a guide for being better able to engage the world with our full, potent strength that is free of aggression, to tap into genuine unconditioned feminine power that is grounded in wholeness, and to invite a fresh partnership with the authentic masculine. The journey into the mandala gives birth to a renewed expression of the feminine that draws on ancient wisdom, but is tailored for this time and place. I have mainly used the feminine pronoun and examples involving women in this book for this reason. However, though not exclusively, there are some examples of men as well, and men have a great deal to gain by reading this book and doing the practices in it.

In Part 1, I open with stories of my journey to the East. I will tell you about how I journeyed to Kathmandu overland from Europe, became ordained as the first North American Buddhist nun in the Tibetan tradition, and first encountered the mandala and dakini. Chapters 2 and 3 then go into more depth and detail about the mandala—its purpose, meaning, and use as a powerful tool of transformation. It's important to have an understanding of the mandala principle as a meditation tool, the foundational structure from which we will work with the five buddha families and wisdom dakinis.

In Part 2, I continue the thread of my story: my decision to disrobe as a nun and become a mother, and how I came face-to-face with a dakini, the great female Tibetan master from the eleventh century, Machig Labdrön. In Chapters 5 and 6, we take a closer look at the dakini principle and the reawakening of the sacred feminine. We will explore how we can achieve spiritual integration and wisdom through embodiment of the empowered feminine. The spiritual path then becomes meditation in action, enlightenment through how we live our everyday lives by harnessing the dakini within.

Part 3 focuses on the five buddha families and the wisdom dakinis—buddha, vajra, ratna, padma, and karma—describing their unique characteristics and personalities. You will discover to which family you belong, and see how the five families apply to so many areas of your life. Most important, we will look at each family's encumbered emotion and its wisdom counterpart. Lastly, in Part 4, I will guide you through step-by-step meditations of the Mandala of the Five Dakinis and Journey with the Dakini, along with other practices to integrate and embody the dakinis in your everyday life, such as how to create a dakini altar, make a mandala drawing, create a mandala in nature, or work with a mandala in sandplay. I also suggest how the mandala can be used for life passages and ceremonies, such as birthdays, marriages, and funerals.

PART 1

Meeting
the Mandala

1

MY JOURNEY TO WHOLENESS

*God is an infinite sphere, the center of which is everywhere and the
circumference nowhere.*

—LIBER XXIV PHILOSOPHORUM

When I was a teenager, I liked to wander around Harvard
Square, where students and professors rushed across the
bustling traffic on their way to classes. At that time it was a neighborhood center with bookstores, a grocery store, a hardware store, a deli
with huge hot pastrami sandwiches on sourdough rolls, a restaurant
to which my grandfather walked every day to eat fresh fish, and an
ice cream parlor that had the best peppermint ice cream with little red
peppermint candies melting in it.

My maternal grandfather had long since retired from teaching
philosophy and business at Harvard, but he continued to live with
my grandmother, a fellow philosopher and also a former professor, in
a small white house in Cambridge at 8 Willard Street. I visited them
on weekends from my boarding school on the outskirts of Boston,
a great getaway from dorm life to their eccentric little house with
uneven colonial wide-board wood floors, and the Greek vases he col-

lected perched precariously on a rickety table in the small, dark living room.

During one of my visits, when I was a senior in high school, I was wandering in the book section of the Harvard Coop when I came upon a big hardcover volume called *Man and His Symbols* edited by Dr. Carl G. Jung. It had numerous illustrations and photographs, and it was unlike any book I had ever seen. A Tibetan mandala graced the cover, and there were many more mandala images within the book. I was so magnetized by the mandalas that I immediately bought it.

I took it back to my grandparents' house, went up to my small guest bedroom, and leaned back on the pillows on the old horsehair mattress, opening the book to find Tibetan mandalas and all the other representations of mandalas from various cultures around the world. Looking at a Tibetan mandala, I held my gaze steady, concentrating on the mandala's center. A luminous dimension opened up. I felt a deep stillness within me. No piece of art had ever triggered such a powerful experience. I had an eerie feeling of familiarity combined with fascination about what had happened to me and what these paintings were. Throughout the next years, I carried the book everywhere with me and contemplated the mandalas.

In the book, Dr. Jung introduced the mandala in many forms, not only traditional Tibetan, but also the mandalas in architecture, city planning, Christian art, stained-glass windows, tribal art, and indigenous ceremonies. But I was particularly drawn to the Tibetan mandalas: their depth and intricate symmetry resonated and called to me. I sensed they were not mere paintings. They emanated a mystical energy that made me wonder what truths lay within them. Their power was derived not from cognitively knowing their meaning, as I do now, but from direct contemplation of the mandalas themselves. It was this first encounter with Tibetan mandalas that became the catalyst for my budding spiritual search.

I was inwardly drawn to Buddhist culture, particularly toward Tibet, but had few resources available in New England. It was a time before the Internet, Google, Facebook, and YouTube; communication took place only via telephone and snail mail. To find something out, you had to read a book, speak to someone knowledgeable, or go to the source yourself. I read about Tibet in my parents' encyclopedia, but other than that couldn't find any books on the subject. Around this time my maternal grandmother gave me *Zen Telegrams* by Paul Reps, a book of Zen haiku and calligraphy. The short poems combined with brushstroke paintings inspired what I would now call my first meditation experience, an insight into an "awareness of awareness," or what I called at the time "consciousness of being conscious."

I was at our summerhouse on a lake in New Hampshire. I had been reading Reps's book in my upstairs bedroom, a rustic space with unfinished pine board walls and open beams. I decided to crawl out the window in my sister's bedroom and sit on the porch roof. In front of the house were four towering white pine trees. A soft breeze was blowing from the lake as I sat in silence. Then I heard pine needles falling on the roof, a barely perceptible sound. At that moment, I was aware of my consciousness, and simultaneously I experienced the gentle breeze and falling pine needles on the roof. I did not fully understand what I experienced; I had no context, no spiritual teacher, and it was nothing my friends would have understood, yet it was something I would never forget, a profound sense of awareness and peace.

These early experiences and others inspired me to become a spiritual seeker, and this longing came to dominate my life. After I graduated from high school, I went west to the University of Colorado, but I found nothing in school that provided me with the inner wisdom I was seeking. Then one day in the autumn of my sophomore year, while meandering through the stacks in the university library, I spotted a book that drew my attention. It was one of the first books published in English about yoga, *The Hidden Teaching Beyond Yoga* by Paul Brunton. I quickly checked it out and brought it back to my dorm room.

After reading it for a while, I grew sleepy and then put the book down and turned onto my stomach to take a nap. As I lay there, I had the sensation that my body was being lifted off the bed, and I was floating up above it at the level of the ceiling. My experience was that this was actually happening. It was so real, and it terrified me to be floating, I forced myself to open my eyes, finding myself back on the bed. This out-of-body experience intensified my spiritual search, and I talked about it with my best friend, Vicki Hitchcock, whose father was at the time the American consul general of Kolkata. Upon meeting during our freshman year, we'd recognized each other as kindred souls, and constantly shared our search and interests in "the mystic East" as we called it. In fact, we have remained friends throughout our lives, and have both ended up following the Tibetan path since we were nineteen.

Our search heated up in the summer of 1967, the Summer of Love. We both dropped out of the University of Colorado and traveled together to India and Nepal. We flew to Hong Kong, where we found an esoteric bookshop and bought every book they had about Tibet. We then took turns reading them as we sailed on an Italian ship to Bombay and then flew to Kolkata, where Vicki's parents were living in a large, old colonial house next to the US consulate. After working for some time in Mother Teresa's home for unwed mothers and abandoned babies, Vicki and I made our way to Nepal.

Lama Tsultrim before leaving India, 1967.

SWAYAMBHU

One morning, while visiting a Nepalese family in the center of Kathmandu, we were invited up to the rooftop of their house to see the view. The valley was covered in low-lying fog, but in the distance were the crystalline peaks of the Himalayas; much closer, about a mile away, like an ephemeral palace on an island floating in a lake, was a glowing white dome topped with a sparkling golden spire. It was one of the most mystical sights I had ever seen, and when I inquired about it, I was told it was called Swayambhu, also known as the Monkey Temple because a troop of wild monkeys lived on the hill, and it was one of the most sacred places in the city.

A few days later, we had the opportunity to join a predawn procession that was going up to this hill. Walking through the darkened streets of Kathmandu was like being whisked back to medieval times. There were pigs, dogs, and cows everywhere, scavenging for the garbage people threw into the streets—a medieval garbage collection service!

We walked through the valley, crossing the river on an old bridge that led to a narrow dirt path between rice paddies, and then gradually made our way up the hill. The path became steeper and steeper, and finally became a staircase going straight up. The morning light began to illuminate our surroundings just as we emerged at the top of the stairs.

Before me stood the white dome, its round golden spire soaring about three stories tall. On the spire's square base were mysterious painted Buddha eyes looking out in the four directions—north, east, west, and south. I later learned that this was an ancient *stupa* (Buddhist shrine) repre-

Stairs leading up to
Swayambhu stupa,
Kathmandu, Nepal, 1967.

senting the mandala, which is the basic structure of the cosmos in the Tantric Buddhist tradition—the circular architecture of the centered enlightened experience, a cosmological representation of the universe. Swayambhu means "self-manifested," because it was said to have been an island in the middle of the lake that was once Kathmandu Valley, and on that island there was a self-existing flame over which the stupa was built.

Swayambhu stupa in Kathmandu Valley, Nepal.

For a nineteen-year-old American girl to encounter this incredible structure, one of the most holy sites in Nepal, in the golden light of dawn was pure magic. Gradually I could see more and more as the sun rose. I began to circumambulate the stupa clockwise, following the Nepalese pilgrims. I saw that at the base in the four directions were five niches with Buddha statues, one in each direction—except for the east, where there are two, one of which represents the center—and they each had different hand gestures, or *mudras*. As I walked around, smelling the pungent Nepalese rope incense and hearing the huge bells ring, I experienced an incredible sensation of familiarity and remembering.

As I sat there that morning, on top of Swayambhu looking out over the valley, I felt that my life had been altered—and as it turned out, it had been. Here is something I wrote about my first encounter with the Swayambhu stupa in 1967. It was the first stupa I had ever seen, and of course, I had no idea at that time that I would return to live there and became a nun.

> We were breathless and sweating as we stumbled up the last steep steps and practically fell upon the biggest *vajra* (thunderbolt scepter) that I have ever seen. Behind this vajra was the vast, round, white dome of the stupa, like a full solid skirt, at the top of which were two giant Buddha eyes wisely looking out over the peaceful valley which was just beginning to come alive.[14]

It became a place I went every morning, sitting in a corner of the monastery at the top of the hill next to the stupa. After a few days, a little carpet appeared in my corner; after a few more days, I was served tea when the monks had their tea during their morning meditation practice. It became my place, my monastery—the outer mandala that I would refer to inwardly for the rest of my life.

LEFT: Lama Tsultrim in Dharamsala for the first time, in 1967, looking a little dusty. She hadn't bathed for three weeks, it was too cold.
RIGHT: Lama Tsultrim with Tibetan woman who dressed her up in Tibetan clothes, Dharamsala, India, 1967.

TRUNGPA RINPOCHE AND SAMYE LING

I returned home and went back to college in Vermont, because my parents wanted me to complete college. But all I could think about was going back to the Tibetans in India and Nepal. So after another year in college, I got enough money together for a cheap ticket to Europe. I went first to Amsterdam, where I heard about a Tibetan monastery in Dumfriesshire, Scotland, called Samye Ling, the first Tibetan monastery in the West. I left Holland the next day, took the ferry to England, and hitchhiked to Scotland straight from the docks.

The very day I arrived, as I was coming down the main staircase of the old Scottish country house that was the seat of Samye Ling (before they built their big monastery), I saw a young Tibetan man in a purple Western-style shirt struggling up the stairs accompanied by young Westerners, several men and a large woman, who were treating him with great deference. I stepped aside, but not before our eyes met and he smiled at me and said, "Well, hello!" in a high-pitched, slightly slurred voice.

It turned out this was the preeminent and unconventional Buddhist teacher, the wild, young, Oxford-educated Chögyam Trungpa Rinpoche, and that day he was returning from a long stay in the hospital recovering from a serious car accident. The accident had occurred when he was driving drunk with his girlfriend. Coming to a fork in the road, he couldn't decide whether to go home with her or go back to the monastery, so instead they barreled straight into a joke shop. The accident left him hospitalized for more than a year, and he remained partially paralyzed on his left side; it also led him to formally decide to disrobe. He had not been keeping his monastic vows for some time, so he decided to let this façade go and no longer depend upon the monk's guise to make his way in the Western world.

I ended up spending six months at Samye Ling. I met Trungpa

Rinpoche several times during my stay and read what were then his only books: his biography, *Born in Tibet*, and the recently released *Meditation in Action*.

The first time I heard the word *dakini* was at Samye Ling. Trungpa Rinpoche had various girlfriends, and my friend Ted, a Scottish rascal with a mop of golden curls, who was Rinpoche's driver and used his role as a perch for his own seductions, said, laughing, "He's looking for his dakini."

I asked, "What is a dakini?"

He looked at me directly with his bright blue eyes and said, "A dakini can be the consort of a high lama, but she also can be a deity, a wild and wrathful manifestation of wisdom, fierce but without aggression. According to Rinpoche, a dakini can simultaneously pull the rug out from under you and encourage you."

Dakinis sounded both fascinating and a little scary to me. But I would always remember that first dakini introduction, as they became a central part of my life. In the meantime, Trungpa Rinpoche gave me a meditation practice text called *The Sadhana of the Embodiment of All the Siddhas* that he had composed during a retreat at an ancient cave cliffside retreat, Tiger's Nest (Tagsang) in Bhutan. I began to practice it daily, chanting it out loud with my friends Craig and Richard at Samye Ling. Every night we sat in the ornate shrine room and read through it, then meditated in silence at the end. Through the sadhana I was introduced to the idea of the mandala and the five buddha families, and even without having in-depth teachings I could feel its power.

At the beginning of the meditation, there is a passage that awakened in me an awareness that the mandala is not a mere painting on a wall or something in a liturgy, but that the whole world is the mandala:

In the boundless space of suchness,
In the play of the great light,

All the miracles of sight, sound, and mind,
Are the five wisdoms and the five buddhas,
This is the mandala, which is never arranged but is
always complete.[15]

I began to see that the mandala is a way of seeing the world. Seeing the world as the mandala meant recognizing the symbolic perfection of the five wisdom energies—all-encompassing wisdom, mirror-like wisdom, wisdom of equanimity, wisdom of discernment, and all-accomplishing wisdom—which manifest in everything. I particularly liked the idea that the mandala doesn't need to be constructed or organized, that our world in all its apparent chaos is actually a spontaneous, ever-evolving mandala. It was with this view that I left Samye Ling and began to travel back to Asia.

OVERLAND FROM LONDON TO KATHMANDU

In late autumn of 1969, I got in a VW van in London as a paying passenger heading for Kathmandu by way of Austria, Yugoslavia, Iran, Iraq, Afghanistan, Pakistan, and India. The driver and VW bus owner was Eric, a Dutch Indonesian, whose parents had migrated to Australia. He was aiming to get home by Christmas, following the overland journey. He planned to sell the VW bus in Kathmandu, using the money to buy his ticket to Australia. We were six in the bus: an innocent young Canadian couple with red maple leaf patches sewn on their backpacks; my dark-haired, bright blue–eyed Australian friend Craig from Samye Ling; a young, blond English guy who had just gotten out of the military and was exploring the world before settling down to a job; Eric; and me.

The back of the bus had been converted into a flat platform of plywood with a layer of two-inch foam. Our luggage was under the platform, atop which we could either sit up or lie down. I made cur-

tains for the windows out of a blue printed cotton fabric to keep out
prying eyes as we traveled through Muslim countries where young
foreigners, especially Western women, were a rarity. The trip took
much longer than Eric had expected. We had to get two entirely new
engines along the way; and in Turkey, when we lost the first engine,
we had to be towed through the mountains for two hundred miles to
Ankara. It took all night over treacherous icy roads.

After that intense experience, I was shocked to see Eric's whis-
kers coming in white instead of black from the strain and fear of
being dragged through the mountains; they had literally changed
overnight! There were stretches of road in Afghanistan that were
unpaved, and we had to lie in the bus and wrap our faces in scarves
to breathe. The fine dust poured into the van, and the bumps were
kidney-rattling and painful, continuing for days on end. After another van breakdown in Pakistan, Craig and I jumped ship and
hitchhiked the rest of the way to Kathmandu. About a week later,
Eric arrived with the van, sold it, and accomplished his mission to go
home to Australia.

We arrived in Nepal about a week before Christmas 1969. The
town was abuzz with the presence of the magical Sixteenth Gyalwa
Karmapa, a great Tibetan lama who was the head of an even more
ancient reincarnation lineage than the Dalai Lama's; in fact, the first
Karmapa had predicted his next life with outstanding accuracy. He
wrote a letter with the names of his parents, a description of the house
where he would be reborn, and even his birthday and year. This
began the whole Tibetan tradition of reincarnate lamas such as the
Dalai Lama, but the Karmapa lineage is the oldest in which the lama
leaves a letter predicting his next rebirth. The Karmapa was in Nepal
for the first time in thirteen years and was staying in the Kagyu monastery next to the Swayambhu stupa, which I had first visited two
years earlier.

My friend Vicki had visited the Karmapa in Sikkim with her
parents before we traveled to India together in 1967. She'd told me,

"He is very fat and wears a big gold watch." I thought that someone could definitely not be fat, have a gold watch, and be spiritual at the same time. I was determined he wouldn't be my guru. I didn't want a fat guru. I wanted a thin, ascetic, spiritual-looking yogi-type teacher, like the gurus in *Autobiography of a Yogi*, who all seemed to be thin and otherworldly. But everyone, all the Tibetans who were pouring in from the Himalayas and all the visiting Westerners, was going to see the holy Karmapa whether he was fat or not, and I decided to go too.

There were the native Ladakhi people with their curly-toed boots matching their stovepipe hats with the curled corners, who looked like they had stepped out of a fairy tale. From the eastern part of Tibet came the wild and fearless Khampa people, and for this auspicious pilgrimage the Khampa women were all decked out. Each had 108 braids interlaced with turquoise, coral, and amber. The amber was stuck in large hunks on top of their heads and looked like antennae. The tall, handsome Khampa men had gold teeth that lit up when they smiled. They wore coral and turquoise earrings, and each had a long braid wrapped around his head with a red silk tassel dangling rakishly off the side. They walked around with their right sleeves hanging almost to the ground to "open" that shoulder like the monks, so that when they circumambulated sacred places and stupas clockwise, the right shoulder was more open to receive the blessings. These native Tibetans looked at everything and everyone, including me, with unabashed directness.

For the occasion, I wore a full-length turquoise and green quilted Afghani coat with long sleeves that hung down way past my hands, paired with a golden-yellow cotton skirt. I had dyed the cotton myself in London. The skirt was fashioned by hand-sewing the piece of cotton into a large tube; I stepped into the tube and wrapped it around my waist, making one big pleat in front, and then tied it in place with a colorful Afghani belt. I wore my long brown hair in braids with thick strands of turquoise and yellow silk threads woven through. I must have looked as odd to them as they did to me.

An air of festivity permeated the area of Kimdol, the village below the Swayambhu stupa, because of Karmapa's presence. New groups of tribal Tibetans were appearing every day. They traveled happily in groups all wearing similar clothes according to their region, teasing each other, laughing, or saying their mantras on small Bodhi seed rosaries in one hand while spinning handheld prayer wheels with the other.

At that time, the Westerners who were around were all young and beginners in Buddhism, but longing to learn more about the spiritual practice that motivated these joyful people emerging from the Himalayans: *What made them so joyful when many were refugees who had lost everything?* I met a couple from California who became my closest friends. Pam was tall and thin, with sparkling green eyes and wild, curly black hair that stuck out in a halo around her head. Jon had long blond hair, gentle brown eyes, a strong jaw, and the body of a mountaineer. We often ate together and spent time wandering around Kathmandu, and they convinced me to go see Karmapa in the Kagyu monastery at the top of the Swayambhu hill, where he was to give the Black Crown Ceremony.

The fact that Karmapa was mentioned often with great devotion in the *Sadhana of All the Siddhas*, the meditation practice I had received from Trungpa Rinpoche in Scotland and recited daily on the arduous journey from Europe to Nepal, also contributed to my decision to see him.

We climbed Swayambhu's long staircase early in the morning, joining the river of Tibetans heading to this ceremony that the Karmapa was known for. When we arrived, we could see him in the distance sitting cross-legged on a throne in front of the huge golden statue of the future Buddha, Maitreya, who is always portrayed seated Western-style in a chair. Karmapa's throne, covered by golden brocade, was positioned in the large doorway of the temple and surrounded by maroon-robed monks, with the Tibetan masses crowded before him in the courtyard. After the lilting, melodious sound of the *jalings* (Tibetan oboes) announced the crown, it was brought out in a hatbox wrapped in silk brocade by a monk wearing a mask covering his mouth.

I turned to Pam and asked, "Why is his mouth covered?"

She whispered, "So his impure breath doesn't pollute Karmapa and the black crown."

Inside the box, the crown was wrapped in layers of antique brocade, which Karmapa unwrapped ceremoniously; then he slowly raised the crown and placed it on his head, continuing to lightly touch it with his right hand. My friend Pam knew more about the ceremony than I did; she had attended it several times, so I asked her, "Why is he holding the crown on his head? Would it slip off otherwise?"

She threw back her head and laughed, then whispered, "No, they say it may fly away, because it's made of the woven hair of the dakinis, who fly through the sky. Their hair would make it fly away. The story is that a hundred thousand dakinis wove their hair into a crown and gave it to his fifth reincarnation. But you couldn't see it unless you had special powers. Then the emperor of China through his devotion had a vision of the dakinis' crown. He had a copy made and offered it to the fifth Karmapa."

The 16th Karmapa Rangjung Rigpe Dorje.

Again I heard that word *dakini*, which Ted had talked to me about in Scotland; from what Pam said, I now knew that they fly in the sky, though it didn't look to me like the crown was trying to fly away. Once he had the black crown on, I saw Karmapa settle into meditation, drawing in a deep breath and steadying his gaze on the distant horizon as he picked up a crystal *mala* (Buddhist prayer beads) and recited a mantra. I asked Pam what he was doing.

She replied, "He's transforming himself into Chenrezig, the Buddha of compassion, and he's saying the mantra *Om Mani Padme Hung Hri* one hundred eight times counting on his mala, sending compassion to all beings."

People were packed around us like groupies at a rock concert, except these were gorgeous mountain people wearing rough wool and embroidered felt boots bound at the tops of their calves. Their deep devotion and rugged physical beauty touched me deeply. They were in the presence of their spiritual leader at a time of great insecurity, when the Chinese invasion of Tibet had caused them to flee their homeland. Here was someone who could offer them solace and spiritual support in a time of great need.

They jostled and pushed with joy as the ceremony ended and the Karmapa began the process of blessing each and every one of the people. Tibetans thrust and shoved toward the narrow side door of the monastery to go before Karmapa. As each person passed, he touched them with a cloth-covered cylinder that hung from a stick, blessing them. Mothers held babies up for the first blessing of their lives. Bent-over old people with canes were led through by relatives. The crowd pressed toward the door. We decided to go too, carried forward by the masses. The smell of old butter, sweaty yak wool, and yak dung smoke filled my nostrils as we surged forward, funneling through a side doorway single file and then emerging in front of Karmapa.

Finally my turn came. I placed my hands in the prayer posture as I had seen the others doing, and as I passed I looked up at Karmapa and saw the biggest smile I had ever seen in my life. A spark of

The 16th Karmapa Rangjung Rigpe Dorje wearing the *Gampopa* hat.

recognition flew between us. He stopped for a moment and whispered something to a man standing near him, who was wearing the traditional Bhutanese men's garb, the *gho*, a striped kind of kimono, belted at the waist, ending at the knees, with long sleeves and wide white cuffs. I did not know it at the time, but he was Karmapa's doctor and translator, Dr. Jigme. I was amazed to see that Karmapa's head was so big his glasses didn't even reach behind his ears. His smile was vast as the sky, emanating joy, warmth, and compassion. I'd never seen a human being with such an expansive presence. His physical size made perfect sense: it was reflective of his largeness as a being. His presence seemed to pervade everywhere.

ORDINATION

In the following days, I began to go to all the initiations Karmapa was giving and visited him in his room at the top of the monastery. I would just walk in and, while the others were prostrating, go straight to him, and give him big bunches of dahlias that I picked in Jon and Pam's garden. He always gave me a huge, warm smile in spite of my unusual behavior.

Over the next weeks I became more and more agitated, because I felt like there was something important I should be doing, but I didn't know what it was. I was sleeping very little, and one sleepless night I was reading the meditation *Sadhana of All the Siddhas*; when I read the line "The only offering I can make is to follow your example . . ."

I suddenly realized that since Karmapa was a monk, to truly follow his example, I had to become a nun. This was the answer to what I was supposed to do.

My body ached as I arose the next morning. In the Kathmandu winter chill, it was cold and damp sleeping on the mud floor with only a straw mat under me and no heat. I dressed quickly and made my way with the crowds up the hill to the monastery and went into the Karmapa's room.

He nodded to me with his usual big smile, and gestured for me to sit down, but I stood in front of him. I took my braids and made scissoring motions with my fingers, indicating that I wanted to renounce the world and take the ordination of a Tibetan nun. He raised his eyebrows and gave a hearty laugh, then asked for the Bhutanese man I had seen him talk to at the Black Crown Ceremony.

When Dr. Jigme came, I said, "Please tell him I want to be a nun."

The Karmapa was looking at me all the while, and after the translator told him what I'd said, everything in the room went silent. The monks gazed at me and then at him. He became very serious and fixed me with a look I shall never forget. His eyes narrowed; then he closed them, then slowly opened them again. He looked at me as though he were seeing my whole karmic stream. Then, just as quickly as he had become serious, he broke into a wide smile and nodded his head and spoke to the doctor.

Dr. Jigme turned to me and said, "His Holiness has said he will ordain you in Bodhgaya in a week. You should get robes and meet him there."

Dr. Jigme took charge of me. First, he told me to get my head shaved. So I braided my hair with gold and blue silk, and put on my Tibetan canary-yellow shirt made out of flannel and the *shantab*, a maroon monastic skirt I had purchased in Kathmandu. Then I went with him into the little town of Bodhgaya, which, in 1970, was a sleepy village with a few chai tea shops, vegetable and grain shops, and one barbershop. The doctor took a picture of me in front of the Mahabodhi Temple, the main temple in Bodhgaya that rises above the Bodhi tree, wearing robes but still with my hair in braids. Then we went to the barber. This was a surreal moment—I was half nun in robes and half layperson with long hair. The robes were made of a heavy, rough Tibetan yak wool, and I didn't know it at the time, but I was coming down with hepatitis, which I had contracted in Afghanistan. So dressed in wool under the sweltering Indian sun and with the illness making me feverish, I felt very strange indeed.

Lama Tsultrim in front of the Mahabodhi Temple just before her head was shaved. Bodhgaya, India, January 1970. *Photograph by Dr. Jigme*

After ordination as Karma Tsultrim Chodrön by His Holiness the 16th Karmapa, 1970.

The barbershop happened to be across the street from the Mahabodhi Temple. So I went in and sat down in the one wooden chair, gesturing to the barber to cut off my hair, with Dr. Jigme translating into Hindi. The barber looked aghast at my request; he had certainly never shaved the head of a Western woman. The shop was open to the street at the front and consisted of a chair, a mirror, and three walls. My braids were the first to go. He cut them off easily: one, two, and brown braids with strands of blue and gold silk interwoven in them fell on my lap. A crowd began to gather around.

The next phase was strange. He cut big clumps of hair close to my head, making me look like a mangy Indian dog. Then he sharpened his single-edge razor on a leather strap, dampened my hair, and began to shave. I felt like I was in a movie, as a gaping crowd of at least thirty men were watching me, and moving closer. They were unabashedly staring at me with something between horror and blank curiosity in their faces. Then the straight edge of the barber's razor scraped my skull—*ouch*—and I snapped back to reality. This was no movie, as I felt the dull razor painfully pull the hair from my scalp.

The razor was not sharp enough, and my head was not prepared well with warm water and soap. I tried not to move or cry, but my eyes were tearing. I waited stoically for it to be over, and before long my head was shaved bare. I touched my scalp with my hand, and it felt like fine sandpaper.

The Indians from the village continued gawking as if I were an exotic animal in a zoo. I felt so exposed, but I felt refreshed at the same time. Losing my hair seemed to clear all the history I carried in it. It was as though everything I had experienced was imprinted in it. I took my braids and wrapped them in a piece of white cotton cloth; I contemplated them occasionally over the next few months, feeling some longing for the life I had left, unsure of what my new life would bring. Ultimately after a few months, when I returned to the monastery in Nepal, I let them go. I threw them over the wall near the stupa into the trees below that cover Swayambhu hill, imagining I was letting go of the vestiges of my past and fully embracing monastic life, and that the birds would make soft linings for their nests from my hair.

RETURN TO SWAYAMBHU

So it came to be that, in a hotel room in Bodhgaya, I was ordained by His Holiness the Sixteenth Karmapa, the first American woman he had ordained. After my ordination, I returned to Nepal. The lama of the Swayambhu stupa, Sapchu Rinpoche, found me a little room on the second floor of a rickety, clay-brick building next to the stupa and set me up with tutors in the Tibetan language.

My room was so tiny I could sit in the middle and touch all the walls. It had two big windows with no glass in them, just ancient wooden shutters. On one side, I made a small shrine from a cardboard box covered with cloth, where I always had beautiful dahlias in small brass bowls from Pam and Jon's garden in Kimdol, down at the bottom of the Swayambhu hill. Along the opposite wall, next to one of the windows, I had my bed, a woven grass mat on the floor covered with a flowered cotton sleeping bag I had bought in Holland. I kept my books in the window niche, and at the foot of my bed was my kitchen, consisting of a round, one-burner kerosene stove and a few aluminum pots.

I studied Tibetan with two Tibetan nuns who lived on the other side of the stupa, and my lessons began at 6:30 A.M. From my little room I could look out the window and see the stupa right there; I could almost touch it. The mysterious eyes on the top of the dome followed me everywhere. Never before had I lived near a sacred structure that was in itself a mandala. The stupa brought hundreds of pilgrims a day to circumambulate it, and by living in the rhythm of the stupa, I became acutely aware of the lunar cycle punctuated by the monks' celebrations, especially during a full moon.

The architectural mandala of Swayambhu stupa has been a central spiritual landmark for me ever since as the first outer mandala that I "lived with." Watching the way the community related to the stupa, day and night, made me aware of how the outer architectural mandala functions as a centering force for the community it serves.

Even today, with the work I've done with the mandala over almost five decades all over the world, whenever I teach or practice the mandala, in my mind I go back to Swayambhu stupa, when I was a twenty-two-year-old newly ordained nun. I can almost smell the red rice and ghee offerings, the rotting bananas, the rope incense placed in the niches of the stupa, and see the crowds of devoted Nepalese and Tibetans who came every day to worship at the stupa. It is my root mandala, and I still draw on the blessings of the stupa. Swayambhu became my spiritual "mother," and I have continually felt the glowing presence of her blessings.

2

WHY THE MANDALA?

*The mandala serves a conservative purpose—namely, to restore
a previously existing order. . . . [W]hat restores the old order simultaneously involves some element of new creation. In the new
order the old pattern returns at a higher level. The process is that
of an ascending spiral, which grows upward while simultaneously returning again and again to the same point.*

—C. G. JUNG

In the mountains of southwest Colorado, where my home and the
Tara Mandala Retreat Center are, we have the beautiful ponderosa pine trees. They are tall and majes-
tic, and after a strong summer rain their
bark smells like vanilla. They are big
enough to create a canopy that prevents
other trees from growing underneath
them, so the ponderosa forests appear
like cultivated parks that you can easily
walk through without following a trail.
The forest floor is ricegrass and medici-
nal herbs, and many pinecones fall every

Mandala form of a
ponderosa pinecone.

year. I collect the pinecones, as they are excellent fire starters. When I gather them, I like to pause and look at the round base of the cone emanating from a center and forming a perfect mandala—one of many mandala offerings from the natural world.

Our spiritual intelligence searches for wholeness, coherence, and attunement to the universe. The mandala is a tool to accomplish this, and thus has continually appeared throughout human history in diverse forms and cultures. And we do not need to travel into the past or to other cultures to experience the mandala in our lives. Once you become aware of the mandala, you will see it in many situations in your daily life. Mandalas will appear when you cut open a cabbage or slice an apple in half. When you look at a lily or a sunflower in full bloom, a magnificent dahlia, or the seeded head of a dandelion, you will find beautiful expressions of the mandala. There are mandalas in the spirals of seashells, the rings of a tree's core, Gothic rose windows, the iris of your eye, and innumerable other places. In the winter in Colorado, we often have snowflake crystals fall, and as I look at them on the dark red sleeve of my jacket for the second before they melt, within each of them is an individual mandala.

LEFT: Complex natural mandalas arise in our daily life: cabbage cut in half. RIGHT: Flowers are naturally arising mandalas: sunflower.

Studies show that infants are born with a desire to look at circles; in fact, it has been shown that infants less than a week old have a preference for curved lines.[16] Babies at three months or even younger prefer simple, complete forms such as circles, rather than complicated shapes.[17] It is presumed that babies seek out circular face-like stimuli to help create a bond with their parents and the mother's breast, but circles are also easier for the eye to process because they are the same all the way around, and the eye itself is circular. So it seems, going back to our earliest visual experiences, that circles bring us to wholeness and primal connection with the source of nurturance. Notes the nature writer Gretel Ehrlich, "Emerson said the first circle is the human eye, but so is the planet. They are linked: the one is always beholding the other."[18]

THE MANDALA TRAVELS WEST

The Western world was first made aware of the potency of the mandala as a psychological healing tool by the Swiss psychologist Dr. Carl G. Jung, who discovered the power of mandala drawings while acting as commandant of a prisoner-of-war camp for English soldiers in Switzerland between 1918 and 1920. Dr. Jung worked to improve the conditions of soldiers stranded in neutral territory and encouraged them to attend university courses, but his role was still emotionally taxing on him.

Admittedly to preserve his own sanity, he began experimenting with drawing personal mandalas daily. Every morning he drew or painted some form of a circular shape with four quadrants in a small notebook. Dr. Jung wrote of this time: "I began to understand that the goal of psychic development is the Self. There is no linear evolution; there is only a circumambulation of the Self. . . . This insight gave me stability, and gradually my inner peace returned. I knew that in finding the mandala as an expression of the Self I had attained what for me was the ultimate."[19]

"Self" as used by Dr. Jung referred not to the egocentric self as it is used in Buddhism, but rather to the Self as the fully individu-ated person. He saw the Self as the revelation of an individual's full potential integrated with the person's emotional shadow or disowned parts. The egocentric self he saw as the center of consciousness, whereas the Self he saw as the center of the whole being, including the ego, consciousness, and the unconscious shadow. This Self was the unification of the conscious and unconscious mind, and this state of integration was symbolized by the circle divided into four quad-rants, which he called the mandala. The Self, he believed, was whole at birth, but it was lost in the development of the ego differentiation necessary to establish oneself in the external world, usually occur-ring in the first half of life.

The second half of life Dr. Jung viewed as a return to the Self through the process of what he called "individuation," a conscious discovery, or a recovery, of the psychic nucleus of oneself. This jour-ney to individuation often began with a wounding of the personality, requiring a reconnection with the greater Self to heal. The mandala, according to Dr. Jung, could play a key role in this process of indi-viduation and reintegration, bringing together what had been splin-tered in the process of egoic differentiation and wounding. His work with himself and later with clients drawing their own mandalas her-alded the entrance of the mandala into Western usage.

Dr. Jung recognized that some form of the mandala could ap-pear in the dreams of his patients who were in states of psychological distress. He saw these dreams as the unconscious mind offering a template of order that could heal the disjointed psyche. He expressed it this way: "Mandalas . . . usually appear in situations of psychic confusion and disorientation. The archetype thereby constellated represents a pattern of order which like a psychological 'view-finder' marked with a cross or a circle divided in four, superimposed on psy-chic chaos so that each content falls into place and the weltering con-fusion is held together by the protective circle."[20]

In his book *The Archetypes and the Collective Unconscious*, where he illustrates the importance of the centering principle, Dr. Jung wrote of the case of Brother Klaus, a Swiss mystic and hermit, who received a vision of a wheel and painted it on his cell wall. Dr. Jung tells us that "the severe pattern imposed by a circular image of this kind compensates the disorder and confusion of the psychic state—namely, through the construction of a central point to which everything is related."[21]

In recent years, the mandala has been used therapeutically, and has also become a generic term for any geometric round diagram with a center that is a symbolic microcosm of the universe. There are now a variety of mandala books, workbooks, T-shirts, posters, and even mandala cell phone cases. There are websites selling paraphernalia related to this interpretation of the mandala, such as mandala tattoos, wall hangings, and painted stones. Mandala coloring books dominated the Nielsen best-seller lists across the United States, Brazil, and the EU in 2016. You can find mandala massages, hotels, restaurants, spas, nightclubs, and magazines, and there are more than a thousand mandala ideas on the Pinterest website. The word also appears in English-language dictionaries and other general reference books.

There is certainly value in these nontraditional mandala drawings, and they are being used effectively in mental health facilities, hospitals, and other psychotherapeutic settings. Mandala drawing has proved to be a centering and healing modality for those recovering from trauma. In fact, mandalas have been used as a therapeutic technique for many psychological issues, such as for HIV-infected children and adolescents[22] and as an assessment tool for women with breast cancer.[23] There have been empirical studies on the healing nature of mandalas for those suffering from PTSD[24] and studies on the effect of mandala drawing on anxiety, to name a few.[25]

All these studies have concluded that mandala drawing and interpretation in a therapeutic setting has a positive effect on a wide range of issues. The wholeness suggested by the mandala pattern through painting or coloring seems to weave together a traumatized psyche and creates an experience of integration and order assisting in healing of trauma, anxiety, or depression. A sense of order is reflected back to the person drawing the mandala, transmitting to the brain an orderly pattern of thought that facilitates psychological recovery.

"A sense of order is reflected back to the person drawing the mandala, transmitting to the brain an orderly pattern of thought that facilitates psychological recovery."

THE TIBETAN MANDALA

The earliest form of the Buddhist mandala appeared in the third century CE, but was more widely diffused during the Tantric Buddhist period between 500 and 1200 CE in India, and its usage followed the spread of Vajrayana Buddhism to China, Korea, Japan, and Malaysia. I have even seen Buddhist mandalas in ancient temples in Bali. But the mandala achieved its greatest complexity and usage in Tibet starting in the eighth century.

The Sanskrit word *mandala* means "the circle"; it can also be interpreted as *manda*, meaning "the supreme or the best," plus *la*, meaning "the marker or completion," combining to denote "the place that holds or contains the ultimate essence." In the earliest Vedic literature, *mandala* already had the meaning of a sacred enclosure or a place for a spiritual practice or ritual. The circle with a seminal nucleus in the center and four quadrants is the basic form of the mandala, and reflects the structure of the universe, from the smallest microcosm to the vast macrocosm.

"The Sanskrit word mandala *means 'the circle';*
it can also be interpreted as manda, *meaning 'the*
supreme or the best,' plus la, *meaning 'the marker*
or completion,' combining to denote 'the place
that holds or contains the ultimate essence.'"

The Tibetan term for *mandala* is *kyil khor. Kyil* means "center" and *khor* means "that which surrounds the center, or the swirl surrounding the center." The Tibetan mandala describes a circular pure dimension surrounded by a protective fire circle that prevents invasive energies from entering. There are hundreds of different Tibetan Buddhist mandalas, and every mandala contains a center, usually a square separated into four sections or directions, from which the rest of the mandala radiates and to which that radiation returns. The Tibetan mandalas symbolize three-dimensional palaces with deities inside.

THE THREE TYPES OF MANDALAS

The mandala principle in Tibetan Buddhism has three aspects: outer, inner, and secret. Of these three aspects, the first is the *outer mandala*, or the mandala of the phenomenal world. The outer mandala sees the world as a mandala: our country, our province, our district, our immediate household, our friends and colleagues, and so on. It is the world of our projections, but shifts and develops order when we see through the lens of a mandala.

The *inner mandala* deals with the process of inner transformation that employs the five families and meditation on the mandala principle using deities like the five dakinis, not with our outer perceptions and projections as the outer mandala does. Through visualization of the mandala, we work with symbolic images, color, sound, and directions to transform blocked emotional energies into wisdom. The inner mandala is based on working with the five buddha families, which are:

* Buddha Family
* Vajra Family
* Ratna Family
* Padma Family
* Karma Family

Each family embodies a specific encumbered emotional pattern, the emotional reactions that are traditionally called the "five poisons," and the transformation of each poison into wisdom. The word in Tibetan for these encumbered patterns is *nyomong*, which literally means "drowsy" or "obscured." *Encumbered* implies a pattern that hides our innate wisdom, and that the energy itself is not inherently bad. I use the terms *poison* and *encumbered pattern* interchangeably throughout this book, in reference to the five blocked emotions.

The third mandala is the *secret mandala*. It is secret not in the sense of something no one else should know, but rather in the sense that it depends on your own understanding of reality, so it is a self-secret. The secret mandala is relating to your own mind as the mandala principle. So anything that arises in your life situation, in terms of the five poisons, is regarded as a potential messenger of wakefulness. What I mean by that is that, instead of emotions being random occurrences that we try to deal with in one way or another, we have the specific knowledge of the mandala and its power of transformation, and we spontaneously and naturally use it as situations arise.

This is the secret mandala, which is never arranged but always

OUTER, INNER, AND SECRET MANDALAS

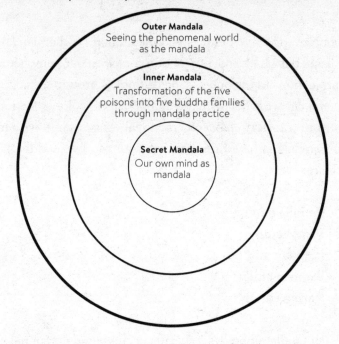

Outer Mandala
Seeing the phenomenal world
as the mandala

Inner Mandala
Transformation of the five
poisons into five buddha families
through mandala practice

Secret Mandala
Our own mind as
mandala

FIVE BUDDHA FAMILIES: INNER MANDALA

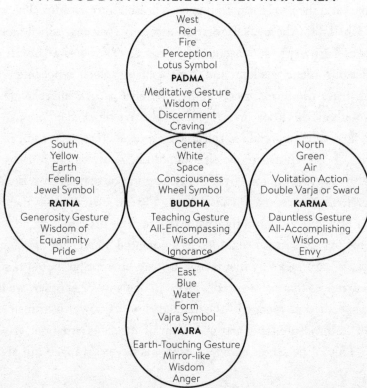

West
Red
Fire
Perception
Lotus Symbol
PADMA
Meditative Gesture
Wisdom of
Discernment
Craving

South
Yellow
Earth
Feeling
Jewel Symbol
RATNA
Generosity Gesture
Wisdom of
Equanimity
Pride

Center
White
Space
Consciousness
Wheel Symbol
BUDDHA
Teaching Gesture
All-Encompassing
Wisdom
Ignorance

North
Green
Air
Volitation Action
Double Varja or Sward
KARMA
Dauntless Gesture
All-Accomplishing
Wisdom
Envy

East
Blue
Water
Form
Vajra Symbol
VAJRA
Earth-Touching Gesture
Mirror-like
Wisdom
Anger

remains complete. It's not based on visualizing a mandala, as the inner mandala is; rather, it's the straightforward process of relating to the poisons and transmuting them directly into wakefulness as they arise. When a fixated pattern arises, we tend to follow it and get hooked, in a sense, to be seduced by it; the secret mandala practice immediately recognizes the pattern and wakes us up to it—we don't fall asleep.

When you get to know the mandala, as you will in this book, you begin to see the world as the outer mandala, you learn to transform your encumbered emotional patterns through the inner mandala, and eventually you will be able to experience the secret mandala. This understanding can be applied to your own life. We each have our own personal mandala, and we are at the center of our mandala, with our family, children, partners, lovers, friends, and so on as our retinue. Our mandala interfaces with others' mandalas, and is often within a greater mandala. For example, students of the same spiritual teacher are all within his or her mandala, but they also have their own mandalas interacting with the mandalas of their fellow students. It becomes a beautiful, pulsating mandala, a matrix of overlaid mandalas. When seen this way, our lives are intricate interwoven patterns.

"Our mandala interfaces with others' mandalas.
It becomes a beautiful, pulsating mandala, a
matrix of overlaid mandalas. When seen this way,
our lives are an intricate interwoven fabric."

INTRODUCTION TO
THE FIVE BUDDHA FAMILIES

At this point, I would like to give a short introduction to the five buddha families so you have a point of reference, and then I will discuss each of the families in more depth as they relate to the dakinis in Part 3. The five buddha families are the various perspectives on the world, five styles of emotional suffering that transform into five manifestations of enlightened energy.

"The five buddha families are the various perspectives on the world, five styles of emotional suffering that transform into five manifestations of enlightened energy."

The word for *family* in Tibetan is *rig*, and in the case of the five buddha families it really means "energetic affinities," aspects of Buddha nature that we possess. Buddha nature does not manifest in the same way for everybody; there are different styles, what Trungpa Rinpoche called the "five different ways to be sane."[26]

When we talk about a family, we're talking about an energetic field, which has in its untransformed state an encumbered pattern or poison, as mentioned before; in its awakened state, this very same energy becomes wisdom. There are certain energetic affinities that are associated with each family: specific core sounds called seed syllables, mudras (hand gestures), seasons, colors, elements, body types, symbols, landscapes, aggregates (the psychophysical component), and so on. (See detailed diagram of the attributes of the five buddha families on page 54.) For the purpose of this book, I will focus on a few core traits and primarily on the encumbered pattern and its wisdom counterpart.

When I was first introduced to the five families by Trungpa Rinpoche, he was teaching the families in a way that brought them into all aspects of life. I learned from him how to see a landscape as ratna or a home interior as buddha, a cooking style as vajra or a way of dressing as padma—even whole countries could be understood as being dominated by a certain family. Through him, the five families were immediately relevant and tangible. Everything seemed workable and had potential for transformation; everything could be used. Everything in life could be met with these dynamic energies as part of the path.

When working with the five families, you don't reject the five poisons; rather, you rehabilitate that energy into its essential wisdom through working with the mandala, in our case the Mandala of the Five Dakinis. Within the mandala you are relating directly to the energies of the poisons, but you are experiencing the energy as sacred and pure. You are working with the tremendous richness of the phenomenal world. You are feeling its energetic luminosity by giving up your "me-ness," your ego, your separateness. (Chapter 3 will discuss in more depth the origins of the five poisons and the path to transform them.)

When we understand the mandala and the five buddha families, our world clarifies itself. Our lives take shape instead of being random confusion. Through the mandala we shift our vision and start to see energies with both obstructed patterns and wisdom patterns; all beings are held in that. Not only the people in our lives, but our homes, workplaces, landscapes, body types, foods, interior decor, seasons, times of the day, and so on are all understood within the mandala. And within ourselves, our disturbing emotions are experienced as energies that, when freed from ego's control and transformed, become the five wisdom energies.

Our consciousness always has the potential of finding its way back to wholeness, just as a child who has wandered away always has the possibility to rediscover and reunite with its mother. When the child does find her, there is absolute certainty: *This is not someone new, this is my mother because she is the source.* Returning to our true nature is like that: the individual practicing within the mandala recognizes his or her own dynamic energy within the luminous structure of the mandala, reaching the state where "other" fades, and returns once again to a state of interconnected wholeness.

"Our consciousness always has the potential of finding its way back to wholeness, just as a child who has wandered away always has the possibility to rediscover and reunite with its mother."

ONE GROUND, TWO PATHS, TWO RESULTS

The entire world of all appearances and possibilities, of samsara and nirvana: one ground, two paths, two results. This is the magical display of innate awareness and the nonrecognition of awareness.

—THE PRAYER OF SAMANTABHADRA

In order to understand the mandala principle, we have to go way back to the beginning, to the basic split. This is the rupture, which created the experience of "I" and "other" and is at the root of our suffering. There is a Tibetan teaching, the *Prayer of Samantabhadra*, that explains how this split happened. It states: "One ground, two paths, two results." Though at first glance this teaching may seem simple, what it describes, in six words, is nothing short of the explanation of our entire human condition.

Let's start by understanding what "one ground" actually means here. One ground is often referred to as the "ground of being," or the Great Mother, meaning literally "the ground out of which all beings and all things arise." Now bear with me; this may be a bit abstract at first, but it's crucial that we understand the profound meaning of one ground as the very base of our existence: the one ground of being is infinite potentiality from which the whole of the universe comes— the source of all creation.

"The one ground of being is infinite potentiality from which the whole of the universe comes—the source of all creation."

This infinite potentiality is formless and so vast that it defies any attempts to conceptualize or limit it in time or space. The nature of the ground of being is pure gnostic awareness—it is the intelligence of the universe, or, put another way, the intrinsically intelligent nature of the universe. Radiant light is the expression of the ground of being, as is stated in the famous Buddhist *Sutra of Transcendent Wisdom* (*Prajnaparamita Sutra*): "The mind is not the mind; the mind's nature is radiant light."[27]

Now, imagine for a moment that the ground of being is the vast blue sky that has no beginning and no end, no center and no edge, and the nature of this space is pure, infinite awareness. Everything arises from this space; its essence is empty; its nature is radiant; it expresses itself as all-pervading compassion. The "two paths" form when the ground of being expresses itself or self-exteriorizes into appearances by radiating its pure, luminous, rainbow-hued light. Here the mystical ground energies move into exteriorization, manifesting as the five lights: white, blue, yellow, red, and green.

At this point the individual awareness either recognizes that pure rainbow-hued luminosity manifesting as appearances as inseparable from itself, or it sees that luminosity manifesting as a separate world of appearances. In that moment, the split occurs and the two paths are created: the one path of liberation, which recognizes the inseparability, and the second path of confusion, which sees appearances as separate, creating fear and anxiety. This path of confusion forms the dualistic barrier and our ego fixation becomes a way to resolve our separation anxiety, and the result of taking this path is called *samsara*, the pattern of grasping that propels us through life, death, and rebirth. This is the path that we all took.

Let me use a simple analogy of how our ego fixation and self-clinging mind works. Like a high-security base, our ego, which forms at the moment of the rupture from the ground, sends out agents to explore the outside world and report back. There are three types of reports or reactions: The first is constantly surveying for potential threats, creating aversion, aggression, or hatred. The second report is concerned with making our ego feel safe—desire, grasping, and attachment are born from this. And then the third report is about neither enhancing nor threatening the ego, producing indifference and ignorance.

Aggression, desire, and ignorance—these three reactions or poisons are constantly taking place within us. The plot lines may flip, and what is at first seen as desirable may become threatening or vice versa, or what at first seems irrelevant may later become something to grasp or to reject. The play of these three fundamental poisons creates two more poisons—pride or arrogance, and jealousy or envy. Those are the origins of the five poisons, which I introduced in the last chapter: ignorance, anger, pride, desire, and jealousy. And the way to transform these poisons into wisdom and return to the one ground is through meditation.

All Buddhist practice is about returning to the unified, ground-of-being state, before the formation of the dualistic split between self and other. This split is extremely painful, and so there's a great longing to overcome it; unfortunately, the way we normally attempt to overcome it—through the five poisons—only increases our suffering.

The process of failing to recognize our inseparability from the one ground creates a self-perpetuating condition, like a kaleidoscopic hall of mirrors, in which we seek to resolve our inherent alienation from the one ground through further projections outward. The ego's plot thickens, moving us further away from the one ground into dualistic confusion. We are all caught in this same dance, a self-perpetuating drama, a vicious cycle that creates chaotic karmic layers of dissatisfaction and suffering over lifetimes.

Meditation practice slows down the reaction patterns of the ego, so that eventually awareness can return to its own source and reunite with the ground from which it has ruptured. When we wake up, we realize there's never been a separation from the ground of being, although the constant activity of the ego has created the illusion of separation—the clear, blue, spacious sky of our being has been obscured. As the ego dissolves and our pure potential manifests, it is like the five rays of light that stream out of a crystal when struck by the sun. These five rainbow-hued lights are the basis of the five buddha family wisdoms.

The key to awakening, then, is recognizing the appearances in the world as the radiance of the essence ground, and our true nature as the vast awaken universe itself. The work with the mandala and the five buddha families returns us to the original luminosity of the ground—we then return home to what is called the Great Mother, the ground of being. The good news is that for all of us who took the second path of confusion, liberation is achievable. All we need to do is stop investing in the dualistic struggle and recognize the true ground of being. The path to liberation is never far from us. We are actually never apart from it. We are simply not recognizing nonduality as our true condition.

"*The key to awakening, then, is recognizing the appearances in the world as the radiance of the one ground, and our true nature as the vast awakened universe itself.*"

Longchenpa, the great Tibetan teacher of the fourteenth century, described the mandala as a "luminous house," a dome of light emanating from the purely latent ground. The mandala is a means by which we return to our essential wholeness. Mandala practice is designed to help us see our patterns. It is the map for returning to the ground of being through transforming the five poisons into wisdom; it is a method of placing the psyche in a template of luminous wholeness. This is possible because, although we have left the ground of being, it has never left us.

There is a deep longing for wholeness in all of us, and from that longing cultures and religions have created mandala-like forms in ceremonies, dances, architecture, temples, churches, stained-glass windows, jewelry, art, gardens, and arrangements of ceremonial food. Although the human body is its own dynamic mandala, with the heart center, the limbs as the four directions, and so on, we often experience the world and ourselves in a fragmented way. This fragmentation is particularly true in modern times when the collective mandalic centering rituals and dances that healed individuals and communities have, for the most part, been lost.

Meditating on the mandala is a tool or template for reintegration and provides a re-centering experience that unites the fragmented psyche and transmutes the five poisons into wisdom. In meditation, the mandala becomes a transformative psychogram rather than a cosmogram. The psyche that has moved into dualistic fragmentation experiences reunion, a return to the ground of being, and is able to shine forth once more from the depths of its true essence.

THE PATH OF TRANSFORMATION

In Tibetan Buddhism, we talk about three different methods for working with the basic split or the dualistic rupture from the ground of being, the fundamental state in which we find ourselves. The first is called the *path of renunciation*, and this is what we associate with the monastic tradition and early Buddhism. The Buddha taught laypeople, but the ideal path was one renouncing worldly life, the path of the monk or nun who becomes celibate and gives up worldly clothes, wealth, possessions, and so on. They do this in order to limit the complications that distract from the spiritual path, to limit the tendency to fall into the five poisonous states.

The second is the method called the *path of transformation*. Now, in this path, the image used is that of a peacock. In the path of renunciation, we don't eat the poison; we avoid it. In the path of transformation, the symbolic peacock is said to eat the poison, and the poison transforms into his beautiful feathers, all those marvelous colors, that incredible translucency. The poisons are used and transformed on the path.

Therefore, in the path of transformation we weaken the hold of the five poisons that have arisen from the basic split, and—working with our body, speech, and mind—we transform the encumbered patterns into wisdom. This is where we find the mandala; we embody the five buddha families, working with the notion of sacred embodiment. The path of transformation has to do with the body, with dance and hand gestures; with speech, in terms of sounds and mantras; and with the subtle energy of sound. The mind comes into play with visualizations, actually seeing and holding certain images. These three essential factors—body, speech, sound—are the tools of the path of transformation.

The third path presented in Tibetan Buddhism is called the *path of natural liberation*, sometimes called self-liberation or inherent liberation. Unlike the path of transformation, there isn't the idea that you take something and turn it into something else. Rather, the path of natural liberation is a method where we experience reality as it is, as perfect, and our state as innately perfected, so that there's nothing to do. We do not need to renounce; we don't need to transform. We are discovering what already is—the self-perfected state.

In this book, we'll be working with the path of transformation, which uses the mandala. As we return to the luminous template of the mandala, we heal the rupture from the ground of being. Through the path of the mandala, we break the cycle of wandering by reversing the outflowing, grasping patterns of energy created at the time of the rupture. Once we know "the inexhaustible treasure" we have been sitting on, the treasure of our radiant true nature, there is a longing to dedicate oneself to it. There is nothing more precious than this.

PART 2

Meeting the Dakini

4

FINDING THE EMPOWERED FEMININE

Traditionally, the term dakini has been used for outstanding female
practitioners, consorts of great masters, and to denote the enlight-
ened female principle of nonduality, which transcends gender . . .
a very sharp, brilliant wisdom mind that is uncompromising, hon-
est, with a little bit of wrath.

—KHANDRO RINPOCHE

After being away from home in Europe and Asia for three years, I began to miss my family and long for familiar places. My sister had had another baby, and her children were growing up without their aunt ever meeting them, and my parents were getting older. After living in Nepal for a year, I had traveled to India and lived in Darjeeling, where I studied with the great master Khabje Kalu Rinpoche, then went down to the sacred places on the Indian plains, Bodhgaya and Sarnath, where the Buddha delivered his first teaching, outside Varanasi. I spent the winter there and then went back to the mountains and settled in the Himalayas, in Himachal Pradesh, near a small town called Manali, where I studied with a great yogi named Apho Rinpoche, who was married and had four children. I lived in a retreat cabin near his house, with vast views that stretched to the nearby snow peaks. I wasn't sure it would be a good idea to leave the Himalayas, where I was supported as a Buddhist nun, living in a culture that understood what this was and respected it. Because of my indecisiveness, I asked Apho Rinpoche to do a divination and decided I would follow whatever the results were.

I waited with great anticipation, feeling the decision would set me on a new course. Tibetans have many methods of divination: using a mirror, using small balls of dough with different answers hidden in them, watching the flight and calls of ravens, counting off beads on a mala, dreams, signs, and intuition. My teacher did the divination using the small dough balls placed in a skullcup. Following a ritual, one dough ball would be chosen, and tucked inside would be a small scrap of paper with the answer: yes, no, or it's the same one way or the other.

I anxiously awaited the results for several days, really not sure what would happen. Finally, the day came and my teacher called me up to his room. I went in and sat down, and his wife offered me Tibetan tea in a shallow wooden bowl. Then he told me my divination: it was the same whether I stayed or went home. This was a letdown for me because I really couldn't decide and wanted a definitive answer; but since I wanted to see my family and the divination said it was the same either way, I decided to go. Who knows what would've happened had I remained in India? In any case, I let my parents know and they were overjoyed, and I began to get excited as I traveled down from the Himalayas to Delhi by ancient Indian buses with hard wooden seats jammed together so you couldn't hold your knees straight. My knees had to be at an angle, even though I'm not very tall. I arrived in the bustling city of Delhi, where beggars followed me and the noise was deafening to me, having been in solitude at the mountain hermitages for several years. I began to wonder if my decision to leave Manalie and Apho Rinpoche was a good one, but I had made up my mind and was truly looking forward to seeing my family.

After staying several days in a cheap hotel near Connaught Circle in Delhi, I boarded a plane for Boston wearing my maroon Tibetan robes and feeling a bit self-conscious among all the Indians and Westerners; at least my shaven hair had grown out a bit, so I wasn't completely bald. It was December of 1972, just before Christmas, when I landed in Boston. I was about to be the only Tibetan Buddhist nun in the United States, Western or Tibetan.

Soon I was in the arms of my anxiously awaiting parents. They loaded my green canvas Indian luggage into their white Chrysler and drove me north to our old colonial house in Keene, New Hampshire. I had been gone three years; our only communication during that time had been through the aerogram, a light-blue one-page letter that was folded up and glued closed with the stamp embedded in it. Our aerograms traveled back and forth; round-trip took six weeks if you wrote back the same day a letter arrived, which we usually didn't.

For six months of my three years abroad, I had been in Scotland at Samye Ling, and the rest of the time I'd spent in Nepal and the Himalayan region of India, and at the sacred sites of the Buddha on the Indian plains. Now, as I came back to the United States, the Vietnam War was winding down, the Paris Peace Accords were about to be signed, friends had died in Vietnam, and a close childhood friend had committed suicide to stay out of the war. Buddhism had been introduced in a few places in America, brought back from Asia by my generation, who had moved from psychedelic experimentation to Buddhist meditation practice. The Hare Krishna movement had begun, and its practitioners were around the big cities and in airports. Vets were coming back and being met with disdain by antiwar protesters.

Our country was wounded, but also there was the excitement of the change that my generation had started, a change that broke out of the rigid structures of our parents, and this included their religion and ideas of spirituality. While others of my generation had been in school and following conventional lives, many had woken up to spirituality outside the Western mainstream, traveling to India or other places in Asia. I had been with Ram Dass, Daniel Goleman, Krishna Das, and friends in Bodhgaya when they started learning Buddhist meditation. Now they were also returning home around the time I did.

I had no idea how I would move forward with my life as a Buddhist nun in the West or how to understand Tibetan Buddhism in the Western context. I had vows not to sleep on a high bed, so I made a kind of encampment in the corner of my old bedroom, surrounding myself with my Tibetan shrine and practice objects, sleeping on a mat on the floor. My parents didn't want me to go downtown in my robes; how would they explain me to the people in our small town?

I had heard while in India that Trungpa Rinpoche had moved from Scotland to Canada and then to the United States, starting a center in northern Vermont, not far from my parents' home, and that he was teaching in a way that made the Tibetan teachings more accessible for Westerners. I was eager to hear him teach and to meet him again, and hoped he might give me some guidance in how to be a monastic in the West.

After Christmas, an old friend from childhood gave me a ride to Trungpa Rinpoche's center in northern Vermont, Tail of the Tiger, later renamed Karmê Chöling, near Saint Johnsbury. I walked into a seminar being held in the Barnet Town Hall, and as I sat in the back row I saw my two worlds—the traditional Tibetan teachings I had studied and practiced in Nepal and India, and my background as a Westerner—coming together in his presence. The teachings I had received were opening into something useful in the West.

I was immediately fascinated and moved by the way he was

teaching to Westerners in their own language with such insight into the Western psyche. He was dressed in a suit and tie and sat in a chair with the town hall's tapestry of a prosaic country scene hanging behind him. He was making the very foreign, complex, and ancient teachings from Tibet comprehensible and digestible for the West. It was incredibly exciting to hear him teach Buddhism in such a lively and meaningful way.

After the talk, I was invited to meet with Trungpa Rinpoche privately. I told him I would like to come and study with him, and he welcomed me warmly and suggested I go into solitary retreat until he returned in the spring. So I spent the winter in a log cabin in Kirby, Vermont, that had previously only been used in the summer. The cabin was deep in the forest, a mile walk (or snowshoe) from the road. Once I got settled and my friends who had dropped me off had left, night fell and the wind whistled through the places where the chinking between the logs had fallen out. It was desolate and lonely. I was cold day and night, but I did a lot of meditation and studied Trungpa Rinpoche's books. It was then that I became deeply aware of his teachings on the five buddha families and the mandala.

When I came out of retreat three months later, the snow was gone and it was spring. After consulting with Trungpa Rinpoche, I moved to Boulder, Colorado, where he was living and had established a center called Karma Dzong and a mountain retreat called Rocky Mountain Dharma Center, which later became Shambhala Mountain Center. At the time, he was working on a film about the venerable yogi and poet Milarepa, which was never completed, but served to introduce his students to the visual ideas of the five buddha families as the base of his cinematography. He also held a seminar on filmmaking in which he elaborated on the five families. Here is a description about how he was teaching the five Buddha families through filmmaking, from the introduction to *The Collected Works*

of Chögyam Trungpa, Volume 7 written by Carolyn Gimian, who
worked closely with Trungpa Rinpoche:

> "He also talked about specific scenes and shots. To con-
> vey the desolation that Milarepa felt in retreat when he
> longed for his teacher, Trungpa Rinpoche suggested that
> the movie might 'work with desert, something completely
> open, and find one human footprint or maybe the footprint
> of an animal, a horse, and maybe horseshit. There could
> be a snowstorm and at the same time sand is blowing.
> The cameramen as well as the directors should develop
> an absolute relationship with sand and storm, not just try
> to entertain.' The study of the five buddha families was
> intended to shape how the film was shot, from five differ-
> ent perspectives representing the different energies of each
> family. Rinpoche talked about how tension and audience
> involvement would come from changing the buddha fam-
> ily perspectives throughout the film. . . ."[28]

In this introduction discussing how he began to see differently
after working with Trungpa Rinpoche on this film project, the filmmaker Baird Bryant is quoted as saying:

> "I remember thinking, so Tibetans see it differently, and
> how come? I know that, since that time, I have never been
> able to see a rotten log lying in the forest without thinking,
> there's the symbol of the Ratna Family. Likewise green
> buds bursting into fresh leaves say Karma Family in my
> head. The deep blue sky speaks of Buddha, graceful seduc-
> tive curves in whatever medium represent Padma, and in
> contemplating the physical world I see it as the great Mudra
> of the spiritual universe: the complete Vajra Family, and in
> my world Trungpa Rinpoche is enthroned therein."[29]

Trungpa Rinpoche became my greatest influence in learning about the mandala and the five buddha families, which began with their application to his artistic pursuits. Once I had received the teachings, I could see landscapes, people, buildings, cities, countries, in short, everything as the mandala of the five families. And when I began to focus on teaching the mandala in the Dakini Retreats in the late 1980s, it was on his explanations that I based my teachings. Trungpa Rinpoche was brilliant at leading the Western mind into an experience of the Tibetan teachings in a way that we could feel it was our own, not something foreign.

Chögyam Trungpa Rinpoche at Tail of the Tiger (currently known as Karmê Chöling), 1972. *Shambhala Archives*

DECIDING TO DISROBE

When I returned to America, I was twenty-five years old and not sure I wanted to remain a nun the rest of my life. It was very alienating and lonely. I was the only Buddhist nun, actually the only monastic, in Trungpa Rinpoche's community. His community was not what you might imagine a Buddhist community to be, with everyone quiet and focused on meditation. There was heavy partying every night, a lot of sexual activity, dancing, poetry, and in general an atmosphere that was not conducive to monastic and celibate life.

I also was not someone who had always wanted to be a nun; I became a nun because of the inspiration of Karmapa and my time at the Swayambhu stupa. In Nepal, being a nun was good for me because it allowed me a kind of independence and spiritual development that I

wouldn't have had otherwise. In my first book, *Women of Wisdom*, I
wrote about this time:

> I now see the time I spent as a nun as an invaluable experi-
> ence. I think it is important for women to have the experi-
> ence of living a "virgin" existence. I mean virgin in its true
> sense: a maiden alone, complete unto herself, belonging to
> no man. . . . This time gave me a chance to develop myself
> without the inevitable drain that comes with relationships.
> As I was only twenty-two at the time of my ordination, I
> was not formed enough myself to resist being swept away
> whenever I fell in love. The robes and the celibacy that
> went with the ordination served as a protective shell in
> which I could grow and find myself. But once this process
> had been established, holding on to this form would have
> become repressive for me.[30]

After a year back in the States, I began to really struggle with the
decision of whether to keep on trying to be a nun or to let my vows
go. It was difficult; I couldn't see it working in America at that time.
Being a nun in Nepal and India made sense with the cultural support
of Buddhist monasticism, but I didn't want to live in Asia for the rest
of my life. A monastic lifestyle is traditionally practiced in groups
with support given by others holding the discipline, and I was alone
as a monastic in America.

Sexuality also played a part in my decision, as I was becoming more and more aware of my sexual energy, and I felt it wasn't
going to be healthy for me to try to repress that part of myself. How
could I be sexual *and* spiritual? Was there any model for this? I was
stimulated and excited by what Trungpa Rinpoche was teaching and
by being in his community, but felt restrained by my robes. I was
trying to find a role in my tradition that would allow me to be just as
dedicated as I was as a nun, but without the vows. I didn't want to be

a part-time practitioner, or to slip away into a middle-class life as a mother driving carpools and thinking about what to put in my kid's lunchboxes. At the time, I knew of no other female role models; I did not yet understand that the dakinis could offer me guidance for the way of living I sought.

During this time, Trungpa Rinpoche sent me back to India, carrying an invitation to Karmapa, inviting him to visit the United States for the first time. After delivering the message, I spent three months in Tashi Jong, a Tibetan refugee community in the Kangra Valley, receiving the Dam Ngag Dzod empowerments from the great Dilgo Khyentse Rinpoche, with about five hundred Tibetans and a few Westerners. He had been requested to give the empowerments by the leader of Tashi Jong, Khamtrul Rinpoche.

Empowerments in the Tibetan tradition are rituals that transmit a seed experience of a particular sadhana practice, which allows the recipient to develop that connection when they actually perform the sadhana. It's the transmission of the power of that practice and creates a link to it. The empowerment is essential, along with the hearing transmission called the *lung*, and the explanation of how to do it is called the *tri*. The *wang* or empowerment along with the lung and the tri give you everything you need to practice a sadhana. Great Tibetan lamas at times give a whole series of empowerments and hearing transmissions at once to a large group of people, partially so lineages are not lost, and partly so those who receive those empowerments can develop the practices at a later date, possibly receiving the explanation from another lama.

During the Tashi Jong empowerments I began to dream about a baby—not a newborn baby, but a one-year-old sitting on my shoulders. I had this dream several times while living in the refugee housing at Tashi Jong. Meanwhile I had reconnected with a Dutchman whom I had met in Holland named Paul Kloppenburg, who was also attending the empowerments. In Holland I had suggested to him where to go study Tibetan Buddhism, since I had already been to

Nepal and India and met the Tibetans. I had suggested Dharamsala, where the Dalai Lama lives, and he had gone directly to Dharamsala and had been living alone in the mountains, practicing meditation and studying with a Tibetan teacher there. He had been there for almost four years, and during that time we had exchanged letters occasionally. He had never been ordained like me, but had been living like a monk.

He started to visit my room in Tashi Jong frequently. He was very entertaining and made me laugh a lot. He was tall and lanky, with medium-length brown hair, twinkling brown eyes, and pink cheeks. We started to cook together over a one-burner kerosene stove on the concrete floor. Mostly we made soup, just putting everything into a pot with water and adding some salt, and not even cutting up the vegetables, just loading in whole scallions, tomatoes, carrots, and potatoes. It took too much time to cut things up, as the breaks in the empowerments were short. We then would eat this vegetable soup quickly before returning to the empowerments, and it was actually quite delicious—or maybe we were just really hungry!

During this time I became attracted to him and I became more and more confused about what to do. Finally, I went to my teacher, Apho Rinpoche, who was married, and told him I was dreaming about babies. He sat on his bed and began to laugh so hard he started to drool, hitting the bed he sat on with his hand. I sat there feeling embarrassed, not sure why this was so funny. Then he said, "All nuns should have babies!" And then continued to howl with laughter.

I did manage to ask him what he meant, and he said, "Of the twenty-five main disciples of Guru Rinpoche, the great yogi who brought Buddhism to Tibet, only a few were monastics. It is not necessary to keep your ordination in order to keep practicing seriously. Look at me—I have four children, I'm increasing the dharma practitioners in this world!" And again he began to laugh.

Right at that moment, Paul came in and sat down. His face was glowing and his eyes were glistening. He was smiling at the joyful atmosphere in the room, not knowing what we were talking about. I took this as a sign, and decided to return my vows the next day. In the Tibetan tradition, if you do not want to keep your vows any longer, it is possible to return them to someone who holds them purely. And so I returned mine to the great teacher Khamtrul Rinpoche, who was hosting the empowerments. He was a pure monk and accepted my vows gently, suggesting I dedicate the merit of the time I had held the vows to benefit all beings and that I do a purification meditation practice to clear any negative karma from breaking the vows. It was the spring of 1973. After the empowerments finished, Paul, Apho and his family, and I all returned to Manali, a two-day journey into the Himalayas, where Lama Apho Rinpoche lived. Paul lived in a hut above mine. It was there that we consummated our relationship, and shortly afterward conceived our first child, Sherab.

The night of her conception we were sleeping in my cabin together for the first time. It was a wooden cabin with storage underneath and a low slate roof. We arranged our two sleeping bags, one under and one above, and added a few wool shawls and made pillows out of folded clothes. It was so strange to sleep with a man after four years alone, and that night I woke up experiencing myself as the dakini Vajra Yogini, a famous red dakini from the padma family who governs fire and passion. The feeling of bliss was so intense I woke Paul up and said to him with great intensity, "I am Vajra Yogini burning with unbearable bliss!"

He grunted and held me close, and we fell back asleep; but when we woke up in the morning, I said, "I just had a very intense dream."

He replied, "Me too! What was yours?"

I said, "It was bright and luminous, a large sphere of light, so bright, the top was white with an arch of blue at the center and the bottom was red flecks of light; in the middle was a U-shaped bump where the white and blue penetrated the red."

He listened in amazement and then said, "I had the exact same dream."

We painted it together the next day; it was such an extraordinary experience to have the same dream. That same day a wild iris with two large blossoms that was in a bottle on my shrine shelf built into the wall produced another tiny, perfect blossom. After that, I suspected it was a sign I had conceived. A week or so later I began to feel strange, both nauseated and craving meat after having been a vegetarian for twelve years. A few days later I went to a Tibetan doctor in Manali village who tested my urine and said I was pregnant. Later Stuart Hamill, an American artist and friend of mine who lived in Delhi and had studied Indian miniature painting using mineral pigments, copied our painting of the dream we'd shared of the conception. (See the Conception Mandala on page 2 of the photo insert.)

My oldest daughter, Sherab, who now has two sons of her own, still has that painting. It is an interesting image because in Tibetan Buddhism, the white represents the male essence and the red the female essence. You can see the penetration of the white part of the mandala into the red part like the penetration of the sperm into the egg—the coming together of the male and female essences. It intrigued me that these specific colors appeared in the dream, as dreams are really beyond this kind of conceptual knowledge.

Sometimes I say that I got pregnant five minutes after returning my vows! It was actually a few weeks later, but it felt that quick. We traveled from Manali to Delhi by bus; it was a two-day journey, and I was so tired and overwhelmed with the pregnancy that I fell asleep at the tea stops the bus made. In Delhi, I went to a doctor, and my pregnancy was confirmed. We got married in a dark hotel room in Delhi, and my friend Stuart had a reception for us at her (yes, a woman named Stuart) apartment.

We traveled back through Holland, where Paul was from, and I met his five brothers and sisters and his mother in Breda, in the southern part of the Netherlands, where he had grown up in an aristocratic Dutch family. Then we crossed the Atlantic to my parents' house on the lake in New Hampshire, and they had a wedding reception for us.

As a wedding present, they gave us a compact, forest-green Hornet, a hatchback car made by AMC. After a few weeks with them, we packed up the Hornet and drove across southern Canada to Seattle, camping along the way. We then settled into the berry-picker's cottage on Maury Island, a small island connected to Vashon Island, and prepared for the home birth, which I described in the Introduction.

After Sherab's birth, I went from having all my time to myself to taking care of Sherab, who was a very active baby. She would literally climb walls and rarely took naps even as an infant. I was exhausted, and then at six weeks she developed colic, so she cried for hours on end. The transition from being a nun to being a mother was not easy; there had been little time for living freely without my vows. And for several years afterward, I dreamt about being unable to decide what to wear—whether I should wear my nun's robes or my layperson's clothing. In many of the dreams, I would keep changing back and forth.

All the bliss and equanimity I had experienced as a nun went out the window when I became a mother, and I developed postpartum depression without knowing what it was. I would feel guilty about my sadness and longing for quiet alone time, feeling that I should be happy and grateful to have such a healthy, beautiful baby. Nine months after giving birth to her, I got pregnant with my second daughter, Aloka. She was also a home delivery on the island; but this time the doctor missed the ferry, so Paul and my friend Sally caught Aloka. The doctor arrived an hour later, and I was happily holding our newborn daughter.

When Aloka was a year old, we moved from Vashon Island back to Boulder. I began to teach at Naropa Institute (now Naropa University), and this brought some balance back into my life. In my time in Boulder, I received the empowerment from Trungpa Rinpoche for Vajra Varahi, a dakini mandala with a form of the Padma Dakini in the center. This was important in terms of my relationship with the dakinis, because for the first time I was immersing myself in a dakini mandala and identifying with the energy of the dakinis. It wasn't until I did this practice that I began to feel the potency of the dakinis through identifying with them, spending an hour a day deeply immersed in this mandala. It was a transformative experience, allowing me to access a strong archetype of the feminine that I had been longing for, and I found it powerful and energizing at a time in my life when I was swamped with diapers, night feedings, and chaotic days with little time to myself. Even though I often had to practice with Sherab and Aloka crawling over me and pulling things off my shrine, I managed to concentrate enough to feel the blessings and benefit of the mandala.

5

EXPLORING THE DAKINI PRINCIPLE

The Matriarchs served as conscientious guardians of the mystery, just as the stratum of matriarchal consciousness coming alive at present contains a treasure—a trove of well-guarded secrets, a welter of psychic seeds: a quiver, a bow, a cauldron, a spindle, a spoon, masks, mirrors, wreaths of string. . . . If the feminine link with the past is recovered, the old wise man, the worn Patriarch, can retire, leaving us face to face with the future.

—NOR HALL

When I was eleven, I ran home on the last day of school and tore off my dress, literally popping the buttons off, feeling simultaneously guilty and liberated. I put on an old, torn pair of cutoff jean shorts, a white T-shirt, and blue Keds sneakers, and ran with my sister into the woods behind our old colonial New Hampshire house. We went to play in the brook burbling down the steep hill over the mossy rocks, through the evergreens and deciduous trees, the water colored rich red-brown by the tannins in the leaves of the maple trees. We would play and catch foot-long white suckerfish with our hands, and then put them back because we didn't want to kill them.

Sometimes we swam naked at night with friends at our summerhouse in the spring-fed lake fifteen miles away, surrounded by pine,
birch, spruce, and maple trees. I loved the feeling of the water caress-
ing my skin like velvet, with the moon reflecting in the mirror-like
lake. My sister and my friend Joanie and I would get on our ponies
bareback and urge them into the lake until they were surging up and
down with water rushing over our thighs and down the backs of the
horses; they were swimming with us as we laughed, clinging onto
their backs.

When violent summer thunderstorms blew through, instead of
staying in the old wooden house, I would run and dance outside in
the rain and thunder, scaring my mother. I liked to eat with my fingers, gnawing on the pork chop bone and gulping down big glasses
of milk, in a hurry to get back outside. I loved gnawing on bones.
My mother would shake her head, saying in desperation, "Oh, dar-
ling, please, please eat with your fork! Heavens alive, I'm raising a
barbarian!"

Barbarian, I thought, *that sounds great!* I imagined women with
long hair streaming out behind them, racing their horses over wide
plains. I saw streaked sunrises on crisp mornings with no school,
waking up outside, and night fires with charred meat and lots of
bones to gnaw on. This wildness was so much a part of me; I could
never imagine living a life that didn't allow for it.

Now that I was a wife and mother raising two young daughters,
that wild young barbarian who'd connected so naturally to the dakini principle seemed lifetimes away. Paul and I had been married
for three years when we decided to move from Vashon Island back to
Boulder and join Trungpa Rinpoche's community. It was wonderful
to be in a big, active community with many young parents. However,
the strain of the early years, our inexperience, and our own individual growth led us to decide to separate and collaborate as co-parents.

In 1978, I had been a single mother for several years when I met
an Italian filmmaker, Costanzo Allione, who was directing a film on

the beat poets of Naropa University. He interviewed me because I was Allen Ginsberg's meditation instructor, and Allen, whom I had met when I was a nun in 1972, introduced me to Costanzo. In the spring of 1979, we were married in Boulder while he was finishing his film, which was called *Fried Shoes Cooked Diamonds*, and soon thereafter we moved to Italy. I got pregnant that summer while we were living in a trailer in an Italian campground on the ocean near Rome, and that fall we moved into a drafty summer villa in the Alban Hills near the town of Velletri outside of Rome.

When I was six months pregnant, my belly measured the size of a nine months pregnant woman's, so they did an ultrasound and discovered I was pregnant with twins. By this time I knew that my husband was a drug addict and unfaithful. I couldn't speak the native language and felt completely isolated. In March of 1980, I gave birth to twins, Chiara and Costanzo; they were a little early, but each weighed over five pounds. I buckled down to nursing two babies, caring for my other two daughters, and dealing with my husband's addiction, erratic mood swings, and physical abuse, which started during my pregnancy when he began to hit me.

My feelings of overwhelm and anxiety increased daily, and I began to wonder about how my life as a mother and a Western woman really connected with my Buddhist spirituality. How had things ended up like this? How had I lost that wild, independent girl and left my life as a nun, ending up in Italy with an abusive husband? It seemed that by choosing to disrobe, I had lost my path, and my self.

Then two months later, on June 1, 1980, I woke up from a night of broken sleep and stumbled into the room where Chiara and her brother Costanzo were sleeping. I nursed him first because he was crying, and then turned to her. She seemed very quiet. When I picked her up, I immediately knew: she felt stiff and light. I remembered the similar feeling from my childhood, picking up my small marmalade-colored kitten that had been hit by a car and crawled under a bush to die. Around Chiara's mouth and nose was purple bruising where blood had pooled; her eyes were closed, but her beautiful, soft amber hair was the same and she still smelled sweet. Her tiny body was there, but she was gone. Chiara had died of sudden infant death syndrome (SIDS).

Following Chiara's death came what I can only call a descent. I was filled with confusion, loss, and grief. Buffeted by raw, intense emotions, I felt more than ever that I desperately needed some female guidance. I needed to turn somewhere: to women's stories, to women teachers, to anything that would guide me as a mother, living this life of motherhood—to connect me to my own experience as a woman and as a serious Buddhist practitioner on the path. I needed the stories of dakinis. But I really didn't know where to turn. I looked into all kinds of resources, but I couldn't find my answers.

At some point in my search, the realization came to me: *I have to find them myself. I have to find their stories.* I needed to research the life stories of the Buddhist women of the past, and see if I could discover some thread, some key that would help unlock the answers about the dakinis and guide me through this passage. If I could find the dakinis, I would find my spiritual role models—I could see how they did it. I could see how they made the connections between mother, wife, and woman . . . how they integrated spirituality with everyday life challenges.

"If I could find the dakinis, I would find my spiritual role models—I could see how they did it. I could see how they made the connections between mother, wife, and woman . . . how they integrated spirituality with everyday life challenges."

About a year later, I was in California doing a retreat with my teacher, Namkhai Norbu Rinpoche, who was teaching a practice called Chöd that involved invoking the presence of one of the great female masters of Tibetan Buddhism, Machig Labdrön. And in this practice there is an invocation, where you visualize her as a young, dancing, sixteen-year-old white dakini. So there I was doing this practice with him, and for some reason that night he kept repeating it. We must have done it for several hours. Then during the section of the practice where we invoked Machig Labdrön, I suddenly had the vision of another female form emerging out of the darkness.

What I saw behind her was a cemetery from which she was emerging. She was old, with long, pendulous breasts that had fed many babies, golden skin, and gray hair that was streaming out. She was staring intensely at me, like an invitation and a challenge. At the same time, there was incredible compassion in her eyes. I was shocked because this woman wasn't what I was supposed to be seeing. Yet there she was, approaching very close to me, her long hair flowing, and looking at me so intensely. Finally, at the end of this practice, I went up to my teacher and said, "Does Machig Labdrön ever appear in any other forms?"

He looked at me and said, "Yes." He didn't say any more.

I went to bed that night and had a dream in which I was trying to get back to Swayambhu hill in Nepal, where I'd lived as a nun, and felt an incredible sense of urgency. I had to get back there and it wasn't clear why; at the same time, there were all kinds of obstacles. A war was going on, and I struggled through many barriers to finally reach the hill, but the dream didn't complete itself. I woke up still not knowing why I was trying to return.

The next night I had the same dream. It was slightly different, and the set of obstacles changed, but the urgency to get back to Swayambhu was just as strong. Then on the third night, I had the same dream again. It is really unusual to have the same dream again and again and again, and I finally realized that the dreams were trying to tell me I had to go back to Swayambhu; they were sending me a message. I spoke to my teacher about the dreams and asked, "Does this seem like maybe I should actually go there?"

He thought about it for a while; again, he simply answered, "Yes."

I decided to return to Nepal, to Swayambhu, to find the stories of women teachers. It took several months of planning and arrangements, a key part being to seek out the biographies of the great female Buddhist teachers. I would use the trip to go back to the source and find those yogini stories and role models I so desperately needed. I went alone, leaving my children in the care of my husband and his parents. It was an emotional and difficult decision, since I had never been away from my children; but there was a deep calling within me that I had to honor and trust.

Back in Nepal, I found myself walking up the very same staircase, one step after another, up the Swayambhu hill, which I had first climbed in 1967. Now it was 1982, and I was the mother of three. When I emerged at the top, a dear friend of mine was there to greet me, Gyalwa, a monk I had known since my first visit. It was as though he was expecting me. I told him I was looking for the stories of women, and he said, "Oh, the life stories of dakinis. Okay, come back in a few days."

And so I did. When I returned, I went into his room in the basement of the monastery and he had a huge Tibetan book in front of him, which was the life story of Machig Labdrön, who'd founded the Chöd practice and had emerged to me as a wild, gray-haired dakini in my vision in California. What evolved out of that was research, and eventually the birth of my book *Women of Wisdom*, which tells my story and provides the translation of six biographies of Tibetan teachers who were embodiments of great dakinis. The book was my link to the dakinis, and it also showed me that there was a real need, a longing for the stories of great women teachers, from the tremendous response the book received. It was a beautiful affirmation of the need for the sacred feminine.

In the research I did for *Women of Wisdom*, I looked more deeply into the dakinis. There is a section in the book called The Dakini Principle in which I write:

> Certain women are said to be emanations of the dakinis, and they have certain signs by which they can be recognized. Because wisdom is an inherent part of the energy, not a separate thing, which follows on a linear pattern, the enlightened aspect might escape from the surveillance of the ego at any moment and therefore everyone has the possibility of becoming a Buddha or a dakini on the spot. We could have little gaps in the claustrophobic game of dualism, and the clarity could shine through. Therefore even an ordinary "unenlightened" woman or situation could suddenly manifest as the dakini. The world is not as solid as we think it is, and the more we are open to the gaps, the more wisdom can shine through and the more the play of the dakini energy can be experienced. The primary way to relax the ego's grasp is to practice meditation. All Tantric visualizations and mantras are geared to freeing the energy of wisdom, which is being suffocated under the solidified fantasies of dualistic fixation.[31]

HISTORICAL CONTEXT OF THE DAKINI

During the process of writing *Women of Wisdom*, I had to do research on the history of the feminine in Buddhism. What I discovered was that for the first thousand years in Buddhism, there were few rep-

resentations of the sacred feminine, although there were women in
the Buddhist *sangha* (community) as nuns and lay householder devo-
tees, and the Buddha's wife and the stepmother who raised him had
a somewhat elevated status; but there were no female buddhas and
no feminine principle, and certainly no dakinis. It was not until the
traditional Mahayana Buddhist teachings joined with the Tantric
teachings, and developed into Vajrayana or Tantric Buddhism in
the eighth century, that we began to see the feminine emerge with a
larger role.

Before we continue, I want to distinguish here between neo-
Tantra and more traditional Tantric Buddhism. Most people these
days who see the word *Tantra* think about neo-Tantra, which has developed in the West as a form of "sacred sexuality" derived from, but
deviating significantly from, traditional Buddhist or Hindu Tantra.
Neo-Tantra offers a view of sexuality that contrasts with the repres-
sive attitude toward sexuality as nonspiritual and profane.

Buddhist Tantra, also known as Vajrayana (Indestructible Vehicle), is much more complex than neo-Tantra and embedded in
meditation, deity yoga, and mandalas, yoga with an emphasis on
the necessity of a spiritual teacher and transmission. I will use the
words Tantra and Vajrayana interchangeably throughout this book.
Tantra uses the creative act of visualization, sound, and hand gestures (mudras) to engage our whole being in the process of meditation. It is a practice of complete engagement and embodiment of
our whole being. And within Buddhist Tantra, often sexuality is
used as a metaphor for the union of wisdom and skillful means. Although sexual practice methods exist, Buddhist Tantra is a rich and
complex spiritual path with a long history, whereas neo-Tantra is
an extraction from traditional Tantric sexual practices with some
additions that have nothing to do with it. So here when I say Tantra
or Vajrayana, I am referring not to neo-Tantra but to traditional
Buddhist Tantra.

"Tantra uses the creative act of visualization, sound, and hand gestures (mudras) to engage our whole being in the process of meditation. It is a practice of complete engagement and embodiment of our whole being."

Tantric Buddhism arose in India during the Pala Empire, whose kings ruled India primarily between the eighth and eleventh centuries CE. Remember that Buddhism had already existed for more than a thousand years by this time, so Vajrayana was a late development in the history of Buddhism. The union of Buddhism and Tantra was considered to be in many ways the crown jewel of the Pala period.

Although the origins of Buddhist Tantra are still being debated by scholars, it seems that it arose out of very ancient pre-Aryan roots represented in Shaktism and Saivism combining with Mahayana Buddhism. Though there is still scholarly debate about the origins of Vajrayana, Tibetans say it was practiced and taught by the Buddha. If we look at the Pala period beginning in the eighth century, we find a situation where the Buddhist monks have been going along for more than a thousand years, and they have become very intellectually astute, developing various schools of sophisticated philosophy, Buddhist universities, and a whole culture connected to Buddhism that is very strong and alive. But at this point the monks have also become involved with politics, and have begun to own land and animals, and to receive jewels and other riches as gifts from wealthy patrons. They also have become rather isolated from the lay community, living a sort of elite, intellectual, and rather exclusive existence.

The Tantric revolution—and it was a revolution in the sense of a major turning point—took place within that context. When the Tantric teachings joined Buddhism, we see the entrance of the lay community, people who were working in the everyday world, doing ordinary jobs and raising children. They might come from any walk of life: jewelers, farmers, shopkeepers, royalty, cobblers, blacksmiths, wood gatherers, to name a few. They worked in various kinds of occupations, including housewives. They were not monks who had isolated themselves from worldly life, and their spiritual practice reflected their experiences. There are many early tales, called the *Siddha Stories*, of people who lived and worked in ordinary situations, and who by turning their life experiences into a spiritual practice achieved enlightenment.

There are also some stories of enlightened women practitioners and teachers in early Buddhism. We see a blossoming of women gurus, and also the presence of female buddhas and of course the dakinis. In many stories, these women taught the intellectual monks in a very direct, juicy way by uniting spirituality with sexuality; they taught based on using, rather than renouncing, the senses. Their teachings took the learned monks out of the monastery into real life with all its rawness, which is why several of the Tantric stories begin with a monk in a monastic university who has a visitation from a woman that drives him out in search of something beyond the monastic walls.

Tantric Buddhism has a genre of literature called "praise of women" in which the virtues of women are extolled. From the *Candamaharosana Tantra*: "When one speaks of the virtues of women, they surpass those of all living beings. Wherever one finds tenderness or protectiveness, it is in the minds of women. They provide sustenance to friends and strangers alike. A woman who is like that is as glorious as Vajrayogini herself."[32]

There is no precedent for this in Buddhist literature, but in Buddhist Tantric texts, writings urge respect for women, and stories about the negative results of failing to recognize the spiritual qualities of women are present. And in fact, in Buddhist Tantra, the fourteenth root of downfall is the failure to recognize all women as the embodiment of wisdom.

In the Tantric period, there was a movement abolishing barriers to women's participation and progress on the spiritual path, offering a vital alternative to the monastic universities and ascetic traditions. In this movement, one finds women of all castes, from queens and princesses to outcasts, artisans, winemakers, pig herders, courtesans, and housewives.

For us today, this is important as we are looking for female models of spirituality that integrate and empower women, because most of us will not pursue a monastic life, yet many of us have deep spiritual longings. Previously excluded from teaching men or holding positions of leadership, women—for whom it was even questioned whether they could reach enlightenment—were now pioneering, teaching, and assuming leadership roles, shaping and inspiring a revolutionary movement. There were no institutional barriers preventing women from excelling in this tradition. There was no religious law or priestly caste defining their participation. As Professor Miranda Shaw's book *Passionate Enlightenment* notes:

> Tantric yogis and yoginis assembled in a network of pilgrimage sites throughout India, where they met other Tantrics and practiced their outer and inner yogas, and staged elaborate rituals. In this open and freewheeling religious setting, there were no formal barriers to the participation of women. Tantric sources express no prohibition of women's full participation alongside men or assumption of leadership and authority over men.[33]

At the same time, the Tantric Buddhist movement shows powerful partnerships between men and women as co-practitioners on the spiritual path, with intimacy as one key component on the path to enlightenment. Below is a passage from the *Candamaharosana Tan-*

tra, in which Vajra Yogini describes how she should be worshipped in the context of a yogi and yogini practicing together that reflects a gynocentric-erotic experience written from the female point of view. In this yogini teaching, the text alternates between the third person and the first person, indicating the shift from the personal to the transpersonal experience that they both are having.

The couple are directed to go into seclusion; they gaze into each other's eyes until their concentration is one-pointed, and then she pulls him to her, saying that he should worship her and obey her. She then draws him to her to kiss him, and directs his mouth between her thighs and guides him to offer her pleasure:

> *Constantly take refuge at my feet dear . . .*
> *Be gracious, beloved, and*
> *Give me pleasure with your diamond scepter.*
> *Look at my three-petaled lotus,*
> *Its center adorned with a stamen.*
> *It is a Buddha paradise, adorned with the red Buddha,*
> *A cosmic mother who bestows*
> *Bliss and tranquility on the passionate.*
> *Abandon all conceptual thought and*
> *Unite with my reclining form;*
> *Place my feet upon your shoulders and*
> *Look me up and down.*
> *Make the fully awakened scepter*
> *Enter the opening in the center of the lotus.*
> *Move a hundred, thousand, hundred thousand times*
> *In my three-petaled lotus*
> *Of swollen flesh.*
> *Placing one's scepter there, offer pleasure to her mind.*
> *Wind, inner wind—my lotus is the unexcelled!*
> *Aroused by the tip of the diamond scepter,*
> *It is red like a bandhuka flower.*[34]

He is instructed to be free of discursive thoughts and lust, and to maintain a clear state of concentration, to worship until she is fully satisfied. Then he can refresh himself with wine and food after he has served her as his goddess. The text also describes a variety of positions of erotic pleasure and is imbued with a sense of unashamed sensuality and mutual pleasure. This kind of intimate offering is called "secret offering" or "secret worship" to activate her sexual fluid, which he drinks as nectar; the term *sukra* is used for both the male and female sexual fluids, although previously it was always given as semen in androcentric translations. The female nectar is also called "flower water" or *madhu*, which means "sweet, honey, nectar, or wine."[35]

As I mentioned before, the word for *dakini* in Tibetan is *khandro*, which means "she who moves through space," sometimes called a "sky dancer" or a "sky goer"; this refers to the energy that integrates itself with emptiness—not emptiness in the sense of an empty pocket or empty cup, but the emptiness of self or emptiness of ego. It's the feminine energy that enters emptiness, moving through it, a messenger of it. The dakinis thus became messengers of wisdom, embodiments of wisdom, and energies that practitioners could invoke and with whom they could create a positive relationship. As Miranda Shaw writes:

> Terms used to designate female Tantrics are all honorific titles denoting the religious seriousness and meditative attainments. Foremost among the terms are yogini, *dakini*, messenger, and heroine. "Yogini" means a female practitioner of yoga or ritual arts, a female being with magical powers, or a type of female deity. The term *dakini* eludes precise definition but is translatable as "sky-walker," "woman who flies," or "female sky dancer," highlighting the flights of spiritual insight, ecstasy and freedom from worldliness granted by realization of emptiness. Female

Tantrics are sometimes called "female messengers" because they deliver success in all endeavors, both trans-
worldly and mundane.[36]

When the Tantric Buddhist ideas of the dakinis migrated to
Tibet in the eighth century, the energy of the feminine was firmly
embedded in the wisdom dakini principle, becoming a prominent sacred manifestation of the feminine. Their powers as guides, protectors, messengers, and enhancers of spiritual experience increased in
Tibet, where a relationship with the dakini became key for both male
and female practitioners.

Another interesting aspect of the worldly dakinis, which has rel-
evance in today's world, is the way they protect the environment and
react wrathfully when it is polluted, causing pestilence and illness,
because worldly dakinis do not have the level of realization that the
wisdom dakinis hold. In *The Hundred Thousand Songs of Milarepa*
there is a story about Milarepa healing a worldly dakini who is ill. She
explains her malaise as a reaction to the polluting smoke and that she
vengefully had caused illness in the village. She is a worldly dakini
who has become Milarepa's student, and this experience occurs during her training. He admonishes her not to be so revengeful. After
she tells him what rituals will heal her, he goes to the villagers and
tells them that the pestilence in their area was caused by a local dakini whom they had offended with their smoky fires. He gives them
the instructions for rituals and offerings that the dakini requested,
and through the power of these prayers and blessings the pestilence
and the dakini are rapidly cured. This story illustrates the effect of a
reciprocal relationship between the dakinis and humans.[37]

Her story makes me think about all the pollution creating cancers
and lung diseases we have today, and the disrespectful way the earth
has been treated: "According to the reciprocal-relation principle of
the Law of Causation, when we recover from a disease, so will the
people. It is the common oath of all worldly dakinis that if one of

us has been made unwell or unhappy, we are all offended and the Devas and spirit support us, throwing the world into confusion."[38] The idea of interdependence expressed in the statement "if one of us has been made unwell or unhappy, we are all offended" is relevant to the interconnection of illness, weather, disruption, and toxins in the environment.

The climate change crisis is actually a crisis of relationship; we have been in an abusive relationship with life on earth. As in the story of Milarepa's student, the wrathful dakini, we are experiencing the revenge of the worldly dakinis. However, as this story also illustrates, it is possible to come back into right relationship with the earth through the dakinis, and if we do so, we will be healed.

THE DAKINI'S SYMBOLS AND ORNAMENTS

Another important part of the Tantric practice is the use of symbols surrounding and being held by the deities. (See the Five Wisdom Dakinis Thangka image on page 140.) These symbols have specific meanings, which the practitioner is familiarized with through his or her teacher. The Tantric practitioner holds these symbolic meanings in mind while doing the visualization. Although we won't go into each of the symbols associated with the dakini mandala specifically in each of the meditations that follow, I'd like you to know what they are so you can keep them in mind, because the symbolic meaning is a very important part of the visualization. I wrote this in *Women of Wisdom* about the dakini:

By consciously invoking the dakini through the Tantric practices we begin to develop a sensitivity to energy itself. When looking at the iconography of the dakini we should bear in mind that through understanding her symbols and identifying with her, we are identifying with our own energy. Tantric divinities are used because we are in a dualistic state. Vajrayana takes advantage of that, or exaggerates it, by embodying an external figure with all the qualities the practitioner wishes to obtain. After glorifying and worshiping this external deity, the deity dissolves into the practitioner—then at the end of any Vajrayana sadhana there is a total dissolution of the deity into space; and finally after resting in that state, the practitioner visualizes herself or himself as a deity again as they go about their normal activities and dedicates the merit of the meditation to all sentient beings.[39]

The first and probably most commonly associated symbol of the dakini is what's called the *trigug* in Tibetan, the *kartari* in Sanskrit, and in English, "the hooked knife." This is a crescent-shaped knife with a hook on the end of the blade and a handle that is ornamented with different symbols. It's modeled from the Indian butcher's knife and sometimes called a "chopper." There are two aspects of this knife: the handle and the blade. The handle can have a variety of symbols at the end of it—in the case of the five dakinis, the handle bears the appropriate symbol for the particular buddha family: a wheel for buddha family, a vajra (thunderbolt scepter) for vajra family, a jewel for ratna family, a lotus for padma family, and both the double vajra and sword for karma family. As we go through the practices that follow, you'll see that each dakini has her family's symbol on the handle of her knife.

The hook on the end of the blade is called the "hook of compassion." It's the hook that pulls sentient beings out of the ocean of suffering. The blade cuts through self-clinging, and through the dualistic split into the great bliss. The cutting edge of the knife is representative of the cutting quality of wisdom, the wisdom that cuts through self-deception.

To me it is a powerful symbol of the wise feminine, because I find that often women tend to hang on too long and not cut through what needs to be cut through. We may hang on to relationships that are unhealthy, instead of ending what needs to be ended. The hooked knife is held in the dakini's raised right hand; she must grasp this power and be ready to strike. The blade is the shape of the crescent moon, and the time of the month associated with the dakini is ten days after the full moon, when the waning moon appears as a crescent at dawn;

The *trigug* with a vajra handle in Tibetan, the *kartari* or "hooked knife" in Sanskrit, a crescent-shaped knife that symbolizes cutting through self-clinging into the great bliss. *Photograph by Clinton Spence*

this is the twenty-fifth day of the lunar cycle and is called Dakini Day in the Tibetan calendar. When I come out early on those days and it is still dark, I look up and see the crescent moon; it always reminds me of the dakini's knife.

The second symbol associated with the dakini is the skull cup. The skull cup holds the nectar of nondual knowledge. It's a symbol of emptiness, and serves as the cauldron of transformation. In centuries past, yogis and yoginis lived in the charnel grounds, where corpses were brought and cremated or fed to the jackals. They would make huts out of skulls, and musical instruments and ornaments out of bones. They would eat and drink out of human skulls as cups. So you can see this is a very primal image of impermanence. When you are eating out of a skull cup, somebody else's skull, you're very much reminded of your own vulnerability, of your own inevitable death, which could come at any moment.

To us this might seem a bit gruesome, but there is something powerful about facing that which we tend to avoid and making it an ornament—a powerful transformation of repressed fear and attachment. Death tends to be hidden, sanitized, and denied in our Western culture. Often doctors with terminal patients won't even say the word "death" to their patients.

In Buddhism, death is faced and acknowledged, in order that we make the most of our time here and can face death with no regrets. One of the core Buddhist teachings is: We are all going to die, but we do not know when, how, or where. This meditation on impermanence goes back to the time of the Buddha, when he would send the monks into the charnel grounds to sit with corpses and meditate on impermanence.

The skull cup takes us to the immediacy of this reality. It is also the cauldron of transformation. The cauldron has a long association with the feminine. The womb cauldron that magically creates life. Women work with the liquids of blood and milk; the liquid in the skull cup is often blood, symbolizing the transformation of our "blood" karma, what we have karmically inherited through our blood, our genetic history.

In some images, we find the knife held above the skull, as though the dakini is chopping. This represents her grinding and chopping negativities and transforming them into this nectar of bliss and emptiness. And then she shares the contents with others from the skull cup. Even today, if you go to a traditional initiation, at the end of the initiation you'll be served from a skull cup, a nectar that will probably have a base of something like red wine or whiskey infused with blessed substances. This again symbolizes the blood of transformation. When you drink from the skull cup, it symbolizes that you're taking in the wisdom, which represents the feminine. And you'll also be served food, which always contains some

The skull cup symbol of impermanence holds the nectar of nondual knowledge, a symbol of impermanence and the transformation of desire.
Photograph by Laura Vitale

kind of meat, symbolizing the masculine—skillful means. And the reason for the meat and wine is that this is the Tantric path of transformation—of consuming the poisons and transforming them into wisdom.

The Tantric feast is a very important part of the Vajrayana practice because, once again, we're in a practice that uses all the senses. And we are in the alchemical process of transformation of what is considered to be impure into equal value, or really going beyond concepts of pure and impure, as the Tantric feast illustrates. Tantric methods were created to cut through conventional ideas of purity that were prevalent in India at the time, to shock or repel, to invoke the hidden limits that we don't admit. Foods that would have been considered impure or forbidden, such as meat and wine, were essential components of the Tantric feast.

At the feast, spontaneous poetry would be recited with insights into the nature of reality often masked in metaphor or sometimes language with hidden meaning called the "twilight language" or the language of the dakinis. The type of poetry that was composed at these elaborately arranged feasts, with yogis and yoginis sitting in circles and practicing mandala meditations while eating and drinking, was called the *doha*. Sometimes the poems were enigmatic, like this one from a dakini called Tree-Leaf Woman:

> *Who speaks the sound of an echo?*
> *Who paints the image in a mirror?*
> *Where are the spectacles in a dream?*
> *Nowhere at all—*
> *That's the nature of mind!*[40]

The effect of the doha is to create a mental paradox, a state of confusion where logic is defeated, and we must enter through another way of knowing. This is the gate to the mysterious home of the dakini through language.

Top of *khatvanga* staff, symbol of the inner consort. Under the *vajra* (at the top), which symbolizes the masculine, are three human heads: The top one symbolizes formless enlightenment (*dharmakaya*); the second symbolizes the body of enjoyment, the dimension of luminosity (*sambhogakaya*); and the third symbolizes the dimension of embodied enlightenment (*nirmanakaya*). *Photograph by Matthew Cannella*

The dakini also holds a staff in the crook of her left arm. This symbolic staff is called the *khatvanga*. Its essential meaning is that of "hidden consort" or "inner consort." It represents the dakini's inner masculine, and at the top of the staff is a vajra symbolizing the phallus. The staff is an interesting metaphor because it can be a tent pole, a protective spear, or a walking staff. With it, she has the power to stand alone; she has internalized the masculine.

Under the vajra at the top there are three human heads. The top one is a dried skull. This symbolizes the *dharmakaya*, which is the formless body of enlightenment. The second head on the staff is several weeks old. This symbolizes the *sambhogakaya*, or the body of enjoyment, which is the dimension of luminosity. The third is a freshly severed human head. This is the *nirmanakaya*, which is the embodied enlightenment that we find in this dimension, in our world, such as the Buddha or the Dalai Lama. This is a good example of how in Tantra things that sometimes appear disgusting or impure have the opposite meaning. For example, these three skulls are conventionally considered to be repulsive, but the meaning is quite the opposite, describing the three spiritual dimensions, or the three *kayas*.

Under the three kayas, there is what's called a double vajra, or double *dorje*, symbolizing indestructibility.

The khatvanga staff also has two scarves on it. The scarves represent the union of Mahayana and Vajrayana: the Mahayana path of compassion and the Vajrayana path of transformation. So essentially the function of this staff is as a support, a spear that protects, and a stake. This is the dakini's impersonal yang energy, her masculine, which makes firm, which nails down; this is the strength of skillful means and compassion, which she has integrated into herself. I find the khatvanga a really important and potent symbol for women: it shows the integration of a woman who can give and receive in relationship, because she's coming from a stance of wholeness. She does not need to find the masculine outside herself; she holds it within. So she's not Sleeping Beauty waiting to be awakened by Prince Charming. She's already awake, she's dancing, she's empowered, and she has her staff. Having this integration helps her to avoid indiscriminate and unwise relationships. Her mind can be turned within, resting in the ultimate nature, experiencing the union of wisdom and compassion. When my husband David died, my son had a magnificent khatvanga made for me depicted in these khatvanga images. He said, "Mom, this is so you know you have Dave near you always."

The other thing about the dakinis is that they are dancing. So this is an expression when all bodily movements become the expression of enlightened mind. All activities express awakening. Dance is also an expression of inner ecstasy. She has her right leg raised and her left leg extended. The raised right leg symbolizes absolute truth. The extended left leg rests on the ground, symbolizing the relative truth, the truth about being in the world, the conventional truth.

She's also naked, so what does that mean? She symbolizes naked awareness—the unadorned truth, free from deception. And she is standing on a corpse, which symbolizes that she has overcome self-clinging; the corpse represents the ego. She has overcome her own ego. And again, it also refers back to the charnel grounds.

The dakini is wearing a crown of five dried skulls. This symbolizes that although each dakini embodies one of the five wisdoms, each one really contains all five. The last feature of the dakini is her bone jewelry, gathered from the charnel ground bones and carved into ornaments: she wears anklets, a belt like an apron around her waist, necklaces, armbands, and bracelets. Each one of these has various meanings, but the essential meaning of all the bone ornaments is to remind us of renunciation and impermanence. She's going beyond convention; fear of death has become an ornament to wear. We think of jewels as gold or silver or something pretty, but she's taken that which is considered repulsive and turned it into an ornament. This is the transformation of the obstructed patterns into wisdom, taking what we fear and expressing it as an ornament.

THE DAKINI FEMININE ENERGY

At the time when I first learned about the dakinis and the Mandala of the Five Dakinis, I started doing a meditation practice from Sapchu Rinpoche, the lama from Swayambhu Kagyu monastery whom I studied with after my ordination, that involved Vajra Yogini and the four retinue dakinis, representing the four directions of the mandala.

Since I had only heard about the dakinis a few times in a cursory way, I asked Sapchu Rinpoche, "What is a dakini?"

He replied, "There are many kinds of dakinis, both worldly and wisdom dakinis. The wisdom dakinis are the same level as buddhas; the worldly dakinis can have enlightened aspects but also worldly aspects. Sometimes the dakinis operate as messengers, sometimes as guides, sometimes as protectors. In the dakini practice we develop a way to access the unique and powerful energy of the wisdom dakinis."

I asked, "What kind of messenger is the dakini?"

Sapchu Rinpoche paused for a moment, and then replied, "The dakini is a messenger of emptiness and also appears in dreams to guide the meditator, and she might appear in real life as a woman with certain wisdom qualities and marks on her body, like a mole in a certain place on her face. The dakini is a force of truth . . . wherever we cling, she cuts; whatever we think we can hide, she reveals."

As I began to practice the dakini mandala, I began to sense a power within myself that I had not ever allowed myself to feel. The idea of an enlightened, sacred feminine energy that was also naked, dancing, and fierce was something I had never experienced, and it touched me deeply. I couldn't put into words the effect it had on me, but it was something significant and new.

In this book, I've chosen to work with the fierce dancing dakinis, who embody and activate the powerful and transformative energy of the feminine. When you think about it, we really don't have that kind of image of spiritual enlightenment in our world. We have a figure like the Holy Virgin Mother, who is peaceful and nonthreatening, but we don't have many reflections of female divinity that are active, dancing, fierce, free, and wild. So by activating the dakini power within us, we will have an inner resource that should never be underestimated. What we're really doing is taking a part of the psyche that's been relegated to the unconscious, the fierce, powerful feminine who has become repressed, and we are bringing that energy forward and exploring that energy's potential for enlightenment.

The dakinis tend to push us through blockages. They appear during challenging, crucial moments when we might be stymied in our lives; perhaps we don't know what to do next and we are in transition. Maybe an obstacle has arisen and we can't figure out how to get around or get through—then the dakinis will guide us. If in some way we're stuck, the dakinis will appear and open the way, push us through; sometimes the energy needs to be forceful, and that's when the wrathful manifestation of a dakini appears.

"The dakinis tend to push us through blockages. They appear during challenging, crucial moments when we might be stymied in our lives; perhaps we don't know what to do next and we are in transition."

Often the dreams of the dakinis will come at dawn, or they will appear in cemeteries at sunset or dawn—cemeteries being very important symbols of the liminal space between worlds, the twilight hour, which is in fact why the language of the dakinis is a symbolic one called the twilight language. As I wrote in *Women of Wisdom*: "Twilight is the time between waking and sleeping, the conscious and the unconscious. It is a time when the switchover takes place, so there could be a gap, a crack in the wall of the ever-protective ego structure where significant communication from something beyond could take place. At dawn we are still beyond the limiting forces of the conscious mind, yet the heavy veil of deep sleep has lifted. We often find the dakini at these transitional points, when we are open to the 'twilight' language."[41]

There's a wonderful example of a dream at dawn that came to Machig Labdrön's mother at the time that she conceived Machig, who was born in 1055 and became one of the greatest Tibetan female teachers. In her mother's dream, four white dakinis appear, surrounding her and carrying four white vases. They pour the vases of water in through the crown of her head and it descends through her whole body, and she feels purified; then other dakinis of various colors come around her and say, "Honor the mother, stay well, our mother-to-be."[42]

When Machig's mother awoke from this dream, she had a sensation of bliss in her body and had no pain, and she felt that her life had been altered. Then she realized that she was pregnant. This is an example of a very important dream. We might not have dreams that are as dramatic as this, but we may have dreams that signify a transition, where something is being pushed through an obstacle.

Another important aspect of the dakini's feminine energy, which I have touched on before, is how they cut through notions of pure and impure, clean and unclean, what you should do and shouldn't do; they break open the shell of those conventional structures into an embrace of all life in which all experience is seen as sacred. If we look at the early stories of Tantric Buddhism, there are all kinds of examples of situations where people are presented with something they perceive to be impure, and then a dakini appears and cuts through that and says, "If you're seeing this as pure or impure, you're clearly not understanding the point."

There's a story of the monk Abhayakaragupta, an accomplished Hindu scholar. He has not yet become a Buddhist when a low-caste woman appears at his door, asking him to have sex. Horrified, he tells her he can't touch her, never mind have sex, or he will be defiled. He chases her away, afraid someone will see him talking to her and he will be criticized for having contact with a low-caste woman. Before she leaves, she tells him to go to a certain place to receive Tantric Buddhist initiation, but he doesn't follow her suggestion.

Then after he becomes a Buddhist monk, a young girl comes to him and offers him raw meat. He is disgusted by this offer and refuses. Sometime later when he is already in his Tantric apprenticeship, he has a third encounter. His guru's female attendant, who usually brings him his water, comes to his room and offers to do a Tantric feast with him. When he turns her down, she orders him to do so, giving him another chance. But he is oblivious of who she really is and refuses again. Then she chastises him and tells him that since he has failed to recognize Vajra Yogini three times, he has missed his chance to attain enlightenment during this lifetime.

The wisdom dakini Vajra Yogini sent her emanations to him three times; but, caught in ideas of pure and impure, he failed to recognize her. Her tests challenged his preconceptions and prejudices to recognize the dakini, but he failed. He was worshipping the divine feminine in his meditations, but did not recognize and honor her human manifestation.

You can see here how, although this happened many, many years ago in India, it's not that different in our lives now. We're always encountering situations in which we're liking or disliking things. We like or dislike foods. We like or dislike places. We like or dislike people. We think something is pure or something is impure; something is dirty or something is clean. These beliefs of duality are all things that the dakinis break through, even those golden rules of celibacy and vegetarianism practiced by the monks. They open and embrace all phenomena, recognizing all phenomena as "one taste," as equal.

Practicing Tibetan Buddhism more deeply, I came to realize that the dakinis are the undomesticated female energies—spiritual and erotic, ecstatic and wise, playful and profound, fierce and peaceful—that are beyond the grasp of the conceptual mind. There is a place for our whole feminine being, in all its guises, to be present.

6

ENLIGHTENMENT
THROUGH EMBODIMENT

*As the psychically enclosed, sanctified space in which enlighten-
ment unfolds, the mandala can also refer to the vulva of the female
consort or the drop of sexual fluid held at the tip of the phallus of
the male consort. These bodily mandalas are also sites for ritual
practice, because they are "locations" for traversing the higher
reaches of the perfection stages, the threshold of Buddhahood.*

—MIRANDA SHAW

My old friend Jetsunma Tenzin Palmo, an Englishwoman ordained as a Tibetan Buddhist nun a few years before me, studied under the great Lama Khamtrul Rinpoche, who oversaw the
Tashi Jong Tibetan refugee community in the Kangra Valley, near
Dharamsala where the Dalai Lama settled. She and I met in 1972
when I was a nun and attending the annual three-day Lama Dances
in Tashi Jong. Later, she did a twelve-year retreat in a cave in an Indian Himalayan province called Lahaul, which is known in Tibetan
as Garsha Khandroling, Land of the Dakinis.

Garsha Khandroling was the destination of many Tibetan pilgrims. It is a very blessed place with mountains sacred to the Buddhist deities Vajra Yogini and Chakrasamvara, and other sacred sites. There are certain areas in the Himalayas considered to be densely imbued with the energy of the dakinis, both within the human beings who inhabit the areas and in the spiritual dimensions; Lahaul is such a place.

Lahauli women in their traditional dress.
Photograph by Anil Yadav

When Tenzin Palmo was looking for a place to do her long retreat, she was aided by the dakinis. This story gives you an idea of how the dakinis can act as guides, and it was recorded for the book that Vicki Mackenzie eventually wrote about her twelve years in a cave called *Cave in the Snow*. Tenzin Palmo moved to remote Lahaul to do her long retreat and began living in a hut by the other nuns near the town, but found it noisy and unsatisfactory for the depth of meditation she wished to pursue:

"After six years she had had enough. 'I had gone to Lahaul to meditate, not to have a swinging social life!' she said. 'I decided I had to move out, to find somewhere quieter. So I went up above the monastery to look for a place I could build a small house.' Up in the mountains she called upon the dakinis, those ethereal Buddhist spirits, known for their wildness, their power, and their willingness to come to the aid of practitioners, to come to her aid. She had always had a particularly intimate relationship with them. Now she approached them in her own inimitable way: 'Look here—if you find me a suitable place to do a retreat, then on my side I promise I will try to practice,' she prayed. 'I felt very positive about it, very happy. I was sure something was going to happen,' she commented."[43]

Her story follows that she went to consult with one of the nuns. From the conversation, Tenzin Palmo quickly realized it would be difficult to acquire the money and materials to build her house, so the nun suggested she look for a cave instead. The nun remembered a cave up on the mountain with a source of water nearby. The next day, Tenzin Palmo gathered together a group of people, including the head lama of the monastery, and set off up the mountain in search of the cave the nun had heard about.

Led by her intuition, she found an overhanging rock with a ledge that overlooked the Bhaga River and the valley below, and it had a spring not far away burbling out of some rocks at 13,200 feet above sea level. Straight in front of her at the summit of the mountain was a black rock formation called Lady of Keylong, appearing to be a woman holding a baby to her breast. To the native Lahaulis, she looked like a Black Tara, but to the Western eye like a Black Madonna. Not far from the cave was a sacred place of the powerful Buddhist protectress Palden Lhamo, traditionally depicted riding on a mule. And several years later Tenzin Palmo found mule prints embedded in the snow there, with no footprints leading to or from the holy spot.

The dakinis had brought her to a place imbued with the sacred feminine, and she stayed for twelve years. At one point she almost died when she was snowed in and unable to open her cave door, but she persevered and was eventually able to open it. Then later she founded a nunnery in Kangra Valley called Dongyu Gatsal Ling, leading Himalayan women in the yogini tradition of her teacher, Khamtrul Rinpoche.

Jetsunma Tenzin Palmo, who was guided by the dakinis to the cave where she spent twelve years. *Photograph by Olivier Adam*

Tenzin Palmo was asked to define the dakini: "To me the special female quality (which of course many men have as well) is first of all a sharpness, a clarity. . . . To me the Dakini principle stands for the intuitive force. Women get it in a flash—they're not interested in intellectual discussion which they normally find dry and cold with minimum appeal."[44]

When I was asked the same question for Michaela Haas's book *Dakini Power*, I said, "The dakinis are the most important element of the enlightened feminine in Tibetan Buddhism. . . . They are the luminous, subtle, spiritual energy, the key, the gatekeeper, the guardian of the unconditioned state. If we are not willing to invite the dakini into our life, then we cannot enter into the subtle states of mind. Sometimes the dakinis appear as messengers, sometimes as guides, and sometimes as protectors. . . . Dakinis have a quality of playfulness, expressing emptiness and pulling the rug out from under you. This feminine quality of seduction and play makes you insecure and yet open."[45]

One of the first stories I read when I studied Tibetan Buddhism at nineteen was about the effect of an old hag dakini, who pulled the rug out from under a great scholar, Naropa (1016–1100), a teacher in the Tantric tradition in India. He became the abbot of the prestigious Buddhist University of Nalanda. He was a brilliant intellectual who had become a monk after renouncing his marriage, saying that his wife had faults.

One day he was sitting outside with his back to the sun, studying books on grammar, epistemology, and logic, when a terrifying shadow fell across the pages. Looking up, he saw an old hag. Because of his training in logic, he immediately analyzed thirty-seven ugly features.

She asked him if he understood what he was reading. When he said yes, she asked the key question: "Do you understand the words or the sense?" When he answered that he understood the words, she was delighted and began to dance, waving her stick in the air.

When Naropa saw this, he thought he would make her even happier and said, "I also understand the sense." Hearing this, she began to cry and threw down her stick.

When he inquired why she was so upset, she responded, "I was happy because you told the truth when you said you understand the words, but sad when you said you also understand the sense because you lied!"

Then he asked, "Who understands the meaning?"

"My brother, Tilopa," she answered, and disappeared into a rainbow.

Whenever Naropa made mistakes in his search for Tilopa, which was often, the voice of his guru from the sky would say:

"Look into the mirror of your mind,
The mysterious home of the dakini."

I have always loved this passage, which is repeated several times as he goes through the process of trying to find Tilopa. What is the "mirror of the mind" that is the "mysterious home of the dakini"? This was the question that he was asked to contemplate again and again as he kept missing the point. For example, as he set out to look for his guru, he came upon a mangy dog full of maggots lying in the middle of the road. Naropa was so intent on his search that he jumped over it, and at that moment the dog disappeared into a rainbow in the sky, and he heard a voice that said:

"Look into the mirror of your mind,
The mysterious home of the dakini.
Without compassion you will never find the guru."[46]

The mind is like a mirror because the primordial state of sentient beings, the ground of being, is the unadulterated awareness. It is stainless because it is naturally pure from the beginningless beginning, everything unborn and unstained; this is mysterious because it's beyond our conceptual mind. It does not judge, does not alter itself due to experiences. Nothing can sully it, although it can be obscured, just as the sun may be hidden behind clouds but it never changes and is simply obscured temporarily.

When we can embrace her and surrender to the inner dakini as our own innate wisdom, as an agent of enlightenment seeking to free us from the clutches of ego, she becomes our greatest ally. She becomes a compassionate support, a refuge, and a mother, but she will tolerate no self-clinging, no egocentric fixation, and she is never deceived.

"When we can embrace her and surrender to the inner dakini as our own innate wisdom, as an agent of enlightenment seeking to free us from the clutches of ego, she becomes our greatest ally."

We are culturally at the point when the shadow of the ugly hag has fallen across Naropa's books on logic and epistemology. Our ugly shadow is not only our inner feminine that has been neglected and imprisoned, but is also the betrayal of Mother Earth.

*"Our ugly shadow is not only our inner feminine
that has been neglected and imprisoned, but
is also the betrayal of Mother Earth."*

The shadow of the dakini in the form of old hag has fallen across our land. As the shadow invades us, inundating us with never-before-seen floods, hurricanes, earthquakes, and droughts, we are being called to find the mysterious home of the dakini within us, and also to heal and stop the toxic fumes that are causing her to be sick, as in the earlier story of the worldly dakini and Milarepa. We must look at the ugly dumps of toxic waste we have been hiding from, the carbon emissions that raise temperatures yearly and cause atmospheric conditions that create environmental disasters; we need to look at how we are polluting our rivers and air, poisoning what we eat, causing the dakinis to become ill.

So, like Naropa, we must journey with the guidance of the old hag, making mistakes that undermine our own progress, until she becomes our consort, our beloved. We must face the pain and embarrassment created when we realize how incredibly egocentric humanity has been and how much we have destroyed the beauty and perfect balance of our world. We must raise the old, ugly hag to her rightful, honored place—until she becomes the honored grandmother.

THE DAKINI'S NET

After my divorce from my Italian husband, Costanzo, I left Italy in 1986 and moved with my children to an old Dutch farmhouse about thirty miles north of New York City, up the Hudson River in the town of Valley Cottage. Around that time, I met an old friend, Terry Clifford, who had been close to me when I was a nun in Nepal in the early 1970s. We had stayed together in a cave near Mount Everest in 1970 for six weeks. At that time I was a nun and she was a layperson; now she had been living in retreat, while I was a mother with three children. After her retreat she had returned to her native New York, living in Manhattan and working as a journalist. She also wrote a book called *Tibetan Buddhist Medicine and Psychiatry*.[47]

We began to talk frequently, comparing notes about our experiences: what we had been through over the years and what we had learned, she in her retreat and me in my life as a mother, finding it funny how our roles had switched. We became very close. Then on her forty-third birthday, she was visiting a friend in Woodstock and out of the blue went into what appeared to be an epileptic fit. When she got to the hospital, she was diagnosed with cancer; and shortly thereafter discovered it had invaded her whole body.

Over the next months of her treatment, rapid decline, and the process of dying, we spent as much time together as possible. During one of our many conversations, we talked about what she thought had caused this cancer. She said, "It is unresolved emotional issues. Some sexual things had happened to me in retreat, which I was told to keep secret. The whole experience created so much pain, and that I wasn't supposed to talk about it, made it worse. I believe that this pain and those secrets had made me sick. And even though the spiritual practices helped to transform my mind states, my emotional wounds festered."

One day we were at my house in Valley Cottage, which overlooked the shore of a lake, where sand mixed with clay on the beach. We were taking handfuls of the sand and clay and rubbing it on our bodies to exfoliate, then slipping into the water to wash it off. As we sat there in the water up to our waists, with the low-hanging branches of the trees dangling above the lake around us, the sun sparkled on the water creating little flecks of light. I said to her, "I am beginning to teach retreats called Dakini Retreats that will bring together spiritual practice and emotional work. I have seen in myself and others like you that we can do all these Tibetan practices, but there can be a lack of resolution in terms of core emotional issues. Some deep things are not being touched." Then I described the Dakini Retreats to her. "We will work with each buddha family for two days and its transformation into wisdoms, sandwiching each day with the Mandala of the Lion-headed Dakini practice; then for each family doing co-counseling, regressions (see page 289), mask making, and movement. We will work deeply and closely with each other transforming emotions."

She thought about it and then said, "This is brilliant. If I wasn't so sick, I would come with you. Please, please try to find a way to integrate the teachings with emotional transformation. Please don't let this happen to anyone else. It is really important to try to find a way."

Lama Tsultrim and Terry Clifford shortly after her ordination, 1970.

Terry died in August of 1987, and the first Dakini Retreat took place that fall in Big Indian, near Woodstock, New York. She became my guiding spirit as I began to teach the Dakini Retreats around the world. Her words resonated with my own experience; I felt that in

some ways we were very similar, that although I had seriously practiced Buddhism for many years, still there was a large part of my being
that somehow wasn't really getting transformed. I also observed this
in my friends and longtime Buddhist practitioners. What I wanted to
do was interface some of what the West understood about psychology and emotions with what the Tibetans knew through spiritual
practice. Out of this came the work of the Dakini Retreats and the
Mandala of the Five Dakinis.

In 1989, I was doing a Dakini Retreat with a group of about
thirty-five women and men at the Ojai Foundation in Ojai, California. We had been in retreat for two weeks, during which we'd
spent two full days on each of the five families, and we were doing
Simhamukha, the lion-headed dakini mandala practice, every morning and evening. We worked with a variety of modalities in order to
deeply penetrate our obstructed emotional patterns, beginning with
meditative regression practices, during which we reviewed one of the
five encumbered patterns in our lives, going back all the way to birth.

For example, in vajra family where the encumbered pattern is
anger, we looked at the way anger had manifested in our lives both
as our own anger and as anger being directed at us, all the way back
to birth and then tracking it forward to the present. Then, working
with a partner, co-counseling methods, and mask making according
to the family, we worked through the issues. We made and decorated
a mask for each family. Finally, we worked with movement in the
obstructed pattern, in this case by moving with the energy of anger
and then moving to transform it to mirror-like wisdom.

The retreat was very intense and powerful. We were camping
in the forest or staying in yurts and eating outside under the shade
of trees. Our meeting space was a thirty-foot canvas yurt, where we
sat in a circle, and there was also a very large sacred Coast Live oak
tree, called "the teaching tree," where we sometimes met. During the
retreat we needed to have good weather, so I prayed to the dakinis
to hold the weather so we could complete our retreat. The sun shone

every day at our retreat area, even though in the hills all around us it rained.

The night before the retreat ended, I had a dream of a very brilliant white cloud crossing the whole sky from one horizon to the other: it looked like a large white bow. The next day at the final closing ceremony, held at the teaching tree, we brought together the five masks we'd each made, one for each of the five dakinis, and began the process of putting one on and then moving and dancing with the wisdom of that family. It was a beautiful clear day, when suddenly overhead there was a cloud that stretched from one side of the sky to the other like a bridge, a completely white bridge across the whole sky, exactly like my dream.

From that bridge came a white dakini in the form of a cloud. She was very clear, shockingly clear, with her right leg raised and her left leg extended and her arms in the dancing posture. There she was, right there in the sky in front of us. Then she began to dance: the cloud formation changed, making it appear as though her arms and legs were moving up and down. We all stopped in our tracks and just stared at the sky, watching this display in amazement. We were in such an altered state from the retreat that it seemed almost normal that she would visit us.

This was the first time such a powerful experience of the dakini's presence had occurred in my life. Before, I had thought they were just archetypes, symbolizing qualities of the feminine that we identified

Cloud dakini, which appeared during the closing ceremony of the Dakini Retreat, Ojai, California, 1990.

with in practice. But after this experience I realized the dakinis are real; they have an independent existence. What we visualize, what we create internally, what we embody, begins to manifest externally as the outer manifestation, which is an important point of working with the dakini mandala.

"What we visualize, what we create internally, what we embody, begins to manifest externally as the outer manifestation, which is an important point of working with the dakini mandala."

Over several years, the dakini mandala continued to be the main thread of my life and my teachings, which intensified between 1988 and 1992, and was my main focus in a series of Dakini Retreats I taught. My vision was to create dakini mandalas in various locations around the world—a series of interlinking dakini mandalas that would cover the globe with a protective net.

Around this time, I received a letter from a young woman who was then a Harvard PhD student, Miranda Shaw. She had seen my newsletter in which I spoke of creating Dakini Retreats around the world and connecting the mandalas to create a web. She wrote:

I wanted to let you know that I was amazed to see in your newsletter a description of something recorded in the *Chakrasamvara Tantra*, one of the earliest Buddhist Tantras. It mentions that each place the Dakini Mandala is practiced the mandala remains there and links with all the others in other places the Dakini Mandala is practiced, this is called the net dakinis, or the dakini's net.[48]

A few years later Miranda Shaw's doctoral thesis from Harvard became her book *Passionate Enlightenment: Women in Tantric Buddhism*,[49] revealing the stories of the early women Vajrayana gurus, which she had translated from the original Sanskrit. This book came out around when I had finished the cycle of Dakini Retreats, and to read the stories and poetry of the ancient yoginis was like finding my long-lost sisters. They had wild names like Blissful Diamond, Tree-Leaf Woman, Wings of Breath, Dakini Lion-Face, and Corpse-Raising Woman.

When I conducted the Dakini Retreat in Bali, I had a mystifying experience that was a confirmation of the need to work with obstructing emotions and meditation simultaneously. When we arrived in Bali a few days before the retreat, we stayed in the town of Ubud in a small guesthouse. At 3 A.M. on the first morning, my family and I found ourselves wide-awake, standing outside on the porch of our little guesthouse. So we decided to go for a walk. We walked into town, and everything was silent except for dogs barking. And then we kept walking into the countryside and as dawn broke, we came upon some people who were chopping massive amounts of cauliflower, carrots, and cabbages on the middle of the road. It turned out that they were preparing for the funeral of an important woman, the mother and grandmother of many. In Bali, funerals are very elaborate and take place over several days. Because of the jet lag, we kept waking up early and returning to this same spot, eventually making friends with the family of the deceased, and were invited to the funeral.

The dakini practice that I was doing intensely during the Dakini Retreats and had planned to teach in Bali was Lion-Headed Dakini Simhamukha. In her mandala, the central dakini is the color blue.

When we attended the funeral, an Austrian woman came up to me, looking at me very oddly, and she said, "Why do you look blue?"

I said without skipping a beat, "Perhaps because I'm here to teach a retreat with Simhamukha, the blue lion-faced dakini."

Her mouth dropped open, and she said, "I can't believe this. I am from Vienna and received the empowerment for that mandala from a Tibetan lama in Austria. I came to Bali to find a place to do a retreat of Simhamukha. I came here looking for an isolated house. Meeting you is definitely a strong sign. Can I join your retreat?"

I answered, "Yes, it's a strong sign. You can join us if you would like, but it won't be an ordinary Buddhist retreat. We will work intensively with the emotions as well as the five wisdoms in the mandala principle."

She looked a little disturbed and replied, "My Buddhist teacher said the emotions are just like waves in the ocean of the empty mind. I don't see any point in working with the emotions. I think we should just focus on the wisdom mandala."

I looked her straight in the eye and said, "In my experience, although that is true on the absolute level, on the relative level we need to work with our emotions and transform them in a tangible way."

This woman, Ingrid, had a strangely armored look: she was wearing a large gold necklace that looked like a breastplate, and large, thick gold bracelets cuffed her wrists. She was very tan, with green eyes and wavy light-brown hair. She ended up coming to the retreat with some hesitation.

We had a gathering the first night of the retreat in the pavilion on the beach. It was a large covered space that usually held the restaurant of the hotel. But for our retreat they cleaned it all out, and we made a big circle in the middle of the space. After our opening circle, we retired to our rooms. We were spread out in two hotels that were next to each other, with the pavilion in between. There were about forty people attending the retreat from several different countries, but mostly we were Americans.

As I was in my room getting ready for bed that night, my friend Virginia from Louisiana, who was assisting me with the retreat, rushed into my room and told me Ingrid had fallen two stories when she was climbing a ladder to her second-floor room in a Balinese-style bungalow. Virginia was very upset; she said, "It was a terrible sound when she hit the concrete patio below, a splattering sound, and now she's really out of it and can barely move."

It turned out Ingrid had a severe concussion. She was projectile-vomiting and could not walk. I wanted to get her airlifted to Australia, to the closest good hospital, but she refused, saying she wanted to stay at the retreat.

She was lying on a bamboo couch with her head on some pillows outside in the pavilion. I sat next to her and took her hand and said, "I am very concerned about you. That was a very bad fall and you are really not well. We will try one thing, but if it doesn't work, I'm going to have to have you taken to a hospital."

I continued, "I want to do the Chöd practice, which is a healing practice I have taught for many years, begun by the eleventh-century Tibetan master Machig Labdrön. It's a core practice connected to feeding your demons that can get at deep illnesses and trauma and heal them.[50] It's done with a bell and a drum and sung in Tibetan; the thighbone trumpet is also used. This is the only thing I think could help you now. Otherwise, you have to go to the hospital."

She agreed, so I gathered some of my most experienced Chöd students to practice with me. We sat under the open veranda right next to the beach, five or six of us practicing with about forty people sitting around observing. It was evening and there were a few lights on in the pavilion. You could hear the sound of the waves lapping on the beach. The smell of jasmine filled the air.

We sat in a crescent shape around the couch Ingrid was lying on. I closed my eyes and began the practice. We began to sing and play drums; the melodies are ancient and the sound of the drum is like the heartbeat. After the preliminary part of the practice, the body is

offered; I visualized offering my body as nectar and invited whatever
was in her body out to feast from the nectar. We continued to practice Chöd with the rhythmic sound of the bell and drum going out
into the hot Balinese night. With my eyes closed, mentally scanning
her body, I saw long, white, thin ghostlike beings coming out of her
sexual area and then moving up and coming out of her body through
her throat. They were terrible looking and had a kind of sticky, slimy
texture. They seemed to be choking her as they exited her body. But
they were leaving, so I kept going until they had all been fed. Then
we completed the practice.

When I opened my eyes, Ingrid was sitting up and smiling. She
held her hands together at her heart and was bowing. She had been
almost unable to move at all before and certainly not sit up.

Ellen, one of my students from New York, had done the practice
with her eyes open. She came over to me and said, "She went into
what appeared to be a seizure, and she was writhing around. It was
weird and really scary to watch. I considered asking you to stop, because it was so violent. But I decided to just let the process continue."

Then I went over and sat on the couch and spoke to Ingrid privately. I said, "I saw the energy coming from your sexual area up
through your body to your throat, and it seemed to choke you. Then
it all went out of your throat. It took a long time. It was very intense. I must ask you, have you ever experienced sexual abuse or
molestation?"

She looked at me, shocked, her beautiful green eyes filled with
tears. She said, "I am adopted, and I was sexually abused by my adopted father. It went on for many years but I never told anybody,
because I was afraid the family would reject me, and I would be out
on the streets. Eventually I got old enough to leave the house and go
to university. I never told anybody about it. Since then, I have tried
to ignore my history and to avoid my emotions. I was able to do that
with Buddhist theory, but now I see I need to face these things."

By this time tears were streaming down her face and she was

crying hard. There was so much in her to be released, so much pain and so many repressed feelings of anger and grief, and so much fear too. We talked for a while, and then she was able to get up stiffly and walk to her new room, which was on the ground level. This experience opened her to the retreat, and she did some very powerful work; it was like a dam breaking, so much emotion came out, but the container of the retreat could hold her. She went on to do the whole Dakini Retreat, working with a lot of repressed emotional material. When she returned to Austria, she continued to practice the dakini mandala along with seeing a therapist, and experienced deep emotional healing and spiritual development.

PART 3

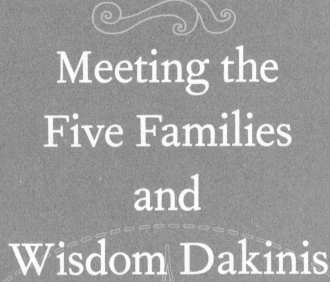

Meeting the
Five Families
and
Wisdom Dakinis

7

THE FIVE FAMILIES

By working with the five Buddha families, we are trying to de-
velop some basic understanding of how to see things in their abso-
lute essence, their own innate nature. We can use this knowledge
with regard to painting or poetry or arranging flowers or making
films or composing music. It is also connected with relationships
between people. The five Buddha family principles seem to cover a
whole new dimension of perception. . . .

—CHÖGYAM TRUNGPA RINPOCHE

After the Sixteenth Karmapa ordained me, I returned to Swa-yambhu hill and lived on the other side of the stupa. Every morning I would walk around the stupa, circumambulating clock-wise as is customary for Buddhists. I would look at each of the stat-ues in their niches, the shrines of the five male and the five female buddhas, and try to remember their qualities and meaning. Inside the niches, there would often be a monkey looking back at me at eye level, feasting on a pilgrim's offering: tiny Nepalese bananas and cooked rice tinted red.

Gegyen Peyjam, a bright, energetic Tibetan lama of about fifty years old, was the head teacher of the monastery under Sapchu Rinpoche, and also knew all about Tibetan herbs and medicine. He would often join me on my morning walks, and as we circumambulated he would take my hand. It was he who first taught me about the five buddha families—buddha, vajra, ratna, padma, and karma—and the mandala, using my fingers.

As we walked past the statues, he took my middle finger and indicated that it represented the buddha family, the center of the mandala, connected to the transformation of ignorance into all-encompassing wisdom. My index finger symbolized the vajra family, the indestructible family connected to the transformation of anger into mirror-like wisdom in the east, which was the front of the stupa at the top of the steep stairs where there was also a huge golden vajra (thunderbolt scepter) on a pedestal. My ring finger stood for the ratna family, the jewel family connected to the transformation of pride into the wisdom of equanimity in the south, which faced the small clay-brick building where I lived. As we walked by the statue of Amitabha on the west side of the stupa, he touched my thumb, which represented the padma family and connected to the transformation of desire into the wisdom of discernment. My pinky represented the karma family in the north, the transformation of envy and jealousy into all-accomplishing wisdom.

He said each finger on my right hand was one of the five male buddhas and the left hand was for the female buddhas, pointing out the statues of each as we walked. He showed me that when I put my hands together in prayer at my heart, it symbolized the joining of the male and female buddhas in union. I was pleased to learn that sexual union of enlightened beings, called yab-yum, was a highly revered spiritual image with deep symbolic meaning. In Tibetan Buddhist tradition, the pinnacle spiritual experience is described as the union of the feminine, symbolizing wisdom, with the masculine, symbolizing skillful means. So sexuality, which had been presented in my culture as a profane thing, was a path to enlightenment, and this resonated with me. I had never been able to buy the idea that sex was somehow shameful, and to find a religion that embraced it as sacred was remarkable and inspiring.

"In Tibetan Buddhist tradition, the pinnacle spiritual experience is described as the union of the feminine, symbolizing wisdom, with the masculine, symbolizing skillful means."

As I walked with Gegyen Peyjam past the niches topped with gilded roofs containing the five male and five female buddhas, I studied their details, the different-colored garments, and the hand gestures of each one, and the mandala imprinted itself indelibly in me. I learned that the mandala is a cosmological system, a worldview through enlightened eyes. It embodies the five types of consciousness, the five types of wisdom, the seasons, the times of the day, the elements, the senses, and the chakras, and is a map of transformation.

In Chapter 2, you learned that there are three types of Tibetan mandalas—outer, inner, and secret—and how we would be working with the inner mandala and the path of transformation. Enlightenment is achieved through the inner mandala by meditating and working with the five buddha families. Remember, each family has in its untransformed state an encumbered emotional pattern or poison, and once awakened, this very same afflicted energy, with the self-clinging mind released, becomes a source of wisdom. There are also certain characteristics associated with each family: seed syllables, colors, elements, body types, symbols, and so on.

All of us belong predominantly to one or more of the five buddha families, and a few of us are evenly all five; we each also have a particular family we use as our "exit"—the way we get out of uncomfortable situations. Very few people are equally all five families, though we all have elements of each one; we should bear in mind that they are not separate but are all one principle radiating five colors or aspects, five aspects of our energy. The families might seem like another system of categorizing ourselves and others, similar to astrology or the enneagram, but they are actually ways to see the world and to work with our own energies and those of others. They are guidelines to perception or, as Trungpa Rinpoche called them, "reference points for perception."[51]

On top of the five families, each mandala is associated with three types of deities: peaceful, wrathful, and joyful. The deities are not like external saviors but are messengers of your true nature, your own energy embodied to aid in transformation. The deities embody the wisdom aspect, and it is through identifying with the deity and what it represents that the transformation happens. This might seem complicated—but we *are* complicated! We aren't simple and one-dimensional. Tantric Buddhism works with the very juice of that complexity.

These deities are, in a way, archetypes that we attune to in order to accelerate our spiritual transformation; however, that may be an oversimplification, because Tantric Buddhism always involves *transmission*—a living stream running from teacher to disciple, unlike a mere archetype. This book obviously cannot offer transmission, but serves as an introduction and meeting with the mandala principle that can then be developed with a teacher or may stand alone as a transformative method to work with in your personal experience.

We will be working with the five wisdom dakinis through the Mandala of the Five Dakinis, so the five buddha families are now being experienced in this particular aspect of the sacred feminine. Therefore, each wisdom dakini embodies the same traits as one of the five buddha families—the same symbols, seasons, body types, colors, and so on—now in the fierce feminine context. Alongside these family traits, each wisdom dakini is specifically connected to one of the five elements: space, water, earth, fire, and air. The ground is the creative feminine and sometimes referred to as the Great Mother, because it has the potential to give birth to everything; yet it (she) is not a "thing" in itself (herself). The five lights arising from the ground of being, the mother of all phenomena, become the five elements.

In the process of Tantric Buddhist practice, these symbols and the specific meanings surrounding them are kept in the mind as we visualize the mandala. The impact of the symbolic meaning ignites the intuitive experience not dominated by logos, and thus can impact the psyche in a nonverbal, direct way, so that we know the *meaning*, not just the words. The Tantric Buddhist path of transformation is said to be very rapid—one can reach enlightenment in one lifetime. Basically this is true because the poisons can be used rather than renounced, so we are transforming anger into wrathful enlightened energy, ignorance into peaceful enlightened energy, and desire into joyful enlightened energy, rather than denying or trying to repress these energies.

"The Tantric Buddhist path of transformation is said to be very rapid—one can reach enlightenment in one lifetime."

As we learned about the teaching of "one ground, two paths, two results" in Chapter 3, the process of straying from the one ground

PADMA

Seed Syllable: NI
Direction: West
Symbol: Red Lotus
Element: Fire
Color: Red
Obstructed Pattern: Craving, Compulsive Seduction, Lust, Longing, Desire
Wisdom: Discriminating, Awareness, Wisdom
Aggregate: Conception
Time: Sunset
Season: Spring
Landscape: Soft, Rolling Hills, Mossy Glens
Shape: Upward-Pointing Triangle
Body Type: Perfectly Proportioned, Well Toned, Very Seductive
Sense Perception: Hearing

RATNA

Seed Syllable: RI
Direction: South
Symbol: Wish-fulfilling Jewel
Element: Earth
Color: Yellow
Obstructed Pattern: Pride, Inadequacy
Wisdom: Wisdom of Equanimity
Aggregate: Feeling
Time: High Noon
Season: Early Autumn
Landscape: Jungle, Fertile Valleys
Shape: Square
Body Type: Generous, Large, Statuesque
Sense Perception: Smell & Taste

BUDDHA

Seed Syllable: BAM
Direction: Center
Symbol: Wheel
Element: Space
Color: White
Obstructed Pattern: Ignorance, Delusion, Depression, Spacing Out
Wisdom: Dhamadhatu Wisdom
Aggregate: Form
Time: No Time, Totality of Everything
Season: Winter
Landscape: White Sky in Wintertime, Big Sky
Shape: Dot, Bindu
Body Type: Plump, Relaxed, Round Body
Sense Perception: Mind

KARMA

Seed Syllable: SA
Direction: North
Symbol: Sword
Element: Air
Color: Green
Obstructed Pattern: Envy, Ambition, Speediness
Wisdom: All-Accomplishing Wisdom
Aggregate: Volitional Action
Time: Midnight
Season: Summer
Landscape: Complicated, Windy Place
Shape: Half Circle
Body Type: Thin, Wispy, Seen in Profile, Always Moving
Sense Perception: Touch

VAJRA

Seed Syllable: HA
Direction: East
Symbol: Vajra
Element: Water
Color: Blue
Obstructed Pattern: Anger
Wisdom: Mirror-like Wisdom
Aggregate: Consciousness
Time: Dawn
Season: Late Autumn
Landscape: Rugged Mountains, Icy River
Shape: Circle
Body Type: Thin & Hard, Clean-Cut, Sharp Features
Sense Perception: Sight

creates a self-perpetuating condition of suffering, and we seek to resolve our inherent alienation through further projections and grasping at "other." This cyclical process is always unsuccessful because
we are attempting to resolve the situation of dualistic clinging by
moving further into dualism, away from the source, instead of returning to the source and entering into union with the one ground.
This unsuccessful resolution creates a pervasive condition of dissatisfaction and anxiety, and continues to build chaotic layer upon layer, a
wild variety of fragmented impulses and subconscious currents leading us from one situation to the next, and one life to the next.

The process of working with the mandala principle directly addresses this issue by returning awareness to the pure, luminous energy of the mandala, which radiates directly from the ground. The
good news is that we have never been separated from the ground—
we are simply failing to recognize its all-pervasive presence, somewhat like a fly buzzing itself to death against a window when an open
door is right next to it.

EXIT FAMILY

A word about the exit family. The exit family describes how you get
out of a situation; the exit can mask your primary family or may be
the same family. You might be of one family, but your way of exit-
ing a situation may well be through another family, through another
encumbered pattern. It is as if you enter a house through the grand
front entrance, but exit through the back kitchen door. The exit family can be slippery and be more hidden than the primary family or
your subfamily(s).

Let's look at some exit family examples:

If you take a buddha family exit when you are upset, you might
go into your room and not want to talk to anybody, not want to eat,
and just close yourself off. Or you might get depressed and procras-

tinate. Another buddha exit would be to forget, or to get confused when confronted with a situation you want to remove yourself from.

A vajra exit would be to get angry, to rage, to manifest very icy anger or hot fury. You might yell at someone or write an angry e-mail.

The ratna exit might have to do with bragging or posting some self-enhancing photos on social media, or you might go shopping when you don't need anything and buy useless things in an attempt to stabilize yourself with retail therapy. A ratna exit might also involve binge eating or drinking.

A padma exit would be to try to seduce somebody or, more subtly, to try to engage a friend to listen to you and convince them of your point of view. You would try with the padma exit to develop the pleasure and security that comes from magnetizing someone else into your life, into your story. A padma exit could also be watching porn as an escape, or compulsively searching for online partners.

A karma exit usually involves throwing yourself into work. It could mean staying late at work and not taking breaks. You might start cleaning your house or organizing your kitchen or office. You're upset, so you just work and block out the feelings. You work harder, do more, become more speedy, and then have another cup of coffee until you are distanced from the original trigger.

You could be, for example, a karma person and use the karma exit. But alternatively, you could be padma but do a buddha exit, or you could be ratna and stage a vajra exit—or really any combination of any of the families. Exits are an interesting thing to think about. What do you do to get out of situations or feelings that make you uncomfortable? As we explore the families, try to find yourself, and also look for your exit style. Your main family or families might be completely different from your exit, but they could be the same.

EMBODYING THE FIVE WISDOM DAKINIS

Now we will dive into a chapter-by-chapter exploration of each wisdom dakini and her family, with some meditations to help you make a personal connection. Each chapter will begin by painting a portrait of the family, along with the dakini's personality traits; then we will look closely at her encumbered patterns and the transformed wisdoms, closing with a set of simple meditations. My suggestion is to take your time with each family—maybe focus on one family at a time for a week or a few days, in order to really feel the energy of it. The idea is to eventually embody each wisdom dakini, so that you feel, see, and sense her presence within you and all around you.

It is important to remember when working with the five families that there isn't any value judgment about which family is good or bad; they each have amazing qualities. It's really about recognizing your own energy and learning to work with it. It also helps sometimes to recognize the five buddha families in others, or in specific situations and places. Look at how you have organized or decorated your home or your office. Or look at how you dress. What family does it represent? You can change these particulars to create the effect of a different family. Let's say you tend to create cluttered, crowded surroundings, a ratna family environment; you could then consciously choose to create a vajra or karma environment for maximum efficiency. You might choose to dress in a more ratna kind of style that encourages bright colors and lots of bold jewelry, or perhaps in one that is more padma if you want a warmer, luxuriant, and sensual feeling.

It could be useful to have a journal by your side, to write down your impressions, thoughts, and feelings of whatever "comes up" as you explore each family. Some questions to consider:

* Which family do I resonate most with? Is there more than one?

* Which encumbered pattern or poison is strongest in me?
* Which family do I least identify with?
* Which family needs to be strengthened, to bring more balance into my life?
* Which family is my exit family?
* Do I dress like a particular family?
* Is my home a particular family type?
* Which families do you notice in the people closest to you?

Remember, when we talk about the encumbered patterns of the five families, the real point is to recognize them within ourselves. We all have elements of each family, although we may predominantly relate to one or two. It is only in recognizing our patterns that we may transform them. Often the family that we least identify with is where our shadow is, our hidden tendencies that we have disowned.

"Remember, when we talk about the encumbered patterns of the five families, the real point is to recognize them within ourselves."

8

BUDDHA DAKINI:
ALL-ENCOMPASSING WISDOM

The supreme method to realize the nature of mind,
Is to unite space and awareness.
When thus mixing space and awareness
You spontaneously purify fixed notions
Such as reality and characteristics, negating and establishing. . . .
—THE GRAND POEM OF PRAJNAPARAMITA BY ARYADEVA

Although all five families are called buddha families, the central one is *the* buddha family, so we will take an in-depth look at this central family first. As we begin our journey through the five families, see where you find yourself. You will probably find several connection points between the various families and your current life situation.

The buddha family is the fundamental family in the Mandala of the Five Dakinis. In a way it permeates all the others, because its element is space. It's the emptiness from which everything springs and to which everything returns. It's the crystal before the spectrum of colored rays springs out of it when it is struck by sunlight, and it's

Buddha Dakini, detail of the thangka of the Five Wisdom Dakinis,
by Lama Gyurme Rabgye, 2016. Acrylic and mineral pigment.
Lama Tsultrim Allione

the crystal after the spectrum returns into it. Space is a precondition
for everything that exists; it's the fundamental level of consciousness
itself.

The symbol of buddha family is the eight-spoked Wheel of
Dharma, the Dharmachakra, representing the Eightfold Path to enlightenment according to the Buddha: right view, right intention,
right speech, right action, right livelihood, right effort, right mindfulness, and right concentration. The Eightfold Path is the most fundamental teaching of the path to enlightenment as described by the

Buddha, and the eight-spoked wheel is one of the most ancient symbols of the Buddha's message. The wheel has three parts: the hub, the spokes, and the circumference. The hub represents emptiness, the pregnant zero, the very center of the wheel that does not move, the still point in the middle; thus the dot, or *bindu*, is the shape associated with the buddha family. The circle of the circumference symbolizes the completeness of the Buddha's teachings.

Dharmachakra: the Eight-Spoked Wheel of Dharma, symbol of the buddha family. Drawing by Robert Beer. Ink on paper.

The family color is white, but a more accurate description would be colorless and full of the potential of all colors. Sometimes this family is associated with blue. Space is experienced within us as consciousness, which is limitless and has no real location, no color, no fixed abode. When this element of space is blue, it refers to the sky and its vastness. The sense perception is the mind, that consciousness that takes in and processes all the other senses. Mind is often compared to the sky, the space in which clouds appear, yet it is not sullied by clouds. The mind is what creates the experience of inner spaciousness, particularly through meditation.

Trungpa Rinpoche defined the space of buddha family in this way: "We are relating with the open space fundamentally and subconsciously. Whatever we're allowed to call it, there's open space constantly, complete open space. And that open space . . . also contains tremendous sparks of light, of matter, otherwise space can never be space; unless there is matter, space is space. It's like if you're going to paint a picture of sky, the only way you can paint a picture of the sky is have a blank paper, and paint two little birds in it."[52]

To get a sense of buddha family–style art, think of the paintings

of the New Mexican artist Georgia O'Keeffe. She painted with a profound sense of simplicity and spaciousness expressed in the forms of
sky, hills, bones, and large flowers of the American Southwest. There
also is a relatively unknown visionary, the Swedish artist Hilma af
Klint (October 26, 1862 – October 21, 1944), whom I discovered, a
mystic whose paintings were among the first abstract art predating
Kandinsky. She knew her paintings were destined for the future, and
she left her work to her nephew, stipulating that her work should not
be seen until twenty years after her death. But it ended up being
forty-two years before her incredible body of work was seen. She was
not seeking to explore abstract mathematical questions with color
and form, but rather to transmit wisdom from higher dimensions received in visions. Many of her paintings are a kind of mandala, offering a transmission of pure luminosity and space. Her paintings were
visual representations of complex spiritual ideas. (See image of *The
Swan*, No. 12, on page 3 of the photo insert.)

Great Sand Dunes National Park.

The Zen brushstroke circle called an *ensō*, made with a big brush
in a completely relaxed single stroke, is also connected to buddha family. In Zen calligraphy, we are working directly with our personal *qi*,

or life force, and with the quality of space we inhabit. How we relate to our state of mind and space is of prime importance in giving our artwork an authentic living expression. This kind of calligraphy practice is perfect for developing the wisdom of buddha family, bringing forth both awareness and the energy of spaciousness.

Ensō by Bankei Yotaku, a Japanese Zen master
from the seventeenth century.

When I think of this family in architecture, I think of the ruins of ancient Greek temples with their white columns open to spacious skies. Buddha family architecture, like its landscapes, inspires a sense of meditative awareness, a natural feeling of quietude. A negative buddha architectural experience would be boring and closed, such as concrete buildings that are all gray, repetitive, and soulless.

The interior space of buddha family would feel comfortable; you could feel cozy and relaxed in this environment. You want to stay there, it's so relaxing, welcoming, and calming. The windows are likely to be big, with views of the sky and long-distance vistas. There is a softness to interior spaces, with white carpets and pale blue designs, white couches, and a pervasive sense of ease and hominess. There is no clutter in these homes, but perhaps some large, white porcelain bowls with white chrysanthemums floating in them. There might be a large woven cylindrical basket holding tall papyrus stalks topped with soft plumes. All the upholstery and fabrics are made of natural fibers.

The landscape perhaps most resonant with this family would be a snowfield with white winter sky against the black branches of leafless trees. It is that blankness, the simplicity and openness found in win-

ter, that expresses the season of buddha family. Although vajra family is also associated with winter, vajra is the sharp clarity of ice, while buddha is the soft curves of a snowfield. It is not only winter-scapes that are buddha landscapes; vast white beaches, sand dunes, and deserts are also included.

Segesta Temple, a Greek ruin in Sicily.

The buddha body type is laid-back and the buddha family person has an open, round face. A buddha woman is sensual in a relaxed way; she is not working to achieve a tight body, but has a feminine, Rubenesque body. As she walks, her blouse slips off her shoulder and her breasts move freely. There is a slight roundness in her belly. There is a feeling that her body is relaxed and free. And this goes for her clothing as well; she prefers to wear simple neutral, flowing, natural garments.

BUDDHA GOES TO A PARTY

Let's imagine you are walking into a party: How would you identify a buddha person? You might look around the room and then notice someone sitting in a corner in a comfortable armchair, wearing relaxed beautiful clothes, quietly observing what's going on. . . . You recognize her: it's Josephine, a fifty-year-old psychotherapist. If she is in the encumbered emotional pattern of this family, she might look disconnected, depressed, or spaced out. There would be an unwill-ingness to engage with others, and she might seem to be isolated in her own world.

If Josephine is, however, in the transformed wisdom state of the buddha family, she would be very open to connecting, taking in what you are saying in a spacious way with a tranquil presence. Being with Josephine would feel relaxing and pleasant. There would be no need for a lot of chitchat; just being together would be enough. If some-body were to bring her a plate of food or a drink, she would be happy to receive it. But Josephine might not make the effort to go and get it herself or to interact with anybody at the party unless she is ap-proached first.

Brian is a buddha family man, an IT specialist; he doesn't par-ticularly want to go to the party, but going is easier than dealing with his wife's reaction if he were to say he doesn't want to go. When they arrive, Brian greets the others quietly, but only after they greet him first. As soon as possible, he finds a quiet place to look at his phone, oblivious to what is happening around him, just waiting for his wife to be ready to go home.

Then Brian wants to go outside onto the back porch at the party, to get away from the noise and look at the sky. He really would pre-fer not to engage in activities like dancing, but his wife comes to get him and he has to dance. Although she wants him to dance with her, he tends to dance alone, making sweeping flowing motions. Brian is kind of a quiet presence at the party, and might want to leave early to get some space and peace.

ENCUMBERED PATTERN: IGNORANCE

The poison or encumbered pattern of the buddha family is a *spaced-out* quality rather than a *spacious* quality. This spaced-out quality is traditionally called "ignorance," or in Tibetan, *ma rigpa*, meaning

"nonawareness." There can be a kind of dullness, making you want
to shake the person and say, "Hey, wake up!" The buddha types
don't initiate activity, and this tendency toward immobility can reveal itself as stubbornness and a lack of awareness of what is around
them. Buddha people can seem insensitive due to not being mindful
of what's going on around them. But it is not insensitivity, rather a
lack of attention as a result of being caught in one's own foggy world.
They may also lack quickness of mind and humor and might be a bit
late to get a joke. This delay is not a lack of intelligence, but a lack of
presence and awareness.

Buddha types tend to wait for things to be different, but do not
do anything about changing them. There may be a kind of discour-
agement that leads to sluggishness and laziness from being disheart-
ened. This pattern also involves denial: they want to get somewhere
safe and protected, to what they deem to be a stable situation. In the
meantime, they play deaf and dumb, not unlike turtles who when
overwhelmed pull in their head and legs. They completely withdraw
and stay like that, waiting for the danger to pass. What is common
in buddha people is what we could consider a kind of frozen emotional space. For example, they do not really want to relate to others, it takes *too* much energy; they just want space. When my three
children were young, they were very intense and active. I often felt
that I just needed space. When certain situations became too intense,
I would space out. My body was there, but I was not *present*.

My children would pull on me and say, "Earth to Mom! Earth
to Mom!"

These buddha encumbered patterns range from being mildly
spacey to going off on a tangent to not being able to focus or keep a
train of thought all the way to complete dissociation and catatonia.
In meditation, a buddha family style of distraction would be blanking
out. For example, a buddha person might find that she has been sitting in meditation for half an hour and has been completely unaware
the whole time. It is not that she has been distracted in an agitated

way, by this thought or that thought. The experience is more akin to being lost in a haze. Her energy feels dense, almost claustrophobic.

Being in relationship with a buddha person can be frustrating for those who want to communicate frequently; you might have the feeling you are reaching through the fog to the buddha person. Although this may create the impression that they are distant, this is not actually the case: they're just not very talkative. They will try to avoid difficult confrontational conversations, and would prefer sweeping things under the carpet to dealing with conflict directly. Buddha people are comfortable with silence and don't feel a need to fill it with music or conversation. The neurotic reaction of the buddha family to the brilliance of the colors of the radiant expression of the one ground is feeling overwhelmed by so many colors, textures, and too many complex things happening.

DEPRESSION

Remember that the element of the buddha family is space; when we get into the family's encumbered pattern, its energy is the solidification of space, which becomes heavy and dense. If you think about the buddha encumbered pattern of depression, it actually has a very dense quality. We feel sort of thick. We can't move. We can't get out of bed. We're immobilized by this solidification of space. There's a sense of disembodiment, disassociation, and overwhelm that causes us to space out. When we feel depressed, we often "check out" energetically. We might feel as though we can't feel anything, and often we do not know why the cloud of depression has come over us.

Depression actually requires a lot of energy; it takes a lot of force to maintain this state. When my infant daughter Chiara died of SIDS at two months, I became very depressed. I would often forget things and not be present with my other children.

A few months after Chiara died, my husband revealed something about a man he was working with and told me not to say anything to this man. Shortly afterward, this man, Paulo, called the house. I told him everything that my husband had warned me not to tell him about a work-related situation.

My husband overheard me on the phone and was furious. I was bewildered and felt terrible, but with grief came forgetfulness; I was lost in the grief. After Chiara's death, my grief was so intense that I felt lost and hardly present. I was fortunate that my depression did not last so intensely for more than a year; for some people depression is a chronic, debilitating state in which they can barely get out of bed.

PROCRASTINATION

The other encumbered quality of the buddha family is procrastination. You put things off. "I'll do the dishes later," while they just keep piling up. "I can't deal with the bills," hoping they will somehow go away. Every time you see the pile of mail, you feel depressed, but you'd rather not deal with it. Procrastinating is usually not a conscious act. You do not *decide* not to open your bills or wash the dishes, to skip over all that needs to be done. Somehow you simply forget them; addressing these life tasks feels like too much effort. Then when you wake up or someone points it out to you, you think, *Oh, how could I have forgotten that?* When we want to remember something, generally we do. We choose to hold it in our minds; when we don't, it slips by. This pattern is associated with the buddha family because of its spacey quality and ignoring of things that need doing.

DENIAL AND DISSOCIATION

Buddha people also have a tendency to be in denial, which is similar to procrastination; the main difference between the two encumbered emotional states is that denial usually involves habits or addictions, not seeing something really damaging that is happening right in front of you. It's the alcoholic who ignores or denies that she is an alcoholic. While everyone else may know, denial steps in and the alcoholic refuses to acknowledge that she has a problem and might say, "I can stop whenever I want to. I just don't want to, because I don't have a problem."

When we are in denial, we unconsciously decide not to know, such as the mother who ignores or acts as though she doesn't see her daughter being molested. No mother would *consciously* allow her daughter to be molested; but unconsciously, through denial, she can allow it. She may even unconsciously put her daughter in harm's way, especially if she has a history of unresolved sexual abuse in her own background. In this way, the buddha person can be extremely destructive and create multigenerational trauma, often paired with alcoholism or other addictions. If you look at someone who's really stuck in this encumbered pattern, they have a kind of glazed-over look in their eyes.

In reaction to an experience of extreme stress or trauma, people often experience dissociation, which could be described as the mind or the spirit "leaving the body." In its mild form, dissociation could take the form of daydreaming or forgetfulness. You are still functioning, and others might not even realize that you are dissociated. A person who is more severely dissociated may not even remember events that occur during the time they are dissociated. This is an extreme buddha reaction, as I said, usually triggered by trauma.

ALL-ENCOMPASSING WISDOM

One winter morning in 1970, after my ordination as a Buddhist nun, when I was living on Swayambhu hill next to the large white stupa, I stood on the terrace that overlooked the Kathmandu Valley. White mist covered the valley, and above the mist the sky was a deep blue. As I gazed at the mist blanketing the valley and the sky above, a feeling of space permeated my whole body. I had been studying the five buddha families and thought: *Ah, this is the wisdom of the buddha fam-*

ily, the wisdom of all-encompassing space. It struck me as paradoxical that this vast emptiness is represented as a tiny point, or bindu, in the center of the mandala, but is actually all-pervading openness.

As we have seen, the encumbered pattern is the untransformed aspect of each family, which, when transformed through sound, visualization, and meditation practices, becomes the wisdom aspect. The good news is that the intensity of the encumbered pattern becomes equally strong when it dawns as wisdom, which is why Buddhists say the Tantric path is the right path for those with strong passions.

"The good news is that the intensity of the encumbered pattern becomes equally strong when it dawns as wisdom, which is why Buddhists say the Tantric path is the right path for those with strong passions."

In Sanskrit, the wisdom for the buddha family is *jnana dharmadhatu.* It is translated in a variety of ways such as "the wisdom of reality's expanse," "the wisdom of total space," or "the wisdom of all-encompassing space." *Dharmadhatu* is one of those words that is really best not translated, because it has layers of meaning that do not fit easily into any one English word, but let's try to unpack it. *Dharma* refers to every "thing" or all phenomena; it can also mean "reality" or "truth." *Dhatu* means "space" or "dimension." We may think of this as the space that includes every "thing," or "all-pervading space."

The space or dhatu is usually discussed in terms of inner and outer space, the space in the body and outside. The expanse is not merely emptiness; it is an emptiness full of dynamic luminosity. So together the two words, dharmadhatu, become a synonym for "the boundless space of totality, the very expanse of reality." When you add *jnana,* the Sanskrit for "primordial wisdom" or "beginning-less wisdom," a knowing beyond the confines of the conditioned reasoning mind, what we knew before the basic split, before our rupture from the ground of being. It is not wisdom gained from accumulated experience or study. It is the recovered, or *re-cognized* wisdom that we get through meditation when we recognize our true condition.

Many meditation teachers and monastics are predominantly from the buddha family, because they have a natural affinity for meditative stillness and serenity. This reflects physically—often their skin glows and their faces appear wide open. They have a predilection for meditation and an open-minded gentleness. They are peaceful and enjoy beautiful tranquil places; they are relaxed and generous, giving off an air of serenity. Buddha people tend to be tolerant and enjoy the simple things in life, not wanting to get overly complicated about anything; in fact, they will resist being overly organized or precise.

Buddha family has tremendous potential in that it is the base of everything, all phenomena, all appearances, and provides the space for the rest of the mandala. If we can get a sense of this buddha family wisdom, we can get a sense of the primary wisdom of the whole dakini mandala, which informs the other four families.

TO KNOW ONE'S OWN FACE

There is a Tibetan expression *rang ngo she,* which means "to know one's own face." It is often translated as "to know one's own nature," but I think it is more accurate to translate it literally as to know one's own face because, paradoxically, our own face is continually with us, like primordial wisdom itself, yet we don't see it unless we look in a mirror. And though our face is continually with us, in a world without mirrors or reflections we would have no way to know our own face except to feel it. It is through meditation, which is a kind of reflection in that we turn the mind back on the outward moving energy, that we begin to know our own true condition, our own true face. There is a Zen teaching by Dogen Zenji (1200–1253) that speaks to this:

> *You should therefore cease practice based on intellectual under-standing, pursuing words and following after speech, and learn the backward step that turns your light inwardly to illuminate your self. Body and mind of themselves will drop away, and your original face will be manifest. If you want to attain such-ness, you should practice suchness without delay.*[53]

As we work with the five wisdom dakinis and their families, we should know that the real meaning of wisdom here is the wisdom of knowing one's original face. In considering the spaciousness of the wisdom aspect of the buddha family, we can see how the family's encumbered pattern has the potential for the wisdom in it. In other words, while the problem you may face in the encumbered pattern is spacing out, the wisdom of this family is actually being *in* a state of spaciousness, while being present and aware. The wisdom is one of total accommodation; there is an incredible vastness—we may call it a sky-like awareness or the wisdom of totality—that is constantly accommodating and holding in the fullest way all our thoughts, feel-ings, sensations, and experiences. Spaciness becomes spaciousness when it is transformed.

"The wisdom is one of total accommodation;
there is an incredible vastness—we may call it a
sky-like awareness or the wisdom of totality."

ROBERTA'S STORY

From who she was until she was eleven years old, she was repeatedly abused by her stepfather, who came into her bedroom at night and sexually molested her. He told her he would kill her mother if she made any noise or told anyone. So Roberta mentally left her body in order to protect herself from being present during the abuse. She would go to "another place" and stay there until it was over and her stepfather left. During this time she became less and less present throughout the day, and her grades went down because she was "daydreaming," according to her teachers. But actually, she was dissociating and no one recognized it.

Dissociation is a mechanism by which the psyche protects itself. This can happen during a single traumatic event or with repeated traumas. It can become an uncontrollable habit. When you are triggered, dissociation happens and you may not even realize it. You may not remember certain things that happen to you because, quite literally, *you* were not there; you were avoiding being present in your body.

In the Tibetan tradition, this kind of dissociation is called loss of the *lha*, or "spirit body." According to the teachings in Tibetan culture, the lha may be lost or stolen. The lha is a subtle energy body that protects the physical body and gives us a sense of confidence and coherence as a person. If through trauma the lha is separated from the physical body, the person feels unwell and out of sorts. The loss of one's lha is an extreme situation. In Tibetan Buddhism, there are certain practices and ceremonies to call back, reinforce, and reestablish the lost or stolen lha in the body.

Roberta had a loss of lha, and what Western psychology would call dissociation. She struggled in school, and when she finally told her mother about the abuse, she didn't believe her. So Roberta had nowhere to turn. Her mother broke up with her stepfather when she was twelve, but the damage was done. She had lost her childhood and her trust in her mother. She suffered from depression and began to drink as a teenager. When she was fifteen, she almost overdosed on aspirin in a suicide attempt. While she was in the hospital, her mother came to see her, and Roberta again told her the whole story; this time her mother believed her and apologized. Her mother had been in a state of denial herself, and had feared losing her relationship with Roberta's stepfather. Roberta went into therapy and became sober. Through Alcoholics Anonymous she was able to stay sober and enter college. She studied psychology and continued with her own healing.

Through her psychotherapist, Roberta discovered my book *Feeding Your Demons* and the Mandala of the Five Dakinis. When working with the five families, the Buddha Dakini and the issues of this family became very important for her. She realized how her whole family lineage was dominated by buddha family neurosis and denial, and she became committed to breaking the pattern. She created a buddha family altar, covering a table with white cloth and fixing an image of the five wisdom dakinis on the wall behind it. She put some pictures of herself as a child on the shrine and found an eight-spoked wheel, which she placed there. She also practiced the Mandala of the Five Dakinis, with an emphasis on visualizing herself as the white Buddha Dakini, sounding the seed syllable BAM when she was stuck in depression or felt herself about to dissociate. She did extensive work with the mandala and was able to stay sober.

Through her meditation practice, she began to experience the spacious wisdom aspect of the buddha family. Roberta grew to love meditation and the quiet openness she experienced through it. She started to go to meditation retreats in her vacation time, and although emotions from her childhood still came up, she began to find a way into the experience of all-encompassing wisdom, the wisdom of the buddha family. Gradually her negative emotional patterns shifted to feelings of spacious, relaxed awareness, and she broke the family pattern of denial and learned how to stabilize the wisdom of the buddha family. Ultimately Roberta went on to graduate school and became a psychotherapist herself, as someone who had been so wounded that she had great empathy and skill in working with others. She continues to do the Mandala of the Five Dakinis practice.

BUDDHA FAMILY MEDITATIONS

NINE RELAXATION BREATHS

Before beginning any of the practices or meditations with the five wisdom dakinis in these chapters, do this breathing meditation:

* Close your eyes and keep them closed as much as possible until the end of the process. You will be doing nine deep relaxation breaths.
* For the first three breaths, breathe into any *physical* tension you are holding in your body, noticing where you feel it; then, hooking that tension with the breath, release the tension with the exhalation.
* For the second three breaths, breathe into any *emotional* tension you are holding, noticing where you are holding emotional tension in your body; then, hooking that emotional tension with the breath, release it, letting it ride out with the exhalation.
* For the last three breaths, breathe into any *mental* tension or worries you are holding, noticing where you are holding mental tension in your body; then, hooking that tension with the breath, release it with the exhalation.

GENERATING THE MOTIVATION

Before beginning any of the meditations with the five wisdom dakinis in these chapters, generate a heartfelt motivation to practice for the benefit of yourself and all beings. You can, for example, say silently or out loud: "It is my heartfelt motivation to practice for the benefit of myself and all beings."

UNBLOCKING THE ENCUMBERED ENERGY

Now, let's take a moment to feel the encumbered buddha pattern in our bodies.

* Scan your body and feel the energy of depression, denial, spaciness, or distractedness in your own body. For example, is it heaviness in the limbs? A cold chill in the belly? A feeling of compression in your heart?
* Feel the encumbered energy. If you don't feel this currently, recall a time, an incident, or a period in your life when you were in the encumbered state.
* Now intensify the encumbered feeling of depression, isolation, or confusion, so that you really feel it deeply and strongly. This gives you a felt experience of buddha family in its blocked state.
* Now sound the seed syllable, slowly in a low voice: BAM. As you sound the syllable, feel the sound go through your body, almost like you are sending the sound into your body rather than projecting it out as we normally do. As you sound the seed syllable BAM, see your body permeated by white light and spaciousness. Feel the obstructed pattern ignorance transform into all-encompassing wisdom. Let the wisdom come from the sound and the light.

* Rest in the wisdom as long as you like. Repeat the seed
  syllable slowly and mindfully, resting after each repetition,
  as many times as you like, always resting in the wisdom
  energy at the end.

You can also do the following abbreviated version of the practice
when a strong attack of the encumbered energy comes up. By attack
I mean when you are suddenly flooded with feelings of depression,
confusion, or spaciness. Perhaps something unexpected happens and
you get very upset, or you take a buddha family exit, meaning you
get away from the triggered emotions by withdrawing.

* First find a quiet place, then either lie down or sit
  comfortably (when you can't sit down, you can do this
  standing).
* Do the Nine Relaxation Breaths described previously; then
  sound the family's particular seed syllable and visualize its
  color as light to release the energy into the wisdom.

You can do this same meditation with any of the other buddha
families in the following chapters; each chapter will give you a seed
syllable and color for that specific dakini, and you can work with the
encumbered pattern of that family in exactly the same way as this.

ELEMENT MEDITATION: SPACE

Because each of the dakinis is connected to an element, it is very helpful to work directly with that specific element as you explore each dakini. Since the Buddha Dakini is connected to the element of space,
this is a meditation practice called "integration with space or sky,"
namkha arte in Tibetan. It is one of my favorite practices, because it
is so relaxing and opens me deeply into a feeling of nonduality. And

it provides a wonderful foundation for an experiential understanding
of the wisdom of all-encompassing space.

* Before beginning this meditation, decide how long you are
  going to practice. I recommend from fifteen minutes to one
  hour.
* Lie on your back outside on a beach or in a field, on a
  rooftop, or in any open area with a fairly unobstructed view
  of the sky. Get comfortable—put a pillow under your head
  if you want to. If you are unable to be outside, find a place
  inside near a window so you have a view of the sky; but
  ideally it's done outside. This can also be done at night, or
  sitting up if you have a big sky view.
* After the Nine Relaxation Breaths, allow your breath to
  settle, and then with open eyes simply rest your mind on the
  sky. Let your mind open, so that there is no *journey* between
  you and the sky, there is no separation. If you get distracted,
  relax back into the spaciousness of the sky.
* Try to avoid fixating on clouds or trees or even the sky
  itself. If you notice you are focusing or straining your
  eyes, relax your eyes and let them go out of focus. It can
  be helpful to think about relaxing the muscles behind your
  eyes.
* When you are finished, sit up, and dedicate the positive
  energy that has been generated to benefit all beings.

After you close the meditation, notice how you feel. Keep the
awareness of that feeling as you go about your day. Do integration
with space meditation as frequently as possible; it will bring palpable
experiences of spacious calmness.

9

VAJRA DAKINI:
MIRROR-LIKE WISDOM

The five upper prongs symbolize the five buddhas and the lower five prongs symbolize their five consorts. The center of the vajra symbolizes that in whatever form the five buddhas and their consorts manifest they are not different than the core essence of the wisdom display. So there is one center connecting them.

—DILGO KHYENTSE

Vajra family represents the first step of the unfolding from emptiness into form. We're moving from the center to the eastern direction. Vajra is sharp and crystalline, vivid clarity, the transformation of anger. Vajra in Tibetan is *dorje* and means "diamond" or "king of stones." As an adjective, it means "indestructible, invincible, firm, and stable." Enlightened wakefulness is indestructible and unconditioned, and cannot be tarnished or harmed; the vajra symbolizes that wakefulness. The Sanskrit word *vajra* is often translated as "thunderbolt" or "adamantine." The thunderbolt references the divine weapon that is impervious and can victoriously cut through any situation; it cuts through the poison into clarity. The adamantine

Vajra Dakini (18th century). Ground mineral pigment on cotton.
Rubin Museum of Art

or diamond-like aspect of the vajra has similarities to a laser, with the laser's astonishing focus and precision in cutting through matter.

The vajra symbol is a scepter, with a central hub with prongs radiating out from it in opposite directions that come to a point on either end; the prongs are the energetic power emitting from the hub. The vajra is a ritual implement, a symbol of power in Buddhism, Jainism, and Hinduism. Just holding it is very powerful. It also symbolizes the phallus, the masculine power of skillful means and penetration; although the family applies to both women and men, many of the characteristics of vajra family are typically considered masculine.

The color of vajra family can be blue or white, but in this book we will mainly use blue. Blue is a cool color, and vajra types tend to be cool, both in terms of their character and also in the slang sense of the word: an aesthetic, hip person. The element here is water. Water is actually a fascinating element when you think about it, because it's the only element that appears in so many forms. It can be steam, liquid, ice, froth, wavy, flowing, or still. Water can be gentle but also destructive. I'm thinking about floods and hurricanes and the burning power of steam. It's a very powerful element. Even when water appears to be gentle, it has a penetrating ability, which you can see in streams where water has been flowing for many years and the rocks have gradually become smooth and round; it will gently eat away something as hard as stone. And think about water moving in a mighty river or in the ocean—when it's turbulent, it has a very powerful and sometimes very destructive ability.

Vajra symbolizes indestructibility, "diamond" or "thunderbolt," and is the symbol for the vajra family. Drawing by Robert Beer. Ink on paper.

I was recently in Nova Scotia staying on Hirtle's Beach in April, and it was still very cold and icy. The beach is in a bay, and behind it are wetlands where muskrats and seabirds feed. The beach had disappeared from the winter surf and was piled high with large rocks tangled in red, brown, and green seaweed, rounded by the intense pounding of the ocean. Where there had been sand, these rocks had been thrown up onto the beach, making it hard to walk along it. The beach had a vajra quality: the sharpness of the cold air, the power that could be felt in the water, and the starkness of the landscape.

The time associated with the vajra family is dawn—that clear moment, just before the sun rises, when it's chilly, and yet there is so much potential. There's a feeling that you can start again. It's very clear and open. The season is late autumn going into winter, that crispness. It's getting chilly, and the air has a tinge of sharpness. This is not the frozen stillness of midwinter that we find with the buddha family, but the sharp, spiky vividness of a late fall morning. There isn't all the complication of everything growing that we have in summer or the rich pungency of early autumn—this time of year has a certain barrenness, where you can see the patterns of things. The landscape that is associated with the vajra family is rugged mountains and icy rivers.

Where I live in southern Colorado at Tara Mandala, there is an old wagon road, no longer in use, leading from the hidden meadow up to a ponderosa-covered ridge and then across the upper meadow. This old road was formed by the homesteaders' wagons. And during the summer, you can't see that there was a road, because it is covered with plant life: small scrub oak trees, grass, artemesia, gumweed, and sage. But once all that dies back in the fall, before the winter comes, suddenly you can see the pattern of the old road emerging, and with it the imprint of those days long ago. Vajra family has that stark skeletal clarity.

The shape for vajra family is the circle, which represents something like a drop of water, a lake, an open space, or a mirror. In Tibetan Buddhism they use a round mirror during initiations to represent the vajra, like the nature of the mind. The sense perception of the vajra family is sight—a visual clarity. This clarity of sight extends to the vajra's intellectual ability to correct any distortion or the vague spacey bewilderment of buddha, with the precision that is penetrating and cutting. The vajra person is scientific and logical, and can analyze something from every point of view. And again, vajra art has that same sharp quality, such as the photography of Ansel Adams, his visual precision.

A vajra interior would exhibit simplicity, similar to buddha fam-

Moon and Half Dome, Yosemite National Park, California, 1960. *Photograph by Ansel Adams.*

ily's, but with harder edges and textures. The Japanese aesthetic is definitely vajra: less is more; simple elegance. The colors of blue and gray would predominate in a vajra interior, with metallic, synthetic, and techy textures. There would be little ornamentation, with more emphasis on simplicity and practicality. A vajra home interior would tend to be modern in sensibility, generally with chrome, concrete, and glass, although it could also have the simple natural textures of wood, woven grass rugs, and Japanese raku ceramics. The stylized simplicity of the Japanese tea ceremony and ikebana flower arrangements would appeal to vajra sensibilities, as would the abstract art of

Mark Rothko. For example, his work in the Rothko chapel in Houston, Texas, the fourteen large black but color-hued paintings covering the walls have a vajra quality. The paintings are essentially black but subtly incorporate other dark hues and texture effects, echoing the stark precision of vajra family. Also, the abstract conceptuality of his art is typical of vajra family. When people enter the chapel they typically ask: *Where are the paintings?* Because at first glance the walls just look like they have been painted black, but as you sit with these paintings, the subtle differences in color and texture slowly emerge.

The body type of the vajra person is thin, well toned, and angular, with sharp facial features. Coco Chanel would be a typical vajra type, and her designs reflected vajra family as well. It's a naturally slim body type, not created at the gym or through diet. The clothes a vajra person likes are simple and tailored, nothing frilly, nothing extra, but high quality and well designed. The colors black, blue, gray, and other neutral tones are preferred.

Steve Jobs, founder of Apple, is a good example of a vajra type: both the positive and the encumbered styles of vajra were embodied in him. He was thin, precise, easily angered, super smart, and creative. He dressed simply in blue and black, and for many years wore a black mock turtleneck and jeans every day like a uniform—but it was no ordinary turtleneck and had been designed by the Japanese designer Issey Miyake. Jobs was volatile, to the point of being accused of "management through character assassination" by his employees. He also actually practiced Zen meditation and liked the Japanese aesthetic.

VAJRA GOES TO A PARTY

If a vajra person goes to a party—of course, they don't much like going to parties to begin with, because, really, what's the point? Andrea, a lab research assistant, doesn't really enjoy communicating or socializing unless there's a reason behind it. If she goes to the party, she wears well-tailored gray slacks and a pressed cotton slim-cut white shirt. Andrea is athletic and runs marathons, and her hair is short and spiky. She arrives at the party punctually and is slightly irritated that people aren't on time. She surveys the scene, noting the details of the furniture, and goes to the bar and requests her usual martini. Gradually, as more people arrive, she starts to mingle. She isn't aiming to seduce or charm anyone, and isn't particularly interested in the snacks being served.

If Peter, who is an entrepreneur, goes to the party, he wears a crisp black designer shirt and black jeans. He goes to the bar and requests his usual scotch on the rocks. Peter thinks, *Well, since I'm here, I might as well not just waste the time. Maybe I could get into some sort of informative conversation about something technological?* He looks around and finds a male friend to connect with, and they chat standing up with drinks in their hands.

He connects in a friendly way to a few people, but has a hard time making small talk. He collects some business cards, makes a few contacts he will pursue later over coffee. Peter would be much more comfortable in a company office having a technical discussion, or even mountain-climbing or riding a sleek racing bike, than being at a party.

If Andrea is in the transformed state, she approaches Peter with an open, reflective presence, and is very clear in her communication, finding the conversation informative. They start dancing; she wants to choose the music and has a very specific idea about what she wants to play. She has suggestions for how to improve the sound system, and if anything did go wrong with the system, Andrea would be called on to help. Her style of dancing is precise, a little choppy, and not particularly sexy, but Peter likes it. Both are drawn to something like a tango that requires precision, skill, and the memory of certain step sequences. They find some tango music and put it on; both enjoy the expertise involved, and amaze the others at the party with their skills.

Let me give you an example of the vajra person in the encumbered state. Alexis travels widely selling medical software. She arrives at a hotel in New York and finds that her registration hasn't been recorded correctly. She starts tapping her foot and becoming agitated. She feels like she is not being greeted properly, that the place is in disarray and clearly not at all as organized as she is! A list of grievances is building inside her, and it is all very logical. When shown a possible room, she's displeased that it is not like the one she booked. They don't have the room she reserved originally, or the conference room where she had planned to hold a meeting. Then the encumbered vajra nature in her expresses itself as a justified, cold hostility, and an inner decision to write a long, negative online review about the hotel.

ENCUMBERED PATTERN: ANGER

Anger is the encumbered pattern of a vajra type, both hot and frigid anger, which is interesting in connection with its water element, since hot anger has a quality like steam. A steam burn is supposed to be one of the worst kinds of burns because you can't see where it's been and yet it burns very deeply; hot anger has that quality. Somebody who is habitually angry often doesn't realize the depth of damage that they do. They blow up, they blow off steam, and then they feel better. But the people who have received their anger are often extremely wounded and it takes them a long time to recover, especially if there's no acknowledgment of the harm that's been done. This hot anger is certainly one of the most destructive energies on our planet. As human beings we are capable of doing great good, but the combination of anger and power can be incredibly destructive, which in and of itself is a formidable reason to transform this emotion into wisdom.

The other aspect of anger is cold anger, passive aggression, which is like ice. We actually use that word—"She's really icy"—so that kind of anger has a cutting quality, a precise quality. Anger can be extremely one-pointed, both in terms of violence and in terms of the ability to really see very clearly the faults of others. It's the energy of the depression that we found in the buddha family turned out, turned toward the other. Anger has a controlling quality. Somebody who gets angry a lot can immediately get the attention of everybody in the room and control them.

Anger can materialize as a pattern of contraction, judgment, and criticism, as well as explosive anger. As you may remember, with the buddha family, we disconnect; but in the vajra family, we forcefully cut off, detaching with a cold intellectual analysis and sometimes aggression. Anger has an aggressive, constantly pushing-out quality; even repressed anger is dying to get out. Anger can trigger physical changes, including an increased heart rate, higher blood pressure, and increased levels of adrenaline and the stress hormone cortisol, preparing us physically for fight-or-flight.

As we do work within the five buddha families, we often find that there is something underneath what initially appears to be the encumbered pattern. Here in vajra, often fear underlies anger; because of this, there is a tendency for vajra types to survey the environment and look for potential threats, so that any threatening situations can be caught ahead of time. For most of us, beneath the emotion of anger is usually something else—vulnerability, an emotion also connected to the vajra family. It is fear and vulnerability that lead us to lash out. Fear is what lies underneath the hot and cold intensity of our anger. Anger is the reaction, the defense spurred by fear.

A vajra person will find that her anger can be triggered by many different circumstances: rudeness, poor service, fatigue, hunger, injustice, infidelity, being bullied, being humiliated, sexual frustration, financial loss or insecurity, unrealistic deadlines, traffic, a feeling of failure, a violation against her, being unwell or having a serious illness, using alcohol or drugs, or withdrawing from substances, to name a few. Grief and/or sadness, the loss of a family member, friend, or other loved one can also trigger anger. Some people are chronically angry and use their anger to control others. Some of us just get angry occasionally. Some internalize their anger, and it may be difficult to see any physical signs. Anger can be short-lived in a burst or held for years. We can develop chronic anger due to oppression or other challenging circumstances we live with, such as racial or sexual discrimination. In Buddhist teachings, they say one moment of anger can destroy the benefits of eons of virtuous action.

The vajra clarity in its encumbered state can become paranoia. There is fear of not having the situation covered, of things getting out of your control. Also there is a fear of humiliation that can lead to coldheartedness, even cruelty. With the encumbered pattern, we can be like the abusive parent who beats their child and hates themselves more every moment, and then continues to beat the child harder, angry at their own anger but taking it out on someone else.

INTELLECTUALIZATION, AUSTERITY, AND CONTROL

The vajra type has a tendency toward intellectualization, disconnecting from intimacy through analysis and being overly conceptual. It is a penchant for getting caught in overly complex thinking rather than being present. All the intellectual traditions such as science, philosophy, and psychology are vajra. A vajra person can see things from all angles and explain things logically—but can have a hard time with intimacy and may find difficulty in being in touch with her feelings. She tends to know what she thinks, but not what she feels.

Vajra sexuality can be sadomasochistic, where violence is eroticized; the vajra person would be the sadist. Another vajra type of sexuality could tend toward an unemotional, detached style, puritanical and somewhat antiseptic when it comes to sex. She wants to keep the barrier up—there is a fear of emotional intimacy and intensity, a kind of coldness.

Connected to this pattern of over-intellectualization is the vajra person's need to be right. Caroline gets into an argument with her partner, Addison, and she really needs to get in the last word. She says, "Okay, this is the way it is. And I'm right about this." Often what is underneath some of her righteous anger is the fear of actually *not* knowing it all. This fear gets covered over by her wanting to talk and talk her way out of an argument so that she has covered all the bases. She thinks: *I've said everything, so nothing can go wrong.* But, as we know, life does not work out this way. Her dominating arguments and her pattern of intellectualization and trying to control everything do not keep her from suffering, pain, or heartbreak. As we have experienced in our real lives, we are constantly reminded that we do not actually have it all covered; we are constantly being awakened by our inability to keep everything under control. However, we desperately want to be in charge. The act of continually trying to establish solid ground is the ego's main activity, and in vajra family it takes the form of logic and control.

The vajra person tends toward austerity. In its extreme form, this can develop into a spartan, cold lifestyle: essentially anti-comfort. One image that comes to mind is that of a Zen swordsman, the kind of crisp austerity that's a combination of clarity and incredible precision. But there's also heartlessness, a disconnection from feeling, rather like the eerie echo of cracking ice. Or just think of the texture of tanks and guns, of all that cold, hard equipment that we take into war. That's the vajra quality in its encumbered pattern. We put so much of our intelligence into defense.

Vajra people may be drawn to a spiritual practice like Zen or Quakerism, in which there is an austere discipline and spare ornamentation. They may run the risk of spiritual bypassing, using the austere form of spirituality in order to avoid emotional wounds. Or on the other side, they can be atheists or agnostics. They might think religion is for fools, since they are being realistic and scientific.

There can also be a tendency to criticize or lean toward excessive precision, to being so very organized that there is little or no room for spontaneity. Vajras like things being just so, and to happen in a certain way. Paula walks into a room where her team is preparing for a special event at the hotel she manages. She looks around, and instead of acknowledging all the work that has been done, she says, "That red chair looks ridiculous there, it'd be much better if you put it in the corner. Whose idea was that anyway?" In the transformed vajra state, she would instead survey the room and say, "You have really paid attention to every detail, everything looks great. It's amazingly clean, and everything looks brilliant—oh, and you might move that red chair to the corner, I think it would look better there."

MIRROR-LIKE WISDOM

The wisdom of this family is a mirror-like wisdom, a clarity like a mirror, and like a mirror this wisdom reflects everything and yet is unaffected by what reflects in it. The base of mirror-like wisdom is space and openness that comes out of the all-encompassing wisdom of buddha family. If you have been on a lake or by the ocean on a calm, misty day, you almost can't tell the difference between the sky and the water. Mirror-like wisdom is like this. Space and water are indivisible. However, we are moving now from space, the total openness of the sky of buddha, into *being* the mirror. In this state, all phenomena appear accurately, with no distortion.

"If you have been on a lake or by the ocean on a calm, misty day, you almost can't tell the difference between the sky and the water. Mirror-like wisdom is like this."

The mirror is an important metaphor in Buddhist teachings. It is a symbol of the nature of mind, because a mirror reflects everything, yet is not altered by what it reflects and does not judge those reflections. If the mind is a mirror, it is not conditioned by what appears in front of it. No matter what happens, the mirror does not react. It reflects, but does not change due to what is reflecting in it. Mirror-like wisdom is vast and precise cognizance, clarity without reactivity, a mind that does not move to judgments. To live within the wisdom of the vajra family is clarity without coldness and the heartlessness of anger; it is a clarity with compassion.

The state of mirror-like wisdom is, in fact, the very same energy that manifested as anger, but now the struggle is removed and the wisdom is revealed. Every disturbing emotion we experience is connected to a struggle of some kind. When the struggle is released, the wisdom is right there, where it has always been. It is the pure energy unencumbered by the struggle of the ego to maintain its ground. The intelligent awareness emerges from the unintelligent encumbered emotion.

They say in Vajrayana that the worse your afflicted patterns are, the brighter your wisdom blazes. The sharp edge of anger can develop, through practice, into panoramic awareness. Instead of being caught in the web of afflicted patterns, in our anger or over-intellectualization or need for control, we can begin to feel in these emotions the pure quality of the energy.

We know from science that energy can be neither created nor destroyed, but it can be transformed. Here the process of transformation is done through sound, light, and visualization. If I am in a situation where anger is arising, I can find the clarity of anger when I release myself from the ego's habitual orientation toward the self and its relentless grasping. In this way, and with practice, we may find that we begin to regard our relationships, our lives, ourselves with the open clarity of a mirror.

"We know from science that energy can be neither created nor destroyed, but it can be transformed. Here the process of transformation is done through sound, light, and visualization."

In 2004, after my teaching tour in Europe was over, my husband Dave and I went to Sicily. On the second night, we were offered a dessert wine after dinner in the beautiful seaside town of Selinunte, in southwest Sicily. It was served in a small glass, an offering from the restaurant at the end of a wonderful meal. The wine was a gold, almost orange in color and the flavor was like liquid gold with notes of apricot and the taste of the southern sun. We were floored by it and asked where it was from. The pleased waiter told us that it came from the island of Pantelleria and that it was called Passito di Pantelleria. Instantly we looked at each other, and we decided we someday had to go to this island that is so far south that on clear days you can see Africa. A few years later, back in Italy and following the scent of the Passito di Pantelleria, we took the short flight from Palermo to

Pantelleria. The next day I asked at the local café about houses for rent, and was told by the owner he had one available on a lake called Lo Specchio di Venere, literally the Mirror of Venus. I instantly loved the name and we decided to see it.

We drove with the café owner around hairpin turns on a narrow road above cliffs that dropped to the cobalt-blue sea. About fifteen minutes from the main town, we crossed a wall of rock perhaps a quarter mile wide that separated the sea from a perfectly round turquoise lake. The lake, in the crown of an extinct volcano with hot springs on one side, was only about five feet deep, with a base of white sand, and perfectly round. It looked unreal, and the house was equally enchanting, a small stone cottage covered with fuchsia bougainvillea vines, with arched doorways, an outdoor terrace overlooking the lake, in a private setting on the edge of a field of flowering caper bushes. We stayed ten days, blissfully wandering between the lake and the ocean. And since that time, whenever I think of the round shape of vajra family and the reflective nature of mirror-like wisdom, I always go back to Lo Specchio di Venere—and, of course, to the taste of Passito di Pantelleria.

Even though a mirror might be very small, say the size of a hand mirror, it can still reflect the moon, or even a mountain range. Mirror-like wisdom refers to this vast reflective presence, being able to accommodate everything and see all with clarity. If you go to a teaching on the nature of mind in the Tibetan tradition, the teacher might hold up a small round mirror, and say something like, "Look right now. This is your mind. This is the nature of your mind." Remember the advice that Naropa got, to "look into the mirror of the mind, the mysterious home of the dakini"? In a reflection on water or in a reflection in a mirror, we realize that nothing is solid, and that everything is illusory. This is another meaning of mirror-like wisdom, recognizing the illusory quality of all appearances. As Prospero said in Shakespeare's *The Tempest*:

Our revels now are ended. These our actors,
As I foretold you, were all spirits and
Are melted into air, into thin air:
And, like the baseless fabric of this vision,
The cloud-capp'd tow'rs, the gorgeous palaces,
The solemn temples, the great globe itself,
Yea, all which it inherit, shall dissolve,
And, like this insubstantial pageant faded,
Leave not a rack behind. We are such stuff
As dreams are made on, and our little life
Is rounded with a sleep.[54]

Knowing the illusory nature of all things, we can fully engage with life without being taken in by illusion's play. We have the clarity in the mirror-like wisdom state that is reflective of what is. And we have clarity without a feeling of separation. When I think of mirror-like wisdom, I think of my teacher Chögyal Namkhai Norbu. There is a vastness about him in every situation, and in this vastness, this immensity, there is also room for me; he takes me into it. It is a vastness that holds it all—life, suffering, the past, the present—like a mirror. Whatever happens, he stays there in that immensity. He talks, he teaches, he writes, he eats, but he is always in the nature of the mirror; it's quite extraordinary. He is also intellectually astute and has written many scholarly books on Tibetan culture as well as books on the teachings; his writings fill many volumes.

However, you have to be prepared for Namkhai Norbu's wrathful manifestations if you are close to him. If students are doing things he feels lack awareness, he will manifest wrathful energy. For example, he teaches *khaita*, a joyful kind of Tibetan dancing done in groups. If he gives an explanation of the steps and then people mess it up, he will call them over and make his point that they have lacked awareness. Then everyone concentrates harder the next time.

I have traveled with him in Tibet and in the West, and have witnessed lots of different situations both positive and negative, but it seems like he never moves from mirror-like awareness; he has the clarity and sharp intelligence of the vajra person.

Sometimes his detachment could feel like coldness; but over time I realized it wasn't coldness, it was just that he didn't react like a normal person—which makes sense since he is a highly realized lama. When my twin baby daughter Chiara died of SIDS, I was living in Italy and had just recently met him. Since he was the only lama I knew in Italy, I called him and told him the news. I expected some kind of reaction like "Oh no, I'm so sorry." But he was just quiet, and then I said, "Rinpoche, are you there?"

He said, "Yes."

Then I said, "What practice should I do?"

He said, "Not very much."

I said, "Will you come?"

He said, "Yes."

When I hung up, I felt sort of disappointed. I didn't feel comforted as I thought I would. But I realized I was dealing with a great lama, not an ordinary person. And somehow his lack of emotionality felt freeing to me as well as disappointing.

A few days later, he came to our house outside of Rome in the Albana Hills with a group of his students, most of whom I didn't know well. I asked him if we could talk privately, and he agreed. He went with me upstairs to the little room above the kitchen where the twins had been. We sat together quietly, and he made an elaborate protection necklace with yarn for the remaining twin, my son. And he gave me a special mantra of protection. But he was never emotional. He was just there, vast and present.

The vajra person can simply be there in the wisdom state without trying to alter what others are saying or feeling, like a mirror. And if you are really present with what is being said, either by someone else or in your own mind, you will find that your presence has the power to defuse anger. Often when we're getting into an argument with somebody, we are thinking about what we are going to say next. And yet, if we are truly present with that person, present without reaction and response, that anger has nothing to attach to because you are not reacting back. You will find that the situation will diffuse. Mirror-like wisdom is an opportunity to reflect all that is present in a situation; it is reflection without feeling like you have to jump in and fix anything.

FIERCE MANIFESTATIONS

In general, anger is something we try to avoid. However, in the Buddhist Tantric teachings, we talk about fierce or wrathful manifestations, which are energies that transform the intensity of anger into compassionate activity. You may have seen Tibetan paintings of fierce deities.

These wrathful deities are often painted in gold on black ground. They are surrounded by swirling flames of fire and have bulging eyes. The energy of the wrathful deities destroys ignorance, rips off the veil of delusion, and clears the way to liberation.

The wrathful manifestations that you see in Tibetan art are different from blind fury. In them there is compassion and no hatred. These deities are manifestations of fast-moving energy; there is no attachment behind it. For example, let's say a child is being harmed or in danger: you might have to show a wrathful manifestation to save that child. It can be likened to the fierceness of a mother lion or a mother wolf. Any mother will become fierce when her young are threatened.

Fierceness in the Tibetan tradition represents a powerful energy. In the Tara Mandala temple, we have life-size statues of the twenty-one Taras in a circle around its circumference. Some of these Taras are fierce, like the seventh, Tara Zhengi Mitubma, who is wrathful and black like dense rain clouds. She stops natural disasters, invading troops, and weapons of mass destruction. She is ablaze with wisdom fire.

The 7th Tara Zhengi Mitubma Unconquerable Fierce One Who Dispels Wars and Natural Disasters, in the Three Kaya Tara Mandala Temple, Pagosa Springs, Colorado. *Photograph by Alan Kozlowski, statue copper gilded with gold by Bijaya Sakya*

Fierce energy is the fastest-moving energy we manifest as human beings, and the fierce deities represent the explosion of energy that destroys limitations and delusion. When you are angry, your blood gets moving, your breath is faster, and you start moving quickly. Fire moves quickly, and unpredictably. So the wrathful manifestations of Tantric deities symbolize energy, a lot of energy, a lot of powerful energy. It is very important to distinguish between a wrathful manifestation and hatred. Even if you have a fierce manifestation, you should not have hatred behind it or underneath it. The paradoxical thing I have found in working with the fierce deities is that practicing them actually makes me feel more peaceful. It is as though by allowing and transforming the fundamental human energy of anger, we are able to incorporate the shadow aspect of that emotion and channel them into a constructive avenue.

"Fierce energy is the fastest-moving energy we manifest as human beings, and the fierce deities represent the explosion of energy that destroys limitations and delusion."

JOHN'S STORY

Let me tell you an example of working with anger. John is a forty-four-year-old psychotherapist and also teaches karate part-time. He started doing mandala work when he was thirty-eight. His father had beaten him severely throughout his childhood, and his mother did little to protect him, sometimes turning him over to his father when he returned from work, reporting John's bad behavior to him. When he grew up, he developed a pattern of taking risks and getting injured and also had suicidal ideation, although he never made a suicide attempt.

Before the mandala work, John had a short fuse and got angry often, and he got angry about little things, like his car not starting or someone being late. He always felt justified in his irritation. Anger was everywhere in his life: his relationships, business, and family; he couldn't get away from it. Others were angry with him; he was angry with them. On and on, anger triggered more anger, so his life became claustrophobic. John also had a sharp precision, a hyperawake quality. When he was angry, he could be extremely cutting and accurate about the faults of others. He developed an interest in martial arts to work with his anger in a more controlled situation, and ended up with a black belt in karate.

John began practice with the mandala meditation after several years of mindfulness meditation practice. Despite his more academic queries into Buddhist teachings, painful psychological and emotional patterns still lurked in his body and mind; residual trauma remained from his abusive childhood. When he learned about the five families, he immediately knew he was vajra.

Two primary developments occurred during his time working with vajra family. John came to see clearly, for the first time, that the intense anger and bitterness he felt toward men, and toward "God" in general, whom he considered a big disappointment, was based on his own inner anger. He had trained as a Catholic brother as a teenager, partly to escape from his home and his father, but lost faith in the church and Christianity and began to study psychology in college.

Secondly, he was able to recognize that much of his anger toward his father stemmed from the deep desire to have a father figure who would protect him, who would have allowed him to claim the masculine in a positive way. He blamed men for not being compassionate, yet simultaneously felt deep resentment and bitterness toward women, because he felt cut off from that strong, nurturing presence when his mother hadn't protected him. During his childhood, his mother, a victim of abuse and abandonment herself, had suffered from depression and, despite her deep love and support for John, was often withdrawn. As John grew up, he began to find unending faults in his mother: her self-imposed isolation, her social oddities, her denial about her own trauma, her anger.

By adulthood, his relationship with his parents had deteriorated and family gatherings were marked with arguments and explosions. John was perpetually frustrated at his own inability to transform the situation. He read Buddhist texts; he tried to meditate on the breath. He knew all the ways he "wanted" to feel about his parents, but felt none of them, and was plagued by a sense of guilt and grief at his fiercely critical mind-set.

Through the work with the five buddha families, and vajra family in particular, John was able to begin the process of accepting positive masculine energy into his life and redirecting the powerful arrows of blame and anger away from his father toward healing. His insights with the vajra family showed so clearly how his distorted view of the feminine, so disparaged in our society in general, had been lumped onto his mother, herself a victim of similar defeating patterns. He also saw that his father was a victim of the same violence that had been inflicted on him, that he had taken the accepted theory of "spare the rod and spoil the child" to the extreme.

The sharp precision and clarity of the vajra family helped John see and feel how futile and defeating the patterns of anger and bitterness were for himself. By accessing the spacious clarity of vajra, he was able to feel the warmth of the feminine he had so dearly needed as a child. He was gradually able to release the expectation that his mother, as an earthly woman with her own pain, would somehow provide him with that sense of ultimate connection.

The healing he experienced around his parents was not what he'd expected. It was not soft or nurturing, nor has it "made everything okay" with them, and he still can't really trust his father. But with the clarity of vajra, he is able to see and release his parents from the expectations of the child. Now he relates to them more as equals, friends who have also suffered. John's work with the mandala as a whole was a deeply transformative re-identification process. He continually experienced a joyful shattering, the loss of hope that the "answer" to life would be found in the same deluded world of the question; instead he has found a true home, a true sense of clarity and peace in himself.

In the "real world," the decision to shift his focus from the obstructive patterns to ones of clarity became natural because of his felt experience and familiarity with the lucid and peaceful clarity of vajra energy. And for the first time in his life, John was able to enter a relationship that he didn't ruin with anger. What was so transformational

Rare Tara Seventeen Deity Mandala, Green Tara embracing her consort
Amoghasiddhi surrounded by the five male and female Buddhas, and
attendant deities (15th century). Ground mineral pigment, gold ink on cotton.
Shelley and Donald Rubin Private Collection.

*Conception Mandala from a dream shared by Lama Tsultrim and
Paul Kloppenburg the night of the conception of their daughter Sherab,
by Stuart Hamill (1974). Mineral pigments in the style of ancient
Indian miniature painting. Lama Tsultrim Allione.*

The Swan *by the Swedish visionary artist Hilma af Klint (1915).*
Oil on canvas. (HaK 160. Group IX/SUW #12. The Swan, 1915.)
Courtesy of the Hilma af Klint Foundation. Photograph by Albin Dahlström,
the Moderna Museet, Stockholm, Sweden.

Traditional Tibetan Architectural Manjushri Mandala (16th century).
Pigments on cloth. Rubin Museum of Art.

Mandala drawn by C.G. Jung, from The Red Book.

*Three Kaya Tara Mandala Temple at Tara Mandala. Design from a dream
by Lama Tsultrim, 2001; built 2008. Tara Mandala Archives.*

Vajra Varahi, an aspect of Vajra Yogini (18th century). Ground mineral pigment on cotton. Rubin Museum of Art.

Seed syllables of the Five Wisdom Dakinis in Tibetan. BAM (center),
(below) HA east, (left) RI south, (top) NI west, (right) SA north. Visualized
as horizontal lotus with syllables standing vertically. Painting by Lama
Gyurme Rabgye (2017). Acrylic with mineral pigment.

Mandala of the Tsogyel Karmo, white Buddha Dakini surrounded by the four retinue dakinis from the Dzinpa Rangdröl lineage practiced at Tara Mandala, by Lama Gyurme Rabgye (2017). Ground mineral pigment on cotton. Tara Mandala.

ABOVE: *Thangka of the Five Wisdom Dakinis by Lama Gyurme Rabgye (2016). Acrylic and mineral pigment. Lama Tsultrim Allione.*

RIGHT: *Buddha Dakini with the wheel ornamented hooked knife, detail of the thangka of the Five Wisdom Dakinis, by Lama Gyurme Rabgye (2016). Acrylic and mineral pigment. Lama Tsultrim Allione.*

*Vajra Dakini with the vajra ornamented hooked knife, detail of
the thangka of the Five Wisdom Dakinis, by Lama Gyurme Rabgye (2016).
Acrylic and mineral pigment. Lama Tsultrim Allione.*

*Ratna Dakini with the jewel ornamented hooked knife, detail of
the thangka of the Five Wisdom Dakinis, by Lama Gyurme Rabgye (2016).
Acrylic and mineral pigment. Lama Tsultrim Allione.*

Padma Dakini with the lotus ornamented hooked knife, detail of the thangka of the Five Wisdom Dakinis, by Lama Gyurme Rabgye (2016). Acrylic and mineral pigment. Lama Tsultrim Allione.

Karma Dakini with the sword ornamented hooked knife, detail of
the thangka of the Five Wisdom Dakinis, by Lama Gyurme Rabgye (2016).
Acrylic and mineral pigment. Lama Tsultrim Allione.

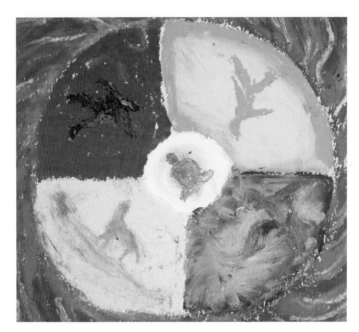

Example of Lama Tsultrim Allione's mandala drawing in oil pastels as described in the chapter "Mandala Work with Your Hands™ and More"

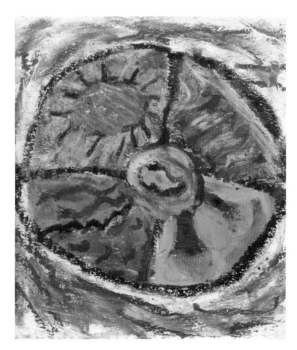

Mandala drawn by Lama Tsultrim's granddaughter, Luna Violet Sands, at the age of eight.

for him in the mandala work was how it *felt*, and how he was able literally to embody the wisdom.

VAJRA FAMILY MEDITATIONS

Before beginning each of the meditations below, please first do the Nine Relaxation Breaths and Generating the Motivation practices as instructed in Chapter 8 on pages 155 and 156.

UNBLOCKING THE ENCUMBERED ENERGY

Let's take a moment to feel the encumbered vajra pattern in our bodies.

* Scan your body and feel the energy of anger in your own body. Is it heaviness in the limbs? A cold chill in the belly? A feeling of compression in your heart?
* Feel the encumbered energy. If you don't feel this currently, recall a time, an incident, or a period in your life when you were in the encumbered state.
* Now intensify the encumbered feeling of anger, control, or coldness, so that you really feel it deeply and strongly. This gives you a felt experience of vajra family in its blocked state.
* Now sound the seed syllable, slowly in a low voice: HA. As you sound the syllable, feel the sound go through your body, and see your body permeated by blue light. Feel the obstructed pattern transform into the mirror-like wisdom. Let the wisdom come with the sound and the light.
* Rest in the wisdom as long as you like. Repeat the seed syllable slowly and mindfully, resting after each repetition,

as many times as you like, always resting in the wisdom
energy at the end.

ELEMENT MEDITATION: WATER

* Before beginning this meditation, decide how long you are
  going to practice. I recommend from fifteen minutes to one
  hour.
* Find a body of water: a lake, stream, pond, fountain,
  waterfall, river, or ocean. Sit near the water and settle
  comfortably with the water in view, getting as close to it as
  you can. If there's none nearby, you can meditate on a bowl
  of water, or take a bath or shower.
* After the Nine Relaxation Breaths, allow your breath to
  settle; rest for a few minutes with the presence of your
  breath, and then bring your eyes to the water. Rather than
  staring at the water, imagine your eyes are reflecting pools.
  Relax your eyes and integrate with the water so there is no
  journey between you and the water, no separation.
* Whenever your mind wanders, bring your awareness back
  to the water; just rest in union with the water. If the water is
  making a sound, as a waterfall does, or a rushing stream, or
  the waves of the ocean, you can integrate with the sound as
  well as the visual aspect of the water.
* When you are finished, dedicate the positive energy that has
  been generated to benefit all beings.

After you close the meditation, notice how you feel. Keep the
awareness of that feeling as you go about your day. I really encourage
you to spend time near some water, next to a stream, a lake, or the
ocean, or even in the bath or the shower, just being very conscious of
that element. This is a very powerful practice. You can do it when-

ever you are near water. When I am by the ocean I like to get up early and go sit near the water and practice integration with the sound and the movement of the ocean. I also like to do it sitting next to the San Juan River, which runs near Tara Mandala. I sit on a big rock on the shore and look upstream, integrating with the sound and the sparkling water as it flows toward me.

10

RATNA DAKINI:
WISDOM OF EQUANIMITY

Were there an inexhaustible treasure in the ground under a poor person's house, they might not know it was there, nor would the treasure tell them, "I am here." Just so, since all living beings fail to realize the precious treasure contained in their minds, the stainless reality, devoid of any negativity to be cleared away or anything positive to establish, they continually experience the suffering of poverty and deprivation in a variety of ways.

—THE SUPREME CONTINUITY, FROM THE *UTTARATANTRA*

R atna family is in the southern direction of the mandala. The word *ratna* means "jewel," and the wish-fulfilling jewel is Ratna Dakini's symbol—a golden jewel like amber set in gold, with a quality of rich, delicious honey. The ratna family was known in ancient times to be ideal for rulers and kings, because it was their duty to provide stability and prosperity for their subjects. The names

Ratna Dakini (18th century). Ground mineral pigment on cotton.
Rubin Museum of Art.

of many ancient rulers in India and Nepal contain the word *ratna*,
indicating this connection.

The Ratna Dakini's color is yellow, not a pale yellow, not a lemon
yellow, but a rich golden yellow. One of the images that's used for
ratna is a rotting log, the kind of golden hue logs get when they rot
with all kinds of things growing out of them, like mushrooms and
moss. And the season associated with the ratna family is early autumn, when the yellow leaves are falling and there's beginning to be
that smell of decomposition that's so rich, sweet, and fertile. And so
we see that the landscape of the ratna family is a fertile forest or jun-

gle with all kinds of rotting logs feeding the rest of the environment, with dense layers of branches and leaves that cover any kind of space. It has this combination of being almost too much and at the same time very rich.

My daughter Sherab lives in the mountains of Colorado, and nearby many mushrooms grow. There is a place that she knows high in the mountains, a forest near a small lake. In the fall, when the aspen trees are turning golden and singing in the breeze, the mushrooms come. It can be earlier in August—it all depends on the rain. Mushrooms have such a magical quality: first they're not there, and then suddenly they are completely there. Mushrooms express the spontaneous richness of ratna family. And when I think about this family, I think about this forest and walking through it with my grandson Otto. His middle name is Ziji, which means confidence, charismatic radiance, and brilliance in Tibetan. He's been mushrooming since he could walk; he has his own mushroom harvesting tool that he wears around his neck and he wears a little cape that flaps in the breeze. So when I see him in the forest with his curly blond hair in the late-afternoon sun and his cape flying, he looks like a little sprite, who just popped up like the mushrooms. He can identify hawk wing mushrooms, boletus, and chanterelle mushrooms. This forest with Otto sprinting from mushroom to mushroom, near the mountain lake which we named "Ziji Lake," with its sparkling water blown by squalls and lit up by the afternoon sun, is to me the essence of ratna.

Jewel symbol of the ratna family. Drawing by Robert Beer. Ink on paper.

The ratna element is earth and the shape is the square. Ziji trans-

mits the qualities of the transformed ratna family. The wisdom quality of confidence in the ratna family is based on the generosity of
the family and the firm connection to the earth. The ratna time is
high noon, when we feel this intensity. Everything is kind of blazing.
There's a potential for growth, a richness. And yet there's almost a
feeling of too much, which could be overwhelming. The senses here,
as one might expect, are smell and taste, the tactile contact of consumption. We can't really consume by way of sight or hearing, but
through taste and smell we can take in and devour. There's a deep
appreciation of food and wine in ratnas. When they taste something,
they savor it and can describe the subtle layers of flavor in a single
bite. They often have highly developed palates, which can lead to
overindulgence and greed.

The figurine of the Sleeping Woman, found inside a womb-
shaped temple on the island of Malta, is a classic ratna image in religious art. She lies asleep on a stone bed, dreaming oracular dreams.
The Neolithic goddess temples in Malta are also a ratna-style architecture, in which the temple is shaped like the body of an obese fertile
goddess, with no corresponding male figures. This led to the theory
that this was a goddess-worshipping culture, and archaeologists pro-
pose that these temples were slept in to receive prophetic dreams. The
temples are entered through what would be the vagina of the goddess.

Sleeping Woman of Malta, a clay figure of a reclining lady, was found
in one of the pits of the Hypogeum in Hal Saflieni, in Malta.

Earth houses all over the world echo the values of ratna, the connection to the stability and warmth of the earth, and the flexibility and organic nature of clay and mud have given us some of the most beautiful buildings in the world. The mud buildings in Africa are among the most exquisite; those in Timbuktu and Djenné in Mali, for example, are both magnificent and practical. A ratna house would have really comfortable furniture with lots of pillows and rich brown alpaca throws to cover you; it would feel very cozy and comfortable, with fresh flowers and wood accents, such as handmade wooden bowls containing fruit and nuts. The house might be made of adobe, rammed earth, straw bale, or wood in a natural finish, and is likely to be packed with things from all over the world.

The female ratna body type is big and full with big breasts. This is a person who likes bright colors, big jewelry (and lots of it), and big patterns. When I was teaching at a university in San Francisco, I met a woman who was a quintessential ratna type. She was racially mixed, giving her a golden complexion. Her body was full and generous in a healthy, strong way. She'd gathered her dreadlocks in a yellow African-print scarf on top of her head, and wore a yellow printed dress and big yellow and black beads. She was very warm and friendly. There was a feeling of richness and creativity around her; almost as though anything could happen when she was around, because there were so many possibilities.

RATNA GOES TO A PARTY

When Clarissa, a dark-haired, statuesque editor, walks into a party, she is wearing vivid colors, a long, large-patterned dress that hangs regally over her generous body. It's set off by bold amber jewelry, a stack of bracelets each a different color of amber—some translucent, some opaque honey-colored, some dark resin—and large dangling gold earrings. Clarissa first locates the food and drink, and hopes there's something delicious and rich to eat. But when she sees the refreshments, she has the tendency to think that there's not enough. This is followed by the thought: *I'd better start eating now or there's not going to be enough.* Clarissa hangs out at the refreshment table, being loud, laughing, and telling jokes and stories.

If Michael, a ratna type, who is a scholar of medieval history, goes to a party, he really looks forward to it, thinking about meeting people and eating and drinking some delicious items. But underneath, he is worried that he's not good enough. He's wearing a bright Hawaiian shirt over his big belly, with loose yoga pants underneath. Once he gets his plate of food stacked high and a big glass of wine, he sits down at a table with some of his friends. He immediately dominates the conversation and begins to talk about some esoteric historical information that he has. Michael wants to be the center of attention and draw as many people as possible into the conversation. He is name-dropping and seeking to collect information. He wants to amass anything that will somehow enhance him—food, drink, contacts—and make him feel important. He is jovial, smiling at everyone, feeling expansive the more he eats and drinks. He talks and eats compulsively at the same time, enjoying everything to its full extent, but with an underlying insecurity.

If Clarissa is in the transformed state of ratna when she goes to the party, she will bring a gift such as some great wine for the host and have some small gifts for others at the party. When she arrives, there's a feeling of a large presence entering the room. Immediately the party seems more exciting. She brings a playful energy, thinks of a creative and fun game for the guests to play that really livens up the party.

ENCUMBERED PATTERN:
PRIDE AND INADEQUACY

The encumbered pattern or poison for ratna family is arrogance, a pride that includes insecurity, creating the need to consume, to shop, to eat, and to hoard—the bag lady syndrome where you find yourself keeping everything, and lots of it. You need to have five of everything in case something happens. And you can't let go of anything because you feel insecure about what might happen; you experience acute fear of there not being enough, which creates a consuming hunger. This hunger is experienced both by ratna types and by those around them, who feel that the ratna is consuming them and taking up a lot of space. There's a neediness and a kind of insistence on love; invasive parents are often ratna types, trying to control their children's lives, force them to eat, direct their social lives, read their journals, and so on.

Trungpa Rinpoche had a great description of the encumbered ratna type: "It is like swimming in a dense lake of honey and butter. When you coat yourself in this mixture of butter and honey, it is very difficult to remove. You cannot just remove it by wiping it off, but you have to apply all kinds of cleaning agents, such as cleanser and soap, to loosen its grasp."[55] Ratnas have a tendency to grab something and hold on for dear life—food, status, material things, alcohol, drugs. It is a kind of greediness in which we find ourselves wanting more, more, and more. This comes from a feeling of insecurity. In the extreme, the ratna can tend toward hoarding, which is rooted in a feeling of anxiety; we think: *I might not have this in the future or I might need it someday, so I am going to keep it.* For ratnas, there is a feeling that if they get more, eat more, or have more, then they'll be safe; but they don't ever feel safe, because they haven't dealt with the underlying problem of insecurity leading to overindulgence in the first place. We call this "poverty mentality," which means that no matter how much you have, you feel poor inside though it may manifest as flagrant ostentatious behavior. If someone brings out the ice cream, the immediate thought is: *Oh no, there's not going to be enough for me.*

They often have a hard time with money and are always feeling financially insecure. Ratna issues could arise from something like a learning disability, or maybe growing up in poverty. If there was shame connected with that, they want to hide it somehow: they're going to pretend to have it all. The ratna reaction might be, "I'm fine. I'm not only fine; actually, I'm great. Everything's going great. I'm actually the best and what I'm doing is superior to others." The encumbered ratna may be overly generous to make a show, perhaps giving everyone on their team or in their class a nicely wrapped gift for Christmas, or giving overly lavish gifts with the need to be seen as generous and lovable. They have the need to inflate themselves with pride, which comes from the fear of not being good enough and not having enough. They feel they aren't good enough in and of themselves, so they need to inflate with such things as more food, more drink, name-dropping, or consumerism. Romantically, this shows up as a desire to be worshipped by their partner with lots of compliments and constant reassurance.

Ratnas can be controlling, blaming, self-absorbed, and so full of themselves they are unaware of the needs of others. They may also be unaware of how they are affecting others, they are so self-involved and in their own world. They may use a variety of strategies to protect themselves at the expense of others. If they get feedback about their behavior, they react by taking up more space and need continual reassurance. Their self-aggrandizing tendencies cover feelings of shame and worthlessness. They usually mask these feelings from others with contrived humility. In the unenlightened aspect, ratna can have a need to be noticed, to perform, to get applause, to be in control.

Consider the ratna element of earth: earth can be very heavy, overpowering, and messy. This neurotic aspect of ratna reminds me of the mudslides that we sometimes have in southern Colorado because of forest fires. In some places where forests have burned and there are steep slopes, when it rains huge mudslides cover everything. The mud rushes into people's houses and into the rivers. One of the saddest things I heard about was that fish were jumping out of the water, suffocating on the shore in an attempt to get out of the mud filling the streams. This domineering aspect of ratna creates a feeling of suffocation for those around them, a kind of crushing quality.

When we look at the encumbered pattern of the ratna family in the broader picture of our world, we see it in corporate greed, that desire to take over, to consume smaller companies, to own the world. Politically this is colonialism, feeling that we must be in everyone else's business. We need to be there to control, to rule, and to get more riches. So even if we have power and riches, we still feel poor, we still feel like we don't have enough, and we have the sense that there is some ultimate experience of consumption that will bring happiness, that will bring peace. But of course it doesn't bring peace, merely builds more compulsive consumption. We see empires built on greed, but they crumble because underneath they're not connected to the earth. There's a literal inflation that is unsustainable and leads to collapse.

WISDOM OF EQUANIMITY

The wisdom in the ratna family is called the wisdom of equanimity or equality. Sometimes it's termed equanimity and unchanging stillness, or equanimity and enriching presence. Equanimity is also about not judging, not valuing one thing over another—in other words, impartiality. So something we would normally consider disgusting and something we would consider beautiful would be held with the same value.

When we stop grasping, this wisdom is there. It is the gesture of generosity based on true richness, which comes from stability, a sense of groundedness, being on the earth, and you can trust that. This is the fundamental reality of equality: that pure and impure are really concepts that we lay on the world. That what's pure to one person might be impure to another. That what's good for one culture is considered bad in another culture. Ratna wisdom is about equality and "sameness," about treating everything with equal value and with the dignity of self-existing completeness. In the transformed ratna, there is a feeling of inherent richness, a feeling that the situation is already rich. You can relax.

"Ratna wisdom is about equality and 'sameness,' about treating everything with equal value and with the dignity of self-existing completeness."

When a transformed ratna person walks into a room, she feels a settled quality; things are just as they are. And yet in that settled feeling, all kinds of things are popping up. The way they pop up appears to be slow, and yet suddenly there they are. Ratna's fertility is like watching crocuses in the early spring. In Colorado, the crocuses spring up while there are still patches of snow on the ground. Their purple, yellow, and white heads are brilliant spots of color among the gray-brown dead grass and bushes. One day they're just there, spontaneously arising gifts. This is the energy of transformed ratna.

Prosperity is connected to ratna, so when you practice the ratna family mandala, your whole prosperity situation can change, and you can boost your resources. While padma is more about magnetizing power and health, with ratna there's an increase of assets and, more important, a sense of trust that creates a feeling of wealth. You can relax; you can open to prosperity rather than feeling like you have to struggle to create it. You can just receive it and feel your richness, just as you are.

To receive the sense of well-being that prosperity can bring, you need to feel that you're worthy of receiving it. If unconsciously you don't feel you are good enough to be supported, you might make money or somehow receive wealth, but you won't have the sense of well-being that could accompany it. You could actually feel impoverished, even if you're rich. So working with prosperity is quite a profound practice, because it does touch deep places within us of insecurity and lack of self-esteem. And prosperity is linked to generosity; when you feel you have enough, you can afford to be generous. All our self-importance, self-advancement, and overbearing tendencies are relaxed and freed from our clinging mind—everything is perfect as it is. There is an experience of innate richness, a feeling that it's not coming from outside. We don't need to consume—and actually, if we stop consuming, we can appreciate the richness of every moment.

This is a generosity based on the Buddhist teaching of the "three empty places": the emptiness of self, of other or the recipient, and of the gift itself. These are empty of any inherent separate existence. If we give in this way, it is truly enlightened generosity. Usually we give with a solid sense of self, recipient, and gift, and with the hope to receive something back. In the case of the transformed ratna, it is more about things being generated from within rather than being consumed. When a transformed ratna person comes into a room, a project, or a team, they bring a feeling of productiveness and creativity, as though anything could happen and all kinds of magic might appear.

Any of the families can be used for practical transformation— buddha family to pacify disturbance, vajra family to remove obstacles, ratna for increase and prosperity, padma for health and empowerment, and karma family to subdue what needs to be subdued. That said, it is important not to use these blessings selfishly. If your motivation is ultimately for the benefit of others, one of the advantages of Vajrayana Buddhism is that it offers the skillful means to benefit others and oneself. Also, it's important to understand that ratna family is not just about prosperity; it is, most vitally, about generosity and equality. The mudra of the Ratna Buddha is that of generosity with the right palm facing out.

Tara's gesture of generosity and giving. *Photograph by Alan Kozlowski*

The wisdom of ratna family is the wisdom of equanimity and enriching presence—a feeling that you don't need more, that what you have is enough. You can practice feeling satisfied, prosperous, and generous. Think about everything you do have, the loved ones in your life, your health, whatever you can think of, and generate a feeling of gratitude and generosity. The more you give away, the more you will receive. And that can be hard to understand when you feel you really don't have very much. Of course, you shouldn't do anything imprudent—just strive to create that sense of movement.

Start by giving small things, and practice feeling trust in the earth to support you. This family is the earth element and involves material things, so working with generosity is a key idea. In the enlightened ratna, there's a sense of trusting the earth. You can sit on the earth. She will provide. You can relax. You can give because there's enough, and because you have Mother Earth to sustain you. So the wisdom of equanimity is that sense of stability, fertility, and of equal value. Everything is okay. You don't need to like it or dislike it. It's simply okay exactly how it is. And the wisdom of equanimity has a sense of unchanging stillness, quietness. In the transformed aspect of ratna, everything feels kind of juicy.

With the wisdom of equanimity, there's also the sense of self-acceptance. You don't need anyone else to approve of you because you're enough in yourself. What you have is enough. You don't need to strive. With enlightened ratna there's the sense of dignity rather than pride, of confidence rather than arrogance, so sharing the abundance is safe because you're not worrying about running out; you can share freely—you don't have to hoard. You let it be.

"With the wisdom of equanimity, there's also the sense of self-acceptance. You don't need anyone else to approve of you because you're enough in yourself."

ANYTHING COULD HAPPEN

When someone embodying the wisdom of ratna is around, they're a large presence, and sometimes a magnanimous one, like the Sixteenth Karmapa who ordained me. The positive ratna personality offers a sense of possibilities, of inexhaustible fruitfulness. They might wear red or gold and a lot of ornaments, but not in an ostentatious way, just expressing the joy of embodiment. Ratna people have a good sense of humor; all kinds of things could emerge—and if nothing emerges, that would be fine too.

The Sixteenth Karmapa, my root teacher and the head of the Kagyu lineage, second to the Dalai Lama among Tibetan lamas, was a ratna being who completely embodied the wisdom of equanimity. He treated everyone from the lowest to the highest rank with the same compassionate presence. And with him, it quite literally seemed like anything could and did happen. He was warm and magnanimous; his smile lit the heart of anyone who met him. He was physically large and emanated an enriching presence. Rumtek, his monastery in Sikkim, was beautifully ornamented with the best frescoes, and it was shaped like a mandala. He taught kings and queens, but also gave loving attention to the youngest monks put into his care.

Back in the 1970s when my friend Stuart Hamill, an artist and photographer, was living in India, she went to see Karmapa at Rumtek and took a Polaroid photo of him; what developed was an image not of him but of a mandala. And not just a vague mandala image, but the precise form of the Mahakala Mandala.

This mandala appeared instead of the body of His Holiness the 16th Karmapa when Lama Tsultrim's friend Stuart Hamill took a Polaroid photo of him. *Courtesy of Naomi Levine. Photograph by Stuart Hamill*

There were so many miracles around him that a book was recently compiled called *The Miraculous Sixteenth Karmapa*,[56] which collected many of the stories from his childhood until he passed away. The Karmapa's magnanimous presence was very ratna. He had great joy and seemed to take enormous pleasure in every experience and every meeting; he loved animals, particularly birds, and his surroundings reflected richness and warmth.

The story of Karmapa is an occasion where the opulent "anything can happen" quality of ratna is brought to full measure. Lesser-transformed ratnas who embody the wisdom of equanimity and enriching presence still bring a feeling of creativity and almost magical presence into a situation.

LIZA'S STORY

Liza had a fascinating experience working with the mandala that suddenly clarified her ratna issues. And what followed was a sudden, almost miraculous shift in her lifelong feelings of financial and work frustration.

Liza is a sixty-year-old mental health consultant. Currently, she works as program director for a large social-service agency protecting against domestic violence, her dream job. Her father was born a Jew in Poland and arrived in America as an immigrant at age five after the war. Her paternal grandparents were also first cousins. She was born in Brooklyn, New York, and lived there with her parents and her sister, who is four years older than she is.

They lived at the less desirable end of an affluent Jewish neighborhood and there was constant worry over finances in her family. Her mother, Miriam, had worked as a nurse and her father, Ben, was a traveling salesman. He frequently changed jobs and had a gambling problem, which was kept secret. Liza was surrounded by a large extended family, but her parents were nicknamed the "poor Goldsteins" by other relatives. Her maternal grandparents lived across the street, while her paternal grandmother, Rachel, lived around the corner with her second husband, Alan, who had replaced Liza's grandfather Aron.

When Liza was a small child, she noticed a snapshot that was carefully placed on her grandmother's desk. It was a picture of a tombstone that had the same name as her grandfather, Aron. She was quickly shut down when she asked about it. All she was told was that it was her daddy's father and not to play with the photo.

Her childhood home was often tense with disputes between her parents. In addition to the money issues, her mother strongly disliked her mother-in-law. As a sensitive child, Liza was affected by the tension, and she developed a tendency to withdraw and "hide" in her room. Her sister also frequently argued with her mother, while Liza was the quiet, well-behaved child.

When Liza was twenty, she was told by her sister that her paternal grandfather, Aron, had been distraught over finances and had committed suicide by jumping off a bridge. They didn't have much conversation about this tragedy, and she never discussed the incident with her parents. When she was forty-three, Liza spent time with her father's first cousin, who came to visit the family from time to time, and during one of his visits he told Liza the story of her grandfather's death.

There had been financial problems in the family, and Miriam wanted to be as affluent as some of her cousins living close by. Aron had approached family members and asked to borrow money, but was denied. He reacted by jumping off the bridge to his death. According to her cousin, the family suspected what had happened when he did not come home. However, they went about their daily lives pretending nothing was amiss, until his body washed ashore a few days later.

Throughout her life Liza has had thoughts of suicide during bouts of depression or anxiety. She always held the thought that she could kill herself if life got too difficult. All through her childhood and adult life, finances were a source of struggle and worry for her; she had a poverty mentality. There were periods when her financial situation improved, but inevitably she would find herself sliding down into a black hole financially, and she believed that financial struggle was somehow her destiny.

Before beginning the work of the mandala, Liza had worked at jobs she disliked even though she had a good education, because she didn't see any other options for earning a living. At times she felt so miserable that suicidal thoughts emerged. As she began to study the mandala, she was able to turn to her meditation practice at these times. But it wasn't until she was deeply immersed in the mandala practice and working with the ratna family that she connected her grandfather Aron's suicide to her lifelong pattern of depression, suicidal ideation, and anxiety over finances. She had not linked this family shadow to her own life in a meaningful way. Remembering this piece of the "secret" family history and connecting it to her persistent financial anxiety and belief that she would never have prosperity, Liza felt a vast sense of relief, freedom, and openness.

Liza was at a crossroads in her career because she felt a strong pull to "return home" to professional work in the violence-against-women movement. She continued to transform the pattern through mandala meditation, and not only did she survive, she thrived. She was offered her dream job, doing the work for women suffering from domestic violence. Liza no longer feels the financial doom that loomed for her whole life; on the contrary, she feels prosperous and that her job is meaningful and provides an emotionally healthy environment. She credits her work with the mandala in the transformation of lifelong, even multigenerational, ratna family issues and the insights gained through the mandala for this significant life change.

RATNA FAMILY MEDITATIONS

Before beginning each of the meditations below, please first do the Nine Relaxation Breaths and Generating the Motivation practices as instructed in Chapter 8 on pages 155 and 156.

UNBLOCKING THE ENCUMBERED ENERGY

Let's take a moment and feel the encumbered ratna pattern in our bodies.

* Scan your body and feel the energy of arrogance, pride, or insecurity in your own body. Is it heaviness in the limbs? A hollow feeling in the belly? A sinking sensation in your heart? What do you feel?
* Feel the encumbered energy. If you don't feel this currently, recall a time, an incident, or a period in your life when you were in the encumbered state.
* Now intensify the encumbered feeling of arrogance, pride, or insecurity, so that you really feel it deeply and strongly. This gives you a felt experience of ratna family in its blocked state.
* Now sound the seed syllable, slowly in a low voice: RI. As you sound the syllable, feel the sound go through your body, and see your body permeated by yellow light. Feel the obstructed pattern transform into the wisdom of equanimity. Let the wisdom of equanimity come from the sound and the light.
* Rest in the wisdom as long as you like. Repeat the seed syllable slowly and mindfully, resting after each repetition, as many times as you like, always resting in the wisdom energy at the end.

ELEMENT MEDITATION: EARTH

* Before beginning this meditation, decide how long you are going to practice. I recommend from fifteen minutes to one hour.

* Earth element meditation can be done anywhere that you can stretch out on the earth. You can lie either facedown or on your back. Facedown, you can feel the earth in a different way than on your back. I like doing it both ways. Put down a thin cloth or towel—this can be done very easily at the beach and no one will even know you are meditating! Or if it's a suitable clean place, lie directly on the earth. I usually begin on my back, then turn over after a while.

* As you lie down, take a moment to feel your connection with Mother Earth. When I lie facedown, I feel I am embracing the earth, but you can choose to either lie on your back or facedown. Let yourself feel the earth, close your eyes, feel grounded, and feel the perfection of everything around you and the wisdom of equanimity. Offer the earth thoughts of gratitude for all she gives. Allow yourself to feel the trust and the support of the earth. Allow yourself to let go and really trust her. Notice how that trust feels. Receive her generosity.

* After the Nine Relaxation Breaths, allow your breath to settle. When you exhale, imagine you become one with the earth. There is no separation. Rest in that experience. It is not you lying on the earth; rather, you are the earth, you are one with her.

* As you inhale, bring her into you. Join with the earth. Integrate with her. Each breath goes deeper into union with her. Remain there as long as you like.

* When you are finished, sit up, and dedicate the positive energy that has been generated to benefit all beings.

After you close the meditation, notice how you feel. Keep the awareness of that feeling as you go about your day. Since we are usually near the earth, it is not difficult to find a situation to do this powerful healing practice that reconnects us with Mother Earth. There is another additional practice I learned from a Native American teacher. In this practice you dig a small hole in the earth with your hands. Then ask permission to give the earth your sorrow. Then say, shout, or weep into the hole until you have let go of everything. Then seal the hole by covering it over with earth. Then press your hands down and see all your grief, anger, and hurt being taken away by Mother Earth, feeling deep gratitude for all she holds.

11

PADMA DAKINI:
WISDOM OF DISCERNMENT

*Mandalas are birth places, vessels of birth in the most literal sense,
lotus flowers in which a Buddha comes to life. Sitting in the lotus
seat the yogi sees himself transfigured into an immortal.*

—C. G. JUNG

We move clockwise around the mandala now from the south into the west. Do you feel the red glow of the sunset? Let's have a glass of red wine as we watch it set, seeing the light of the sun shining through the ruby-colored wine. In padma family, we've moved from the material consumer in ratna—connected to the element of earth, the material world—to fire, desire, heat, and longing in the heart. Having developed dignity and generosity in the ratna family, you become a self-contained magnet in padma family. Here we enter the realm of passion and compassion, the big heart.

The symbol for the padma family is the lotus, a red lotus. The lotus is a very common symbol used in Vajrayana Buddhism to represent our enlightened nature, because while the lotus grows in the

Padma Dakini (18th century). Ground mineral pigment on cotton.
Rubin Museum of Art.

muck, it emerges from the mud completely unscathed and fragrant. It would seem these two realities could not coexist, yet the lotus is ultra-pure and unaffected by the polluted water that provides the fertile matrix from which it emerges. The Sanskrit word for passion is *raga*, which can mean "color," specifically red, and is also a musical piece in Indian music. Each musical raga evokes certain emotions, so the color red is tied to emotions. Brilliant, magnetizing red is padma's color, a blazing red that reflects her element of fire—the fire that helps us to digest, helps the blood to circulate, and warms our body; the energy of the sun, the energy of life.

The lotus is the symbol of the padma family. Drawing by Robert Beer. Ink on paper.

The time for padma is sunset, that warm, red glow. It is time to light the fire, both the literal fire and the romantic fire, so that we can connect with our lover, relax, and feel the glow. And the shape is the triangle, upward-pointing, like a flame. The season of padma is spring, when the rugged intensity of winter gives way to those gentle mild days, a season of transition making way for summer and for new beginnings. It has the quality of freshness, of possibility, the glamour of all those little flowers, the heat rising in the earth. In fact, February, which in Europe is the beginning of spring, comes from the word *febris*, or "fever" in Latin, when the heat starts to return—and Valentine's Day, which we associate with red and passion, was actually formerly a pagan festival recognizing spring, the fever of passion, and the return of the sun.

The padma landscape is soft rolling hills, mossy glens where you could make love, sandy coves, places where animals play. I always think about the garden at Tara Mandala when I think of padma landscape—there are lots of flowers; the whole shape of the garden is curves, round shapes; and there's always a few bunnies hopping around, chipmunks, birds eating the sunflower seeds. Tara Mandala is a place of rolling meadows, lushness, and promise.

The padma sense faculty is hearing. I think about the beautiful music at sunset, or the way a deer perks up its ears when you play a flute or just speak to it. Hearing, of course, can trigger seduction; music can stir the senses and activate the emotions in a way that no other art form can. It is very common to see deer or elk near the roads at Tara Mandala. They are usually in small groups, but I have seen as many as three hundred elk migrating through the land. The ones I see up close are usually mule deer, which have very big ears and

sensitive hearing to protect themselves from predators. Whenever I
see them while driving, often within twenty feet of the car, I stop and
roll down the window. They turn and pause and flick their large ears
back and forth, looking at me with huge, shiny brown eyes. Then
I start to sing the Avalokiteśvara Mantra of the padma family, *Om
Mani Padme Hum Hri* (Om Jewel in the Lotus Hum Hri), in a melodious way. It is the most famous of all mantras, a mantra of great
compassion. I sing it to them to create karmic seeds of connection to
the dharma for their future lives. They always stop and listen for as
long as I sing, and once I move, they scamper off.

The Austrian artist Gustav Klimt could be considered a padma
family artist, with his sensual paintings fusing brilliant pigments and
gold. Klimt's primary subject was the female body, and his paintings
are marked by a frank eroticism, perhaps the most famous being *The
Kiss*. His work has the warmth, the heat, and the swirling energy of
padma.

The Kiss by Gustav Klimt (1908). Oil on canvas.
Austrian Gallery Belvedere.

Other artists who capture this family would be J. M. W. Turner and the impressionist painter Claude Monet. The impressionists stressed precise depiction of light and how it changed over time, as well as open composition, and often painted on the spot. Their style displays the discernment and attempt to penetrate into the deepest visual reality that echoes the discerning wisdom of padma family. In a way, Michelangelo's *Creation of Adam* on the ceiling of the Sistine Chapel is quintessential padma with the magnetizing energy passing between God and Adam, the sensual light, and the vivid color.

While the earthy ratna house might be rich and comfortable, with a tendency toward clutter, the padma home would have an artistic ambience without being as crowded. The padma-influenced home is charming and colorful, neither as opulent as ratna nor as crisp and sharp-edged as vajra. When you enter a padma house, there is an immediate sense of beauty and harmony; everything works together. The colors are warm, with reds predominating. There are soft leather couches with jewel-toned throws and pillows. The master bedroom tends toward the erotic, with low lights, a canopy bed with burgundy velvet curtains, and velvet accent pillows. Candles are displayed throughout the house, some in candelabras, some in single candle-holders, and some on pillar candle stands. The padma house feels warm whether there's a fire going or not; it has a comforting feeling, and the beauty of the environment is soothing.

The body type of the padma person tends to be well-proportioned and very attractive. Padmas emanate magnetism and charm. They are vivacious, warm, and outgoing, as well as athletic and fit. They move with grace and tend to be what we consider classically attractive, with attractive balanced faces and radiant, luminous eyes. They wear solid colors, especially red. The padma looks for form-fitting, good-quality clothes—velvet, silk, garments that feel soft to the skin and luxuriant. Their jewelry is not particularly big or obvious, but very alluring.

PADMA GOES TO A PARTY

We barely even need to imagine the padma personality at a party—because Lila, a forty-one-year-old life coach, is, of course, having the party! She loves parties, so much so that she'll find any little excuse to have one: the first day of spring, the first snow, someone leaving, someone arriving—and of course birthdays and holidays are elaborately celebrated! She enjoys giving parties because, first of all, she loves to win over the guests and entice people to attend. How can she make her party sound really appealing? How can she say the right thing so they want to come?

It's not difficult, because others enjoy Lila's company; it's always fun to be with her. Lila buys fancy chocolate, and then decides to have a chocolate party—the chocolate is a vehicle for relationship. She sends out "come and share some chocolate with me" invitations. For a padma, eating good chocolate alone is no fun! There's a sense of the importance, not so much of the substance itself, but rather of the energy that she can generate around the substance.

She wears flashy red clothes, even some red lingerie to her chocolate party. Lila gets a little tipsy, then effusive, and begins to tell a whole string of guests how awesome they are, all the things that she loves about them. She wants to hug them and maybe even kiss them. She might even force it a little: make them hug her, make them give her a little kiss. But she just feels so good, so warm, so affectionate. And then, toward the end of the night, she needs to find someone to go to bed with. She feels an intense need, and she manages to seduce someone. But when she wakes up in the morning, she wants him out so she can move on to the next conquest.

A padma man, Daniel is a filmmaker. He goes to the party wearing snug jeans with a sexy silver belt, cool running shoes, and a red T-shirt. He's a womanizer. He's talking to one woman while looking over her shoulder and winking at another. Daniel acts like he's really interested in what the woman in front of him is talking about, offers her all kinds of possible connections, and suggests she star in his next film. As soon as possible, he begins some sexual banter and puts his arm around her. But he can't resist looking at the other woman behind her. He speaks very gently; he's so good-looking that he can seduce her even if she recognizes his superficiality. At the end of the evening, he ends up with the last woman he talks to, and leaves in his wake several irritated women who can't believe they fell for him.

In her transformed state, Lila is the life of the party, making everyone feel welcome, but without any personal attachments to anyone or attempts to seduce anyone. There is the quality of warm compassion and joyfulness coming from her. If there's a guest who's having a hard time, she will spend time offering empathy and trying to make the person comfortable. She has a genuine interest in everyone, but no need to seduce, no need to find "the one." If Daniel is in the transformed padma state, when he arrives at the party he begins to see various film shots that he could take of the house, and considers it for a setting for his next movie. He looks around at the people who are there and sees how he could improve the situation by creating more connections among them. So he goes around consciously introducing people to each other who he thinks could benefit, without any personal agenda of his own. He really enjoys the party in a loose, open kind of way but without trying to seduce anyone specifically; he just feels a lot of warmth for everyone.

ENCUMBERED PATTERN: DESIRE AND SEDUCTION

The encumbered mind state of padma is intense desire, lust, and craving. Padma personalities desire to manipulate situations and people through their magnetism. These days someone is evaluated as being attractive or not with the word *hot*. It's a perfect word for padma family, which is based on the element of fire. When you say someone's "hot," it immediately implies they are sexy. Padmas want to be hot—they *are* hot, they can't help it—but they also need the assurance from others that they are. They just want to seduce without concern for genuine communication and heart connection.

There is a compulsive need to be seductive, and they get frustrated when their usual powers don't have an effect and will keep trying persistently to get what they want. Padmas need to draw others in, merging not only in sexual union, but so they feel others agree with their view of reality or do what they want. The padma personality becomes hyperaware of whomever they are trying to pull toward them. They are very discerning about the person they're trying to win over in order to "have" them and feel safe: "What color or brand does this person like? Oh, I think I'll give him that!" Or "What would she like me to wear? Oh, I'll wear that."

There can be a tendency in padma people to start many relationships and then drop them once the initial phase of seduction is over, because they are mainly interested in seduction, not relationship. The animal connected to this family is the peacock; there is probably no other bird or animal in the world that says as loudly, "Look at me! Aren't I gorgeous?" Where I live in Colorado, there are many wild turkeys. They are very similar to peacocks in many ways, only their colors are more subtle in order to blend with the browns and reddish tones of the landscape. In the spring, I often come upon a male dancing with his tail fully spread for a group of females. When the sunlight hits the turkey feathers, all the colors light up: shades of green, bright red, blue, and the browns we commonly associate with turkeys. Sometimes they'll be in the middle of the dirt road that runs up to Tara Mandala. The females are chatting and reacting to the male, but he is in his own world, dancing and moving elegantly for them.

The Zuni tribe nearby here in New Mexico have a turkey dance in which they reenact this performance. The men wear turkey tail feathers as headdresses, with a fringe over their eyes, fringed boots, turquoise necklaces and armbands and bracelets, and aprons of red, yellow, and black, while the women dance behind the men in more subdued costumes. These turkey dancers embody and dance the energy of padma family.

Padma people may have trouble meeting the challenges of deep, intimate relationships, and are therefore put off by the unglamorous demands necessary for true intimacy, like working through communication issues. They want the intrigue of superficial crushes and brief romances. Padma embodies the Don Juan (or Donna Juanita) complex. They are primarily interested in the chase, the lure of the hunt, driven by the consuming energy of passion. They pride themselves on being skilled hunters, and the man (or woman) is simply the prey. They do not really care to know him or her beyond what's necessary for their purposes. During the seduction they are completely accommodating, gentle, and very sexy; they are magnificent and alluring. As soon as the seduction is over, the energy is gone and they move on heartlessly, dropping the person they so ardently pursued. When this passion fizzles, we say it's "gone cold."

Padma types also include the Casanova personality, who loves but can't stop seducing and can't limit himself to monogamy. Let's look at an example of the Casanova type, Paul. He is a fitness trainer working at a gym where lots of women go to work out. He seduces one, professing his deep passionate love; then another catches his eye. Paul finds himself in pursuit of her with intense dedication, while still "loving" the first. Sometimes it gets complicated, but in a job with constant turnover, he manages to keep the pattern going, truly believing he loves all the women. They have the encumbered padma pattern of an inability to go deep, while being caught in passion for passion's sake.

Because padma people often lack healthy boundaries in relationships, they may betray their partners with infidelity, having multiple or serial relationships. In a more extreme manifestation, padmas might become easily involved with people sexually or emotionally regardless of how well they know them, resulting in high rates of

STDs and sex addiction. Because most sex addicts, like others with padma afflictions, fear being abandoned, they might also tend to stay in relationships that aren't healthy. There is a fear of loneliness and feelings of emptiness or incompleteness that arise, and the only "cure" is through a lover (or a new lover). Padmas might try to deal with that feeling through impulsive sexuality or porn activity, and they may also have feelings like guilt, loneliness, and fear.

Padmas have the feeling that if the *right* person could just be magnetized, all their problems would be solved. However, the addiction to the push-pull energy of seduction creates a need to move on once the seduction has been completed. Commitment is a difficult thing for obstructed padma family personalities. They want to go on to the next thing; they're not really interested anymore. In a sense, they consume the other, the way fire consumes its fuel, and therefore they need more, they need another one. Passion is kindled; they burn with it, and then it burns out. Fire doesn't distinguish—it just burns whatever is in its path.

So much harm has been caused by unwise expressions of desire; so much pain comes from cheating and betrayal. I think we have probably all experienced that ourselves or have inflicted it on someone else. Unfaithfulness causes such a deep sense of injury, because in relationship, we open our hearts to fundamental vulnerability. In relationship, there is longing to heal the feeling of separation. Probably the strongest human longing is for love, which is possible through relationship. So there's a combination of the incredible potential for satisfaction and an incredible potential for harm and pain in rejection, which can lead to the creation or destruction of marriages or families. All kinds of things both positive and negative, even violence, can come out of padma-driven relationships. The heat of passion and sexuality are hallmarks of this pattern, and raising the temperature with a longing for sensual pleasure, for love, for union.

Padmas can misuse empathetic intensity, acting sympathetic and connected when there may be some kind of manipulation going on or nothing really backing it up. We see this in salesmen who attempt to develop a personal relationship in order to sell you something. They seem really excited to meet you and to learn all about you and your family, but underneath, their interest in you is motivated only by a desire to sell you something. When it gets really extreme, padma passion can become obsession and turn into something like stalking. Believing that the victim loves and cares for them, stalkers can become violent when frustrated in their quest for this love.

Stalkers refuse to believe that a target is not attracted to them, often believing that the person actually does love them, but just isn't aware of it and needs to be pushed into realizing it. So the padma's need to feel he or she can magnetize turns into a compulsive *need* to magnetize a particular person, which can then develop into a dangerous rage, even murder. As long as the stalker continues pursuing the victim, they can convince themselves they haven't been completely rejected yet; but when they are blocked, they can become deadly, as we see in the numerous stalker murders that occur, a majority committed by someone the victim was once intimate with.

Clearly this is an extreme situation, and there are less excessive forms of this padma affliction. She might start compulsively checking a former lover's social media accounts to see what he is doing and whether he is seeing someone else. She might frequently text, e-mail, or call him even though he won't respond. She might go to places hoping to see him or ask friends about him. When she is caught in the energy of padma obsession, it can feel like the other person has something that she must get, something she must be close to and possess. Another padma problem can be getting involved with unsuitable, unkind, or undependable partners, even abusive ones, and not being able to let them go. This usually happens out of padma desperation and fear of being alone.

My daughter lives in Los Angeles and works at a film company. Having had a chance to watch the dynamics of Hollywood through her, I have decided this city should be called Padma City instead of

Hollywood. Padma definitely dominates Hollywood. First, good acting itself must be magnetizing, and movie stars live or die by their ability to magnetize others, not only fans but directors and producers too. Then stars become dependent on that attention. Once they've had some success, they can become desperate, wanting the high they get from all that attention to continue. With all the padma personalities circulating around Hollywood, it can get ferociously competitive. With fame you get that power, and then when it starts to fall away, it often creates a terrible feeling of fear and loss. When they start to get old, actors literally can have a feeling of insignificance. Most can't get roles anymore, and then there is the need to somehow pump things into their faces or cut things up and put them back together with plastic surgery, Botox, etc. They will do whatever they can to keep alive their power to magnetize. If appearances are your whole identity, it's extremely painful when this changes. The insecurity of the padma family easily leads to addiction and alcoholism. It is the same issue for fashion models or anyone basing their life on being able to magnetize others through their appearance.

WISDOM OF DISCERNMENT

Now let's look at the wisdom aspect of padma family. The wisdom here is called discerning wisdom, or discriminating awareness wisdom. This wisdom has the ability to see the relationship of things in great detail, with investigative discernment. The spaciousness of buddha family's all-encompassing wisdom combined with the mirror-like wisdom of vajra provides a vast reflective presence, while ratna family's wisdom of equanimity grounds and stabilizes awareness; these provide the base for wise discernment of the padma.

This wisdom might seem strange when we've been talking about passion in the encumbered pattern. However, when the ego fixation is gone, as it is when the wisdom emerges, under that is radiant compassion without an object, a discerning compassion. There is an experience of magnetism without effort, seeing all the nuances, but without attachment—enlightened relationship. Here in the awakened state of discerning wisdom, we can love but with a feeling of being free from the need to be loved back; it is contained warmth. It is compassion rather than passion, enjoyment with discernment.

"When the ego fixation is gone, as it is when the wisdom emerges, under that is radiant compassion without an object, a discerning compassion."

The Dalai Lama is a good example of the enlightened padma, and in fact he is considered to be the incarnation of Avalokiteśvara, who is a form of Amitabha, the Buddha of the padma family. He is an emanation, an incarnation of that enlightened family, and he really does embody the energy of warmth and compassion. He has magnetized the whole world; everyone who knows him loves him and he is perhaps one of the most popular people on earth. A Nobel Peace Prize laureate, he is the person who, according to a poll of five countries in Europe and the US commissioned by ICT (International Campaign for Tibet), best embodies the qualities of humility, peace, and nonviolence. He is also extremely discerning and intellectually brilliant, and can be cutting and sharp when necessary, yet His Holiness is nearly always smiling with loving warmth.

Padma family is connected to the aggregate of perception, allowing for the discriminating power of seeing distinctions with great precision, enabling one to create art. The five aggregates, collections, or heaps (*Skandhas* in Sanskrit) are the psycho-physical constituents of a human being: form (the elements that constitute our physical body), feeling, perception, volitional action, and consciousness. These aggregates combine to create the body and mind of an individual. The padma personality is about the perception of relationships, not only between people but between colors, textures, forms, sound, and space, so padma is the family that rules the arts. With a lover you are so aware of every little touch, every detail of what they like to wear, what they like to eat, how they move, that little flick of the finger, that look in the eye. When we're in the neurotic padma energy, the fixation on all those little details is because of our desire to magnetize the person. But in the awakened state, there is clarity that leads to precise attention to detail, aesthetics that enlighten, and also genuine warmth and friendliness without ulterior motives.

An artist needs to be able to work with color, sound, and so on, depending on what branch of art they pursue. A visual artist places objects in different positions and sees their relation to each other, judging the relationship of forms and textures in a discerning way. Maybe it's arranging flowers, or architecture, or graphic design, or just arranging furniture in your house, but for all these fine and applied arts, even if the art is merely a hobby such as knitting, you need discernment to understand the relationships of form and color and perspective, among other things.

The padma's discernment allows for skillful compassionate connections, allowing you to guide others and to see relationships without your personal stake in the situation. When there is discernment, you won't get involved in unhealthy relationships, because you don't have all the padma needs going on underneath the surface, and you're actually able to see: "Who is this person?" Your relationship to them is viewed with clarity. So the awake padma person has a sense of discriminating awareness of what's good for everyone, rather than only what's good for himself or herself.

What's the difference between the encumbered pattern and the wisdom? It is the removal of struggle, the struggle based on ego-fixation. If there is no struggle, there is no self-reference. When there is no striving, no ego-clinging, you still are aware of every detail, like the neurotic padma, and of shape and form and so on, but it's not about yourself and how you can seduce.

A transformed padma is also good at communication and at working with energy, and it's actually a very beautiful, warm energy, with the potential for deep love and compassion. And within that general sense of radiating warmth, there is in the awakened padma a deep and resonating kindness. There is significant research now that tells us that we are biologically wired to feel safer and more at ease if we are in a dependable relationship.[57] Sue Johnson in her book *Hold Me Tight* wrote: "Isolation and the potential loss of loving connection is coded into the human brain into a primal panic response. This need for safe connection to a few loved ones is wired in by millions of years of evolution."[58]

After my husband Dave died suddenly of a heart attack at the age of only fifty-four, I was in a state of shock and overwhelming grief. He died in the night in our home; there had been no sickness or any warning signs. After the cremation I had to leave home, because I couldn't bear to be there without him. I went on a six-month pilgrimage; I couldn't inhabit our bedroom or live in our house for the next six years. I lived in my retreat cabin or my room in the temple. Although I reached out to my adult children and friends, who also loved him, no one could really know the depths of my loss—and I tried not to be a burden to them. I found that our friends, those who had been close to him, were my greatest comfort. Still, I was devastated, grief stricken. I had to stop teaching and remove myself from Tara Mandala for several years.

He had been not only my beloved, but also a partner on every level. We had created Tara Mandala together and he was integral in running it, and suddenly Tara Mandala was in my lap. My son helped for a few years, but in the end it was back to me. Dave was a family man, and every family gathering had been full of his humor and the fun factor that came with him. He was the place I called "home"; if he was present, no matter where in the world I was, I felt I was home. We had been deeply intimate lovers, and this had not diminished in twenty-two years of marriage.

Hardest of all was the loneliness. It was there even when I was with my children and grandchildren, who bring me great joy, or when I was with my closest friends. The loneliness was always there, day and night. As years passed, it did diminish; but every year the anniversary (a strange word for such an event) of his death was like pulling off a scab and starting to bleed again. But I felt I *should* be able to deal with it myself. I *should* be fine by myself. I *shouldn't* need another relationship to be happy. And others said that to me too, things like, "You had twenty-two blessed years with Dave. Count your blessings. Most people don't get that." I gradually realized I did need an intimate relationship, even though I thought that meant I was weak and not integrated or strong.

Then I discovered the work of Sue Johnson in a book called *Hold Me Tight* in year seven after his death. Her work told me through research how the need for closeness, to feel emotionally safe, is wired into us. In a way this is obvious: it has been our survival instinct from primitive times. What a relief it was to let go of the feelings that there was something *wrong* with me because I longed for closeness and felt distressed without it. I no longer had the added judgment of myself as inadequate to deal with, on top of the grief, which was already unbearable. And I began to explore new relationships. It helped immediately, and although I'll never replace Dave, I now accept that needing connection is not the same as neurotic padma craving. This was for me an important lesson in padma, that what I experienced as neurotic padma behavior was a human need for connection, warmth, and intimacy. When I stopped judging myself, I felt the grief heal a little bit more.

The power of the padma family and the padma energy is long life and health, so it's a really good family to invoke if you're weak or if you have an illness like chronic fatigue. You can work with the padma family and magnetize life energy. It's also powerful in the sense that when you want to do something, you have the power and the strength to do it.

In the positive padma experience, there can be subtle, intimate sexuality, which is a nondual union with your partner—based not on seduction but on love, an openhearted depth of connection and presence. Sacred sexuality is intricately involved with energy and the subtle body. To actually have an experience of sacred sexuality, the subtle bodies of the people need to *meet*. So much sex takes place in our world where the subtle bodies are completely separate. Many people have their eyes closed during sex, and so the subtle body doesn't connect. In Tantric sexuality, you involve the padma aggregate of perception in nondual taste, nondual touch, nondual smell, nondual sight, and so on. Then the couple combines this energy, so instead of having the energy in one person, you actually have this energy circulating through both people.

And when you have that experience of nonduality at that level, it's potentially liberating, and that's why sacred sexuality can be a path to enlightenment. The depth of warmth that is generated evokes the transformed energy of padma family. What human experience do we have that is more powerful than sexual union? I love what the great Indian yogi Naropa said: "In the midst of intense pleasure, imagine that you're both no more substantial than clouds in the sky."

In discussing padma wisdom and how difficult it is to touch on all the implications of the Sanskrit word *pratyavekshana*, which embodies the essence of the wisdom aspect of padma family, Francesca Fremantle's book *Luminous Emptiness* sums it up this way: "It is possible all the different implications inherent in the original Sanskrit word may be present simultaneously: not only just the ability to distinguish between different objects of perception, but even more importantly, the capacity to look deeply into each one, appreciating its unique qualities and entering into its unique being with love and understanding."[59]

The wisdom of discernment carries with it a quality of empathetic concern and caring for others and profound insight into the nature of reality. It also has an investigative curiosity, an ability to see deeply into the nature of things. In my mention of subtle sacred sexuality and the integration with the elements practice, we see this deep knowing not through intellect, but rather through experience. There is a deep knowing, beyond ordinary ego-centered knowing, that penetrates into the core of reality. We see the Buddha Amitabha with both hands in meditative equipoise, deep in contemplation. All the other buddhas have their hands in gestures indicating some kind of activity, while only Amitabha tells us he is in deep meditation with no other activity.

"The wisdom of discernment carries with it a quality of empathetic concern and caring for others and profound insight into the nature of reality."

ISABELLA'S STORY

Let's look at Isabella's journey with the padma family as an example of the evolution from the encumbered pattern to the wisdom aspect. Isabella's mother was twenty years younger than her father, Henry, who was originally her mother's professor and was famous in his field of music theory. Her mother, Myra, met Henry when she was his assistant at the university.

Henry was a charismatic person who was, in many ways, larger than life. Because of the age difference and his accomplishment in their field, Myra adored him to the point that she put him on a pedestal way above herself. Even though she was actually quite accomplished in their field, Myra took the backseat to support him. Their marriage was a classic example of the woman feeling she would be completed and defined by her husband. Isabella saw this pattern throughout her childhood, and began to believe that she would need a man in her life who would define and complete her. Her parents' relationship was romantic; however, her father was not an easy person to live with. Due to their great age difference, there were issues later in his life when her mother had to care for him. Henry was egotistical and demanding, and Myra acquiesced. The message Isabella got loud and clear was that you must have a man in your life; a woman is only whole by attaining a man, and you must do whatever it requires to hold on to him.

Isabella unconsciously took this message to heart and married at twenty. She couldn't wait to be married and really thought it would be for the rest of her life. She did well with her husband for ten years. But Isabella was insecure and tried too hard to be the perfect wife; she also had ratna issues of not being good enough along with her padma pattern. Even while she was teaching at the university level, she always cooked full meals for her husband and kept the house clean, and even entertained often. She was so perfect she allowed no space in their relationship; she smothered him with love.

Then one day her husband came home from work and announced, without any warning, that he had met someone else and was leaving her. Isabella was completely shocked. They had experienced challenges, but nothing had prepared her for this sudden dismissal. Since she'd based her own value on her success in the relationship, she felt like a total failure.

After the end of her marriage, Isabella was lost. Without her role as a wife, she did not know who she was anymore and felt insignificant and desperate. She was embarrassed by being left and by being single, and started looking for a replacement right away. This led to another relationship followed by marriage without delay. This time, out of desperation, she chose badly, and even knew on her wedding day she had made a big mistake. It was then that Isabella started working with the mandala, and the padma family work transformed her life. Through practicing the Mandala of the Five Dakinis, she found that the feeling of "I would be complete if I just had the right man" began to decrease; she could see both the encumbered pattern and the potential wisdom. She was a warm, compassionate person. She gradually moved from grasping, clinging, and seduction, to which she had become so addicted, to the development of the wisdom of discernment.

When Isabella came to the end of her second marriage, she looked back at her padma pattern and saw how unhealthy it was. She could see that she was good at seduction and how she used her sexuality to entice someone. But then there would be a sexual cooling-off period after she "had" him in the typical padma way, and then Isabella wasn't interested in sex anymore. When she looked deeper into this pattern, she could see that she was desperately grasping for someone to define her. She needed a man to say she was attractive, desirable, and sought-after, realizing that this was different from actually being loved or loving someone. She'd thought she was looking for romantic love, but she was really looking for acceptance and reassurance.

In her Mandala of the Five Dakinis practice, Isabella started working with accepting empowered female embodiment, learning to feel the strength of the sacred feminine. At one point she went to the woods behind her house and found a branch, creating the khatvanga staff that the dakinis hold representing their inner male consort. She decorated it with symbols that were meaningful to her process with the padma family. When it was finished, Isabella went every day and danced alone with the staff in the woods. In this very embodied way, she developed an awareness of the inner masculine and noticed what it felt like in her body to have the inner consort. She did this until an awareness of the inner masculine felt stable in her body.

At the same time, Isabella decided to take a break from men and dating for a while. She knew it was important to be alone and to be able to be comfortable with herself. She bought a house on her own that she loved and decorated it in her own way with many symbols and colors from the mandala. She planted a mandala garden and tried to be at ease with being alone. Isabella was surprised to find out how fearful she was when she was alone; but over time with daily mandala practices, she found that she could do almost anything by herself. And she enjoyed it! She began to love being alone. This was an important time of mandala practice and inner growth for her.

At that point, Isabella thought she was "done" with men. But as soon as she thought that, she met a man whom she became friends with—just friends. He was also divorced and seeing a few women, and she was casually seeing a few men. They would talk about their dates and share stories and laugh together. It was great for Isabella to have a male friend who was not a lover. She had worked on developing discerning wisdom and didn't need to seduce this man. They could simply be friends and allow things to progress or not.

Eventually, they discovered that they felt more than friendship for each other, and things slowly became more intimate. Isabella found that she was different with him than she had been in other relationships, because of her new understanding from her work with the mandala and particularly with the Padma Dakini. Isabella was no longer defining herself by her relationship and wasn't trying to merge with her new male friend. Rather, she kept her own identity and was able to enjoy her friend without the fear of losing him. They have now been married fifteen years and are still good friends, as well as lovers and partners. The fires of padma still burn for her, and she still finds that she needs approval, but not in the moth-to-a-flame way of earlier in her life. She continues to work with the Mandala of the Five Dakinis to generate wisdom.

PADMA FAMILY MEDITATIONS

Before beginning each of the meditations below, please first do the Nine Relaxation Breaths and Generating the Motivation practices as instructed in Chapter 8 on pages 155 and 156.

UNBLOCKING THE ENCUMBERED ENERGY

Let's take a moment and feel the encumbered padma pattern in our bodies.

* Scan your body and feel the energy of craving or desire in your own body. Is it an ache in your heart? A heat in the belly? Where do you feel it?
* Feel the encumbered energy. If you don't feel this currently, recall a time, an incident, or a period in your life when you were in the encumbered state.
* Now intensify the encumbered feeling of grasping, craving, or longing so that you really feel it deeply and strongly. This gives you a felt experience of padma family in its blocked state.
* Now sound the seed syllable, slowly in a low voice: NI. As you sound the syllable, feel the sound go through your body, and see your body permeated by red light and fire. Feel the obstructed pattern transform into the wisdom of discernment. Let the wisdom come from the sound and the light.
* Rest in the wisdom as long as you like. Repeat the seed syllable slowly and mindfully, resting after each repetition, as many times as you like, always resting in the wisdom energy at the end.

ELEMENT MEDITATION: FIRE

* Before beginning this meditation, decide how long you are going to practice. I recommend from fifteen minutes to one hour.
* To do this, you need real fire. It could be something as small as a candle or as big as a bonfire, or anything in between such as a campfire or a fire in a fireplace. Settle in front of the fire. Fire's dancing and living quality naturally draws people to stare at it for hours on end. Get comfortable and put a pillow under you, or sit in a chair. This can also be done at night with a fire outside.
* After the Nine Relaxation Breaths, allow your breath to settle. Then with open eyes simply rest your eyes and mind on the fire. Let your mind open, so that there is no *journey* between you and the fire; there is no separation. If you get distracted, relax back into the fire.
* Try to avoid fixating on any one place in the fire. If you notice you are focusing or straining your eyes, relax your eyes and ease the focus. It can be helpful to think about relaxing the muscles behind your eyes.
* When you are finished, dedicate the positive energy that has been generated to benefit all beings.

After you close the meditation, notice how you feel. Keep the awareness of that feeling as you go about your day. Fire, more than any other element, seems to naturally draw us into a meditative state, but this practice takes you deeper into a nondual union with fire.

12

KARMA DAKINI:
ALL-ACCOMPLISHING WISDOM

The tremendously active and dynamic energy of karma family with its tendencies toward jealousy, ambition, and paranoia is transformed into the action-accomplishing knowledge, with its ability to overcome all obstructions and achieve all aims.

—FRANCESCA FREMANTLE

As we move clockwise around the mandala into the last family in the north, do you hear the wind blowing? The karma family is air, wind, and movement. The karma family is, in a way, the culmination of the other four families. From what has been built in the process of working through the other families, we are ready to manifest and go into action. This is the action family; in fact, the word *karma* actually means "action."

Karma family has two symbols, first the double-edged sword that cuts through emotional instability and false concepts about reality. The sword has the energy to cut through what needs to be done away with, slicing through negativity and our trapped places. The sword penetrates into truth, cutting through delusion and obstacles,

Karma Dakini (18th century). Ground mineral pigment on cotton.
Rubin Museum of Art.

destroying what needs to be destroyed. And this is interesting—
because why would destruction be connected to accomplishment?
When you think about it, in order to accomplish, we often have to cut
away a lot, to hack away the slack, sever the dead wood. We must let
go of that which is dragging us down, and this is often very difficult.
So it is noteworthy that one of the main accoutrements of the dakini
is a knife, the hooked knife, and now here in the karma family we
find the sword, because often in order to begin afresh, to complete
something, we need to let something go. The other symbol is the
double vajra, a crossed vajra with four prongs symbolizing the four
karmas or the four enlightened activities: pacifying, increasing, mag-

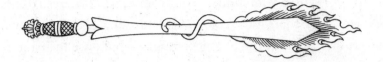

The double-edged sword is a symbol of the karma family.
Drawing by Robert Beer. Ink on paper.

netizing, and subduing, associated with vajra, ratna, padma, and karma families accordingly.

The color of karma family is green and its element is air, which signifies movement. Green is the color of growth, like trees leafing out in spring, but also there is the green of jealousy. We find a connection between the color and the emotion in our Western expression "green with envy." Also interestingly, green in our culture, like the action the family represents, signifies *GO*, green light! The color black is also associated with the wrathful activity of karma family, which includes the fierce removal of obstacles. The shape of the karma family is the half circle. The sense faculty connected to karma family is touch. Air touches us every-

The double vajra is a symbol of the karma family. Drawing by Robert Beer. Ink on paper.

where, all around our bodies. And touch is one of the senses in which we actually do something. We reach out and act, rather than receiving through the eyes and ears, for example.

The American artist Jackson Pollock epitomizes action art and synchronicity. He painted with his whole body moving energetically around the canvas, which was tacked firmly to the wood floor. He moved in all directions, painting from all sides. His full-body movement and the liquidity of the paint created what was called "action painting." He used a mixture of controllable and uncontrollable factors. He could control the colors, his body, and his instruments—stiff brushes, sticks, even basting syringes—but once the paint was released onto the canvas, because of its liquidity and his movements, it was to some extent uncontrollable. The very nature of his painting delivers a feeling of motion, and the violent flinging, squirting, and splattering of paint as well as the large size of his canvases created a completely new kind of painting.

Architecture connected to karma would be practical, with an emphasis on efficiency. Work modules or efficiency apartments would be karma. A karma house would be sparsely furnished and emphasize good organization, allowing movement and activity. It would be airy and likely have green plants hanging from the ceiling and swaying in the breeze coming in from numerous windows. There might be a workout or yoga space in the house, and various things to do around, such as a hover board or an interior swing. Green and black colors predominate.

The time of karma family is summer, when things are most active. In Colorado there are intense thunderstorms with lightning striking all around you in the summer, often followed by beautiful rainbows. Most of our tall ponderosa pine trees are scarred with the vertical stripe of lightning. In summer, there is an incredible green rush when suddenly everything is growing fast. In spring you can see things growing bit by bit, progressing gradually—but there is a certain point when we get into midsummer when everything just takes off. While ratna is the time of harvest and fulfillment, in karma season there's a feeling of competition and speed, of trying to get to the momentum of growth. Everything is growing in the karma family, and destruction is part of creation. There is all that green energy: growth, money, change, and movement.

The time in karma family is midnight: the day has been accomplished and we turn to new beginnings. There is also a real sensation of air at midnight, of movement, possibility; one thing has ended, another thing is about to begin. The karma family landscape is windy places, complicated landscapes, hard-edged and rocky, like the Southwest's mesas. Karma is also the landscapes of cities where there is always bustling and speed, things moving fast, multiple highways crossing each other, traffic, underground transportation, and pedestrians always in motion.

The body type of the karma family person is thin, almost wispy, always moving and seen in profile, because the karma person is always busy going somewhere. The body type is different from vajra, which is also thin: while the vajra body has defined muscles and is trim, the karma body type is more delicate. The karma person doesn't settle anywhere, flitting from place to place, full of nervous energy, whereas vajra settles and concentrates in a firm way. Karma people like their hair short and easy to care for; they wouldn't want to waste time taking care of it. And no useless ornaments either—maybe a highly practical watch, but that's it. Their clothes would tend to be efficient for work and flexible, such as long-lasting, stretchy outdoor garments or yoga clothes, which move with you.

KARMA GOES TO A PARTY

Well, of course the karma person doesn't really have time for a party. Sarah is a blond forty-year-old literary agent. She is busy, but decides to go for a while for work reasons, to network. So she'll arrive right from work, still wearing work clothes, and make it clear that she can't stay long because she really has more important things to do. She'll only go to accomplish some kind of purpose.

When Sarah arrives at the party, she scans the room and is disappointed; she knows there is another, better party going on, one where the real "A-list" crowd is, but she didn't get invited. Then she starts thinking: *Well, why am I at this party anyway? I really think I should be at that other party.* She then launches into thoughts about why she wasn't invited, then gets jealous about that and starts feeling envious of those people who were invited to the more important "in" party.

Therefore she hastens to leave the party, making a few connections and giving out her card on the way out, but she truly isn't interested in the people here since they aren't A-listers. *Why fritter away time at a party when I could be working?* At home, she rides her stationary bike for half an hour, and then works for a few hours before bed.

If we look at the transformed karma state, Tom at the party is fully present; he is not thinking about where there could be a better party happening. He is ready to be active in whatever's happening right here. Tom gets some refreshments (not a lot, since he doesn't care much about food), and then wanders around meeting people. When you talk to Tom, you feel he is very engaged and is not glancing at others, wondering if he should go talk to someone else, someone better. When someone puts on music and dancing starts, Tom jumps in; he is active and spins and moves a lot while dancing, enjoying the movement. He is very dynamic and even offers to organize a follow-up event with the people at the party. He connects with Sarah before she leaves the party and starts a conversation about work because they know each other through work channels, then he invites her to dance; they are a great couple, both really active on the dance floor. After dancing for a while, he invites her to go for a bike ride the next day—not just a normal bike ride, but a mountain bike ride. She accepts because she loves that activity level. They bike up to a high mountain pass and sit in the wind, enjoying the feeling of its movement on their skin.

ENCUMBERED PATTERN: ENVY

The official word in Tibetan for the obstructed emotion of karma family is *tadrel*, which is usually translated as "jealousy"; but the way I understand karma family, it is beyond the love relationship type of jealousy. It is also the process of comparing oneself to others and the feeling of envy and the need to hurry to "keep up with the Joneses." So there is a combination of envy and ambition here. There is paranoid comparison with others, a feeling that maybe there is an in-group and I'm not in it, I'm being excluded. You want to be part of that in-group, but they're moving ahead without you, and so there is the paranoia of being left behind.

We've moved from the discernment in the padma family to action, into doing, with karma family. The obstructed pattern of the karma family is to keep busy in order to not feel the inherent space and emotions that are present when we slow down. There is also a sense of avoidance of heartbreak by staying free in karma family; if you don't commit and just keep moving, you can sidestep the pain that comes with commitment. If you keep busy, you don't feel the disappointment or loneliness. Karmas are always working at something, even on vacation. Holidays become the work of having fun, organizing everyone; there has to be a schedule for the karma type on holiday. When we're in karma energy, we have to keep frantically organizing everyone and everything.

Karma personalities tend toward impulsivity, taking risks, literally speeding, and pushing forward without looking carefully at the dangers. This is accompanied by a fear of losing track of all the plots, losing ground, so control and surveillance are important. We need to control outcomes with a feeling of speediness and force.

The karma family has to do with defending territory and watching what others are doing to be sure to keep up with the competition. We see this intensely in the tech industry. My friend Gena was COO of a tech start-up in San Francisco. It grew rapidly and the board fired the CEO, and she became CEO by default. She did a good job, but it was an incredibly hectic life dominated by speed, and she was trying to raise her daughter at the same time. It was so intense. She was constantly trying to raise more millions to keep the start-up afloat. Millions of dollars were made and lost daily; the speed of change and the ruthlessness of the people involved was shocking. She connected with a man who was also in her company and they became lovers; he seemed like a real friend. Then, behind her back, he gathered enough support from the board to get her ousted. She left at forty-five years old with a "retirement package" that was just enough to live on for a year, while she recovered from the shingles that she'd gotten because of stress. This is a typical karma family environment: very high-stress, breathless, and paranoid.

If we can't keep up, we resent our competition, and that is where the jealousy comes in. We try to bring them down, destroy them. We can become karma neurotics in our spiritual path as well, with the motivation to do a lot of meditation to get to enlightenment before anyone else, to do it all very quickly, to get to the goal and then get famous—this is how charlatans are born. The paradox is that enlightenment is actually the ultimate state of letting go, the goal-less goal, so karma family tactics don't apply.

The neurotic karma person will try to jump to results before the middle part is done, jump to the fruition stage. "Let's just get this done today!" would be their attitude. They send lots of e-mails entitled URGENT. They can jump to making decisions that are not wise because of this sense of urgency. The thing to understand about the karma family is that there is an underlying insecurity that creates a feeling of having to get more done and to get it done faster. The karma family doesn't attach well—they don't really have time for relationships, and they can avoid relationship pitfalls because they don't have time. They're too busy for love.

This is the story of workaholic parents and spouses. Workaholic parents often use the excuse that they are working to make more money for the family, so then they can be together and be happy. For many workaholics, incessant work-related activity continues even after it is clear it's having a negative impact on the person's relationships and physical health. Causes of this stress-producing karma family activity are anxiety, low self-esteem, and intimacy issues. The encumbered karma family person also tends toward perfectionism and has an inability to delegate tasks to others. I have a friend who overworked while neglecting his family; he told me he realized what was happening when, as he was leaving for his office one morning, he said to his wife absentmindedly, "I'm going home now."

I had a karma family experience when I was working on my first book, *Women of Wisdom*. I was living in Rome with my husband and my children, who were three, eight, and nine years old. I realized that I had to go back to Nepal to gather some more biographies of Tibetan women teachers for the book and to check some facts. My children were still little, and I didn't really have a good childcare situation set up. I was leaving them with my Italian in-laws, who treated my daughters somewhat like Cinderellas since they were from a previous marriage. I was anxious about how they would be treated in my absence, and I really felt I couldn't be gone very long. I wanted to just go, get it done, and get back home.

The first thing that happened was I forgot my passport and didn't realize it until I was at the airport, so I had to go all the way back to our house in Rome from Fiumicino Airport, a forty-minute drive back into the city. I missed my flight, so right from the beginning everything was thrown off. I had to reschedule and couldn't get a flight for a few days, so already I had lost valuable time.

In Nepal, you cannot be successful when you are operating with neurotic karma energy, because the country has forty-two public holidays a year, including many that extend for several weeks. And the people just don't live under the kind of pressure we do. Plus there are lots of inconveniences—often no electricity, no water, terrible traffic jams, high levels of pollution, and so on. If you are in a hurry, it just doesn't work; cell phones didn't exist at that time in the 1980s. So I could never check to see if the person I was going to try to see, who lived several hours across the city, would even be there when I arrived. And they weren't! But I kept trying to force things to happen, and they didn't happen. The entire trip was like that, and nothing really worked. I couldn't get much done, and not what I had wanted to accomplish. Finally my time was up, and I went back to Rome, frustrated and disappointed. I'd put my children at risk and hadn't even achieved what I needed to do.

A few days after I got back, I went to see my teacher Namkhai Norbu Rinpoche in his center, Merigar, several hours north of Rome at the base of Monte Amiata. It was in the early days before he had thousands of students, and everything was very informal. We would just hang out with him, eating, talking, and practicing meditation together. When I arrived, I discovered he was sick, so I went to see him in his room in the old yellow house rebuilt from ruins, which was still cold and damp even after the renovations. I offered him some gifts from Kathmandu and then sat down by his bed.

He looked at me and said in Italian, "*Com'é andata?* (How did it go?)"

I groaned and replied, "Well, it really didn't go well. It was really difficult, Rinpoche. There were so many obstacles. Why?"

And he just looked at me and didn't say anything for a while, and then he said, "Maybe too much hope and fear." That was it in a nutshell, too much karma family speed.

If we already have karma family energy, we can add to it by our habits. Let's say you are already speedy and then you drink a lot of coffee: it increases the nervousness, and you become even more consumed by karma energy. Then you have lots of high-speed devices like phones, iPads, computers nearby, and you constantly check them, which leads to more activity. So there is this compulsive work element, together with the competitive emotional element of karma, coming from a feeling that "being" isn't enough, just *being* really isn't valuable. *Doing* is what is valuable.

Often it is a message given to us by our parents, because it is how we are praised. It is what you *do* that counts: what you accomplish, what your grades are, how you perform in sports, and so on. You don't get a sense of being valued for who you are. This pattern gets started very early when parents compliment their kids by say-ing, "Good job!" The child feels like he has to keep doing "good jobs" to get more love. Then, as adults, we can get caught up in our accomplishments and see them as being the equivalent of our lov-ability. Long after we've grown up and think we don't care what our parents think, we have in fact internalized the taskmaster and are still unconsciously working for our parents' approval. It is hard to shift to value *being*, rather than *doing*. How you're seen in the world, your job, your possessions, and your accomplishments are what matters. When we meet someone, we ask, "What do you *do*?" This reinforces the sense that we are only valuable because of what we do, and that creates karma neurosis.

Another aspect of encumbered karma is the disrupted air element and its connection to the mind. The agitated mind is never still; one thing passes quickly into another, and this affects what is called the *lung* or air element in our body. Agitation of the air element through constant busy-ness, caffeine, or too much talking causes air distur-bance, manifesting as nervousness and emotional reactivity. The lung disturbance causes the mind to keep moving. Have you ever tried to stop your mind? It is impossible. When we say that some-body is really driven, that is usually a disturbance of the lung that drives the karma energy. Experienced doctors of Tibetan medicine are able to identify and calm the disturbed winds of the more gross types of wind disorders, using the tools of diet, behavior, medicines, and external therapies; but deeper lung disturbance is hard to cure. What happens with air disturbances is that an energy disturbance is driving you—*you're* not driving, your lung is driving and in charge.

The Tibetan teacher Tsoknyi Rinpoche said in an interview:

> In anything we do, whether during meditation or in any
> situation, lung can be intensified. This can happen when
> we feel overloaded and "stressed out" or when our emo-
> tions get quite strong, even overwhelming. Any practice

we do driven by the wish to perform well or succeed with a corresponding lack of relaxation and lightness increases this intensity and creates restlessness. I am speaking here about the attitude of a forced, driven, goal-oriented practice. . . . Overactive lung confuses and disturbs the subtle body nervous system and becomes increasingly rigid and solidified—and because of this the natural capacity to feel compassion becomes blocked—your innate ability to feel unconditional, unbiased love, warmth and openness. We have to reconnect with our basic nature and relax in that.[60]

SLOW DOWN, YOU MOVE TOO FAST

Like the White Rabbit in *Alice in Wonderland* who says, "I'm late, I'm late, for a very important date. No time to say hello, good-bye, I'm late, I'm late, I'm late, I'm late . . ." there is no time to waste for the karma person. In fact, karma types are often seen in profile, because they are always going somewhere.

These days we really see the speedy tendency of karma more and more with the speediness of the Internet, which is increasing the alacrity of everything. We think that when things are faster, they are better, that we can get more things done and have more time to relax, which is an encumbered karma pattern of thinking. In fact, what happens is we just get busier. And life gets more breathless. So instead of having more time, the actuality is: *speed begets speed*. Our world is really more and more dominated by karma neurosis. We have a plague of hyperactive children, and attention deficit hyperactivity disorder is so common. As recently as December 2015, George Washington University's Milken Institute School of Public Health reported a 43 percent increase in ADHD diagnosis for schoolchildren in the United States.[61] One of the only solutions that we've come up with so far is to give Ritalin to these hyperactive children, which is actually what is known on the street as "speed." Ritalin is a brand name for methylphenidate, which is classified by the Drug Enforcement Administration as a Schedule II narcotic—the same classification as cocaine, morphine, and amphetamines.

I know ADHD does exist and that medication is sometimes in order, but ADHD is one of the fastest-growing and widely diagnosed conditions today and is overdiagnosed for a cluster of symptoms stemming from many other conditions and disorders, dyslexia amongst them.[62] My point is that the prevalence of this diagnosis is part of the pattern of speediness. Speed is not necessarily improving our quality of life, and maybe medicating our children with "speed" is not helping them in the long run. Nowadays if a kid is problematic in school there is a tendency to medicate him, rather than pinpointing a specific diagnosis from among the more than twenty possible causes for the disruptive behavior.

Karma neurosis manifests as speed that pushes us toward some undefined ultimate place, some kind of goal; it is the need to accomplish the "great act," to be the first, the fastest, and the best. And this pattern has an edge of windy paranoia, the fear that we won't be the first, the fastest, or the best. Karma is connected to the dark, stormy energy of the north, which also has an aggressive quality; unlike the anger of the vajra family, karma's aggressiveness is a quality more connected to pushy impatience. The karma energy is aware of everything that needs to be done and destroys anything in the way; however, in the wisdom aspect, it is the energy that clears any obstacle to enlightenment.

ALL-ACCOMPLISHING WISDOM

The wisdom in karma family is referred to as all-accomplishing wisdom. When transformed, the neurotic aspect of karma family becomes the ability to skillfully realize activities and to subdue or cut through what needs to be cut through. This wisdom brings into action what has been developed in the other four families. It requires both vast awareness and the skill to bring something to completion. The buddhas and bodhisattvas must have the skillful means to benefit sentient beings, and in this way all-accomplishing wisdom manifests as dynamic heroic actions.

"This wisdom brings into action what has been developed in the other four families. It requires both vast awareness and the skill to bring something to completion."

The name of the great Tibetan lama Karmapa comes from his enactment of the karma family, demonstrating Amoghasiddhi's fearlessness and skill. It is worth noting that the current Seventeenth Karmapa is embodying these values by becoming an activist in human rights, women's empowerment, and environmentalism, bringing all-accomplishing wisdom into the twenty-first century.

This wisdom gives one the ability to get things done in quite a remarkable way, efficiently, by being in the flow. You see how you can fit things together; you have the bigger view of what's happening and thus can accomplish things without stress. My husband Dave and I used to say to each other, when we were in the middle of the extremely complex building of Tara Mandala, "Let's try to do it all with a feeling of ease." We were building a three-story temple, a residence hall, and the multipurpose community building, as well as keeping track of my three kids and dealing with staff and fund-raising and so on. It was definitely a challenge to do it all with a feeling of ease, but it was good to remind each other to try. With this wisdom, we would change the *Star Wars* salutation "May the Force be with you" to "May the flow be with you."

All-accomplishing wisdom is being there when the wind comes through and picks up the sail and you go, being present but not forcing it, moving with the wind. The stress leaves because we realize that on the absolute level there is nowhere to go. There is no one to compare ourselves to. All-accomplishing wisdom is the ability to connect with the flow of energy to carry out activities, while remaining open to spontaneity along the way. In the experience of this wisdom, you can realize your goals, because everything opens up naturally. Instead of forcing things to happen, when you are *in the flow* people appear at the right time, or a different route emerges if there is an obstacle.

This flow is often accompanied by synchronicity. This term was coined by Dr. Carl Jung, who used it in his 1951 lecture on this topic at Eranos in Moscia, Switzerland, and later wrote a book about it, which also contained a related study by the physicist and Nobel laureate Wolfgang Pauli.[63] Dr. Jung believed that events connected by meaning did not need to have an explanation in terms of causality, because a meaningful coincidence (or series of coincidences) could help to clarify a situation or indicate the way one should proceed. This concept was inspired by a client's case: Dr. Jung was at an impasse in her treatment because her exaggerated rationalism—what he called "animus possession," or the possession of the negative masculine—was holding her back from assimilating valuable unconscious material. For everything he suggested to her, she had a rational retort negating it. He wasn't sure what to do. Then one night, the client dreamt she had been given an expensive piece of jewelry, a golden scarab.

The next day during her psychotherapy session, Dr. Jung was listening to her dream when he heard something tapping against the window behind him. Curious, he got up, opened the window, and caught a large golden beetle that was trying to get into the dark room. Dr. Jung wrote: "I handed the beetle to my patient with the words, 'Here is your scarab.' This experience punctured a hole in her rationalism and broke the ice of her intellectual resistance. The treatment could now be continued with satisfactory results."[64] The startling fact of the synchronicity between the dream and the reality of the gold scarab jolted her out of fixed rationalism.

The ability to interpret outer events as symbolic of inner events and as "signs" indicating the direction one should take is intimately woven into all-accomplishing wisdom. Lamas are always watching for signs, be it through dreams, weather, the flight of birds, passing animals, or the sudden arrival of a guest. Many occurrences can be "read" and used as guidance when one is attuned at a nonrational level of experience. In this way, one can receive guidance in activities or prophecies for the future.

For example, before starting to build the temple at Tara Mandala, I wanted to bury a traditional treasure vase with offerings to the earth and water spirits. This was a large vase about twenty-four inches tall, and it took several days to prepare and seal closed. Just as we were about to begin the ceremony, Lama Tulku Sang-ngag, whom I hadn't seen for several years, stopped by for a visit. I hadn't been sure exactly how to do the ceremony, but had prepared everything for it, and figured something would happen to clarify how to proceed, so this was the first synchronistic event. Of all the lamas I know, he is the most deeply trained in ceremonies such as this one, having been close to the great master Dilgo Khyentse Rinpoche for fourteen years.

Once the vase was ready, Tulku Sang-ngag Rinpoche laid out a thread grid over the circumference of the temple site, with each square along the circumference representing a day of the year. Then the day of the ceremony was marked, and inside the grid below that day, a *nagini*, or female water spirit, was painted on the ground facing the direction of the next day on the calendar (i.e., the future). So she would symbolically carry the treasure into the future. Under her left arm, he told us to begin to dig a hole where the vase would be placed. After the first shovel of earth was dug, he halted the work and went through the earth carefully, looking for predictions about the future of the temple. Sure enough, there was an ancient fossil that formed a clear spiral eye in the dirt. He was very happy with this and told me to keep it. He said the eye represented the wisdom eye, the third eye, and indicated that the temple would develop wisdom in those who entered it.

Usually when synchronistic events occur, it is when we are more open, not going too fast, and we are allowing things to happen without forcing a certain outcome. The wisdom in karma family is trusting in the flow, opening to synchronicity rather than trying to control everything through logic and planning. Actually, you can often get

The "Eye of Wisdom" stone found in the first shovel of earth when burying the earth treasure vase, an offering to earth spirits, at the site of Tara Mandala Temple, 2007.

more done by allowing space, because karma is air—it can be neurotic windiness, or it can be a spacious airy experience, with lots of room to breathe and giving space to the spontaneous fulfillment of endeavors.

If we go through the sequence of the families, karma is the last, the enlightened activity as a result of all the other families. In buddha family there is spaciousness; in vajra we develop intellectual precision; in ratna we cultivate generosity, enrichment, and stability; in padma family we learn wise discernment; and then finally in the karma family we have accomplishment. The wisdom here is a sense of self-existing energy, where there is automatic fulfillment rather than imposing a result, which is actually often the fastest way to get something done. The "already accomplished" aspect of the karma family's all-accomplishing wisdom is the sense that, whatever you are stressing about, you can relax and trust that *it is already done*.

This isn't a matter of not planning or getting well organized or taking proper steps to do something; it is an inner freedom and relaxation that is present.

"The wisdom here is a sense of self-existing energy, where there is automatic fulfillment rather than imposing a result, which is actually often the fastest way to get something done."

CARY'S STORY

Cary grew up in a family in which her father was a high-powered lawyer, and her mother had been a professor of economics, but stopped working when she married and had children. Her parents had a respectful, loving relationship, but her father often worked overtime and when he was home wanted to have his vodka tonic and read the newspaper in peace. He didn't really want to relate to his three children. Cary was the middle child, and in order to get her father's attention she had to impress him in some way with her performance. If she had won a cross-country race or had gotten good grades, he would perk up and praise her. She learned that being loved meant performing.

When she grew up, she went to the Ivy League school her father had gone to and became a lawyer as well. Her mother projected her unmet career ambitions onto Cary, praising her accomplishments and bragging about her daughter to friends and family. So Cary worked very hard and was soon promoted to be a partner in her firm. But she was also impatient with her assistants, pushing things to be prepared in unreasonable time frames.

She married and had two children of her own, but was often delayed at her office and came home late, which caused upset for her children and a frequent turnover among her nannies because the hours were irregular. Her husband did help, but he also was working hard, so the brunt of the childcare went to the nannies. Cary felt pushed to work more and more; she had little intimacy with her husband, took work calls at home, and spent limited time with her children. Her son was showing behavior problems in school and her daughter developed an eating disorder when she became a teen. Through family counseling required by the therapist for her daughter's eating disorder, Cary started to wake up to how neglectful she'd been as a mother. She realized she was doing to her kids what had been done to her, putting work before family.

She also saw that she was living out her parents' dreams, not her own. She went to a retreat to work with the mandala, and recognized herself in particular in the karma family. She started a regular early-morning mandala practice and began coming home on time and spending weekends with her family, refusing to take work calls at home. Gradually things with her kids settled down. She slowly shifted, and she was able to talk to her daughter and son when they were teenagers, explaining what had happened and, basically, apologizing for their early years. The family has been able to heal and deepen their closeness in the process, and Cary continues her mandala meditation.

KARMA FAMILY MEDITATIONS

Before beginning each of the meditations below, please first do the Nine Relaxation Breaths and Generating the Motivation practices as instructed in Chapter 8 on pages 155 and 156.

UNBLOCKING THE ENCUMBERED ENERGY

Let's take a moment and feel the encumbered karma pattern in our bodies.

* Scan your body and feel the energy of envy, jealousy, or ambition in your own body. Is it a winded sensation in your chest? Tension in your shoulder? A feeling of compression in your belly?
* Feel the encumbered energy. If you don't feel this currently, recall a time, an incident, or a period in your life when you were in the encumbered state.
* Now intensify the encumbered feeling of envy, jealousy, or speediness, so that you really feel it deeply and strongly. This gives you a felt experience of karma family in its blocked state.
* Now sound the seed syllable, slowly in a low voice: SA. As you sound the syllable, feel the sound go through your body, and see your body permeated by green light and air. Feel the obstructed pattern transform into all-accomplishing wisdom. Let the wisdom come from the sound and the light.
* Rest in the wisdom as long as you like. Repeat the seed syllable slowly and mindfully, resting after each repetition, as many times as you like, always resting in the wisdom energy at the end.

ELEMENT MEDITATION: AIR

* Before beginning this meditation, decide how long you are going to practice. I recommend from fifteen minutes to one hour.
* To do the meditation on the element of air, it's best to be somewhere there's a breeze, clearly outside, but in a pinch

inside with a fan. However, the idea of element practices
is that you take advantage of the situations in which you
find yourself, such as sitting by a river, lying on the beach,
or sitting by a fire, so that the element practice becomes
spontaneous and uncontrived. It is also meaningful to create
a situation for the practices. So for the air element, sit where
you can feel a breeze or lie under a fan. Get comfortable,
put a pillow under your head. This can also be done at night
outside.

* After the Nine Relaxation Breaths, allow your breath to
  settle. Then, with eyes open or closed, begin to be aware of
  the air on your skin. Notice the way it touches you; don't
  judge it by thinking you like or dislike it. Just be with it.
  If there's a strong wind, there may be a sound as well. Let
  your mind open, so that there is no *journey* between you and
  the air, there is no separation. If you get distracted, relax
  back into the feeling of the air.

* Try to avoid fixating any one place if your eyes are open.
  As the wind touches you, relax into its touch on your skin.
  As your breath, the air literally integrates into your body.

* When you are finished, dedicate the positive energy that has
  been generated to benefit all beings.

After you close the meditation, notice how you feel. Keep the
awareness of that feeling as you go about your day. I love this practice. Even in a strong wind it can be powerful; if you enter a state of
union with the wind, it feels like you are dissolving.

PART 4

Wisdom Rising: Practices

13

MANDALA OF THE FIVE DAKINIS

The medial woman's function is to be of assistance in times of difficult passage. As midwife to the psyche she is constellated in emergency situations where a spirit, a song, an alternative, a new being is emerging—whenever things appear to rise spontaneously from the depths of the unconscious. . . . The medial woman is evocative: she evokes or calls forth the inner spirit.

—NOR HALL

Now we will begin our journey into the actual practice of the Mandala of the Five Dakinis. We have spoken about the theory, history, stories, and meditations to feel and embody each of the five families in a more personal way. It's time now to have your own experience that brings together all the families and wisdom dakinis in one meditation.

KEY POINTS TO REMEMBER IN MANDALA MEDITATION:

* Create a sacred space for meditation. If possible, set up a place in your home where you have an altar and a place to sit in front of it. (See altar instructions in Chapter 15.)

FIVE WISDOM DAKINIS

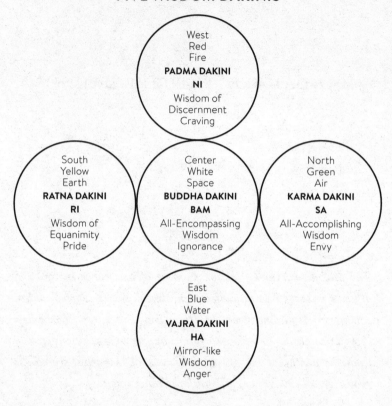

- * Before you begin: imagine this meditation space is protected by a "tent" of rainbow light; this tent is made of interlocking double vajras, so it becomes like a chain-link fence, but these vajras are made of rainbow light. The spectrum of rainbow light includes all the colors, but the colors are pure luminosity. It therefore raises the vibratory field surrounding you and acts as a protection.

- * Set a time when you won't be disturbed; turn off your phone and other devices that might create distraction. The amount of time will vary with each person, and after you practice for a while, you will have an intuitive sense of your own timing.

* Check your intentions: the benefit of your practice is only as vast as your intention. Anything that we do is influenced by our motivation at the outset. If you have a vast intention, you will have a vast result. If you have a limited, ego-oriented motivation, your results will be limited. So create a vast intention for the benefit of all beings.

* When you sound the seed syllables, take a long inhalation and then sound the syllable slowly and deeply, noticing the feeling in your body from each sound. The seed syllables are sacred sounds in Sanskrit coming down from a tradition more than a thousand years old. They are not randomly made up. Sanskrit is a sacred language, and so mantras and seed syllables were not translated into Tibetan or English but have been left in the original Sanskrit.

* Remember that the dakinis are not like human beings with internal organs and so forth. They are humanlike in appearance, but they are made of pure light, and their colors are brilliant and luminous. Remember also the meaning of the symbolic objects that each dakini carries, her posture, her color, and her direction.

* If you need a reminder, go back to the detailed diagram of the attributes of the Mandala of the Five Dakinis on page 134. Don't worry about memorizing all these traits— you will be reminded of them during the meditation—but use the diagram for your own reference, and after a while you will naturally remember these qualities.

Begin the meditation by taking your seat. Find a place where you can sit comfortably either on the floor or in a chair, in either case where you will be able to turn in all four directions without any problem.

Now, wherever you are, take a moment to locate the east direction (most smartphones have a compass). Sit facing east and, just to settle into your body becoming present right here and now, relax. Please keep your back straight so that your breath flows smoothly, but without tension. One of the traditional analogies for the back in meditative posture is to imagine it is like gold coins stacked one upon another. Feel yourself relaxing in this space, and wait until you feel relaxed to begin.

NINE RELAXATION BREATHS

Close your eyes and keep them closed as much as possible until the end of the process. You will begin by taking nine deep relaxation breaths.

* For the first three breaths, breathe into any *physical* tension you are holding in your body, noticing where you feel it; then, hooking that tension with the breath, release the tension with the exhalation.
* For the second three breaths, breathe into any *emotional* tension you are holding, noticing where you are holding emotional tension in your body; then, hooking that emotional tension with the breath, release it, letting it ride out with the exhalation.
* For the last three breaths, breathe into any *mental* tension or worries you are holding, noticing where you are holding mental tension in your body; then, hooking that tension with the breath, release it with the exhalation.

GENERATING THE MOTIVATION

Generate a heartfelt motivation to practice for the benefit of yourself and all beings. Even though this is a personal practice, we are all interrelated, and thus our meditation can benefit everyone, especially those close to us. So let's meditate with the motivation to benefit all beings as our base. Take a moment to generate the feeling from the depths of your heart; this is called generating *bodhicitta*.

Once you've completed these two opening meditations, you're ready to begin your journey through the Mandala of the Five Dakinis. Remember that each direction in the mandala is governed by one of the five buddha families—buddha in the center, vajra in the east, ratna in the south, padma in the west, and karma in the north—and each is connected to a certain poison, or encumbered pattern, and its wisdom counterpart. Let's begin.

BUDDHA DAKINI

We start in the center with the buddha family. The color is white. The element here is space. The symbol is the Wheel of Dharma, the eight-spoked wheel representing the Eightfold Path to enlightenment that the Buddha taught during his first teaching on the Four Noble Truths.[65] And the poison is ignorance, which is a kind of dullness, giving up, just waiting for things to be different. This encumbered pattern also involves depression and denial. Buddha family people are spaced-out rather than spacious in their obstructed pattern.

The wisdom is called the all-encompassing wisdom, in which awareness and emptiness are experienced as one, where your mind becomes like the sky. The Buddha Dakini has a luminous white body. She's dancing with her right leg raised and the left leg extended. In her raised right hand, she holds the trigug, the hooked knife, and its handle is ornamented with an eight-spoked wheel; in her left hand, at her heart, she holds the skull cup brimming with blood, the blood of the transformation of desire. In the crook of her left arm rests the khatvanga staff, her inner consort. She is so intense and fierce that she emanates wisdom flames. She's naked except for the eight bone ornaments.[66]

The seed syllable of the Buddha Dakini is BAM. So what we will be doing is first identifying the blocked pattern of the buddha family in your body; then, through sounding the seed syllable, seeing the white light, and visualizing yourself as the Buddha Dakini, you'll release the obstructed pattern and feel the all-encompassing wisdom.

* Now take a moment to feel the blocked pattern in your body, that energy of depression and dullness in your own body, however the buddha family pattern manifests for you: procrastination, passivity, depression, dissociation, laziness, or giving up. Really feel that for a moment, perhaps recalling an instance where you had experienced this poison intensely.
* Intensify it, feeling it very deeply. Then take a pause.
* And now you will sound the seed syllable, BAM; through this sound, and through the white light, which is clear and radiant, you will become the Buddha Dakini.
* *BAM.* Sound the seed syllable and become the Buddha Dakini. As you sound the first seed syllable, transform your body into the body of the white Buddha Dakini: full-breasted, dancing, naked, wearing bone ornaments, luminous white, feeling the intensity of the all-encompassing wisdom, wisdom of awareness-emptiness. This wisdom is emanating out of you as the dakini with such intensity that it becomes flames. From every pore of your body come wisdom flames; feel the embodiment of her spaciousness, sky-like awareness. Wait until you feel this before sounding the seed syllable a second time.

* *BAM*. Sounding the seed syllable a second time as the Buddha Dakini, send rainbow light out to all the wisdom beings of the universe. This light invites those beings to send their light back; your light rays have hooks on the end that gather the wisdom of those beings.

* *BAM*. Sound the seed syllable a third time. Wisdom-infused light returns and enters the Buddha Dakini. Rest awhile here, noticing how it feels to actually become the Buddha Dakini, emanating all-encompassing wisdom. How does it feel to embody this wisdom? Bask in this energy. When you have an embodied sense of the Buddha Dakini, imagine she stays there as you move to the east direction.

VAJRA DAKINI

From the Buddha Dakini in the center, move forward a few inches still facing east, keeping your eyes closed as much as possible. Take a moment to feel the energy of the east direction. Here we have the vajra family; the color is blue, deep blue like the autumn sky, the color of lapis lazuli. The element associated with vajra family is water and the symbol is the vajra or dorje, which is a scepter with five prongs joined together into a point on either end and a central sphere connecting the two ends; it represents skillful means, and the union of the five female and five male buddhas, as well as the five aggregates transforming into the five male buddhas.

The poison of vajra family is anger, sharpness, a tendency toward austerity and coldness; this can be cold or hot anger, also connected to fear. The wisdom of the vajra family is mirror-like wisdom, the mind being in the state of the mirror in its true condition, reflecting with clarity, not judging or being altered by what passes in front of it. Awareness is like a huge mirror: clear and vast. When we let go of our self-clinging mind, whatever passes in front of us is simply experienced as a reflection without reactivity.

The Vajra Dakini is dancing. She holds the hooked knife ornamented with a vajra on the handle, and in the crook of her left arm she holds the khatvanga staff, her inner consort. She has her right leg raised and her left leg extended in the dancing posture. Her body is luminous blue and surrounded by wisdom flames. She holds the skull cup at her heart and she is burning with wisdom flames, the transformation of anger into the mirror-like wisdom of clarity. Her seed syllable is HA.

* Now take a moment to identify the blocked pattern in your body, the pattern of anger, which can be hot or cold. How do you manifest anger? Perhaps recall an incident in which you've gotten angry recently, or something that happened from your past: feel it in your body. Wait until you feel this before beginning.
* Intensify it, feeling it very deeply. Then take a pause.
* As you sound the syllable, HA, sending forth blue light, your mind state will transform into the embodiment of mirror-like wisdom; through that sound and through the luminous blue light, transform yourself into the blue Vajra Dakini.
* *HA.* Sound the seed syllable and become the Vajra Dakini. As you sound the first seed syllable, feel the anger transform into blueness, it's the element of water transformed into blue light, and you become the blue Vajra Dakini emanating mirror-like wisdom. Imagine you embody this wisdom so intensely that wisdom flames pour from each pore in your body, spreading out in all directions, really feeling the transformation of the emotion into the wisdom.
* *HA.* Sounding the seed syllable a second time as the Vajra Dakini, send rainbow light out to all the wisdom beings of

the universe. This light invites those beings to send their light back; your rays have hooks on the end that gather the wisdom of those beings.

* *HA*. Sound the seed syllable a third time. Wisdom-infused light returns and enters the Vajra Dakini. Rest awhile here, noticing how it feels to actually become the Vajra Dakini, emanating mirror-like wisdom. How does it feel to embody this wisdom? Bask in this energy. When you have an embodied sense of the Vajra Dakini, imagine she stays there as you move to the south direction.

RATNA DAKINI

Leaving the Vajra Dakini in the east, turn to the right into the south. Take a moment and simply feel the energy of the south. This family is the ratna or jewel family. This dakini's color is golden-yellow. The element here is earth: rich, fertile earth. Her symbol is the golden jewel.

The encumbered emotion, the mind state here, is that of arrogance and pride, which covers feelings of inadequacy, not being good enough, not being enough; it creates greed, consuming hunger, consuming of all kinds. The wisdom of the ratna family is the wisdom of equanimity, the reality of equality. It's the release of grasping, judging, likes and dislikes, self-importance, and overbearing attitudes into a relaxed, stable state of equanimity and generosity, like the earth.

The Ratna Dakini has a full, golden body. She has a good sense of humor and loves bright colors. In her raised right hand, she holds the hooked knife ornamented with a golden jewel like beautiful amber. She's dancing naked, with the right leg raised and the left leg extended in the dancing posture. She holds the skull cup at her heart, and in the crook of her left arm the khatvanga staff, the inner consort. Wisdom flames stream out of her body, the wisdom of equanimity and unchanging stillness. Her seed syllable is RI.

* Now take a moment to identify this pattern, this mind state of arrogance and the feelings of "I'm not enough" and "I'm not good enough" that make you want to inflate yourself with pride, haughtiness, and the need to consume more. Allow yourself to feel that in your body. How does this particular poison manifest for you? Perhaps recall an incident in which you've found yourself acting arrogantly due to a deep sense of insecurity.
* Intensify it, feeling it very deeply. Then take a pause.
* As you sound the seed syllable RI, visualize the yellow light, and then you will transform into the Ratna Dakini.
* *RI.* Sound the seed syllable and become the Ratna Dakini. As you sound the first seed syllable, transform your body into the body of the golden-yellow Ratna Dakini: full-breasted, dancing, naked, wearing bone ornaments, luminous golden-yellow, feeling the intensity of the wisdom of equanimity. This wisdom is emanating out of you as the dakini with such intensity that it becomes flames. From every pore of your body come wisdom flames; feel the embodiment of her richness. Wait until you feel this before sounding the seed syllable a second time.
* *RI.* Sounding the seed syllable a second time as the Ratna Dakini, send rainbow light out to all the wisdom beings of the universe. This light invites those beings to send their light back; your light rays have hooks on the end that gather the wisdom of those beings.
* *RI.* Sound the seed syllable a third time. Wisdom-infused light returns and enters the Ratna Dakini. Rest awhile here, noticing how it feels: the fullness of your naked body,

large breasts, radiant golden color, dancing in golden light, emanating the wisdom of equanimity. Embrace the realization that you don't need to have more, that you can rest in what is with equanimity, trusting the earth. When you have an embodied sense of the Ratna Dakini, imagine she stays there as you move to the west direction.

PADMA DAKINI

Leaving Ratna Dakini in the south, turn to the right into the west, keeping your eyes closed as much as possible in order to keep your focus. Take a moment just to feel the energy of the west. The name of this family is the padma or lotus family, and its symbol is the red lotus. The direction is toward the setting sun. The color is red and the element is fire. Padma's poison is compulsive seduction, union through suction, a needy intensity directed at magnetizing others in order to feel significant. There's superficiality here—going for the glitter, from one object of desire or relationship to the next, without any real intimacy or deep connection.

The wisdom of this family is called wisdom of discernment, which is the ability to discern, to discriminate, but without selfish attachment, without your own agenda. This is the wisdom that enables you to see relationships with objects and with people, but without the need to have or to seduce or to magnetize them.

Padma Dakini is ruby red. She holds the hooked knife ornamented with a lotus, and the skull cup of blood at her heart, containing the blood of transformation of desire; in the crook of her left arm rests the khatvanga staff, symbolizing the inner consort. She's dancing with her right leg raised and her left leg extended, emanating wisdom flames. Her wisdom is so intense that the flames pour out of her in every direction. Her seed syllable is NI.

* Now take a moment to identify the blocked pattern: feel its energy in your body, the need to seduce. Perhaps recall an incident where this energy of need and desire has dominated you, taking over your body, pushing you to do things that you might later regret.

* Intensify the encumbered pattern, feeling it very deeply. Then take a pause.

* Now sound the seed syllable: *NI*. Through the sound of the seed syllable and through visualizing the red light, this emotion releases into its wisdom nature of discernment, and you will become the red Padma Dakini.

* *NI*. Sound the seed syllable and become the Padma Dakini. As you sound the first seed syllable, transform your body into the body of the red Padma Dakini: full-breasted, dancing, naked, wearing bone ornaments, fiery red, feeling the intensity of the wisdom of discernment. This wisdom is emanating out of you with such intensity that it becomes flames. From every pore of your body come wisdom flames. Wait until you feel this before sounding the seed syllable a second time.

* *NI*. Sounding the seed syllable a second time as the Padma Dakini, send rainbow light out to all the wisdom beings of the universe. This light invites those beings to send their light back; your light rays have hooks on the end that gather the wisdom of those beings.

* *NI*. Sound the seed syllable a third time. Wisdom-infused light returns and enters the Padma Dakini. Rest awhile here, noticing how it feels to become the Padma Dakini, embodying the wisdom of discernment and open awareness, releasing the struggle of grasping into the embodied wisdom. Bask in this energy. When you have an embodied sense of the Padma Dakini, imagine she stays there as you move to the north direction.

KARMA DAKINI

Now, leaving the Padma Dakini in the west, turn to the right into the final direction, the north. Keep your eyes closed, stay centered, and simply feel the energy of north as it hits you for a moment. The name of this family is the karma family. The color is green and the element is air. Karma's symbol is the sword or the double vajra. The poison is jealousy, competitiveness, speediness, and workaholic tendencies. The karma family tends toward paranoid comparison, and a thrusting movement. Her wisdom is all-accomplishing wisdom, wise action, which sees all karmic strivings to be completed, and trusts self-existing energy, the flow rather than the force.

The Karma Dakini is thin and airy, always moving; she is seen in profile, because she is always going somewhere to do something. She holds in her raised right hand the hooked knife, ornamented with a sword; the skull cup of blood is at her heart, the blood of transformation of desire. She's dancing with her right leg raised and her left leg extended, and in the crook of her left arm is her khatvanga staff, the inner consort. She is emanating all-accomplishing wisdom so intensely that she's surrounded by wisdom flames. Her seed syllable is SA.

* Take a moment to be with the blocked pattern here. The pattern of speed, workaholic tendencies, ambition, jealousy—really feel that. Perhaps recall a time when you experienced this, recently or in the past. Notice how that feels in your body.
* Intensify the encumbered pattern, feeling it very deeply. Then take a pause.
* Now you will sound the seed syllable: *SA*. Feel the encumbered pattern dissolving into the sound and the luminous green light, and you will become the Karma Dakini, emanating the energy of all-accomplishing wisdom.

* *SA.* Sound the seed syllable and become the Karma Dakini. As you sound the first seed syllable, transform your body into the body of the green Karma Dakini: full-breasted, dancing, naked, wearing bone ornaments, luminous green, feeling the intensity of the all-accomplishing wisdom. This wisdom is emanating out of you as the dakini with such intensity that it becomes flames. From every pore of your body come wisdom flames. Rest in the feeling that everything is naturally completed, everything is already accomplished; in the fullness of that trust, you can move with the flow rather than the force. The mind state of arrogance, jealousy, and envy is transformed into wisdom. Wait until you feel this before sounding the seed syllable a second time.

* *SA.* Sound the seed syllable a second time as the Karma Dakini, sending rainbow light out to all the wisdom beings of the universe. This light invites those beings to send their light back; your light rays have hooks on the end that gather the wisdom of those beings.

* *SA.* Sound the seed syllable a third time. Wisdom-infused light returns and enters the Karma Dakini. Rest awhile here, noticing how it feels to actually become the Karma Dakini, emanating all-accomplishing wisdom. Really feeling that already accomplished wisdom in your body, relax, and let go of all striving. How does it feel to embody this wisdom? Bask in this energy. When you have an embodied sense of the Karma Dakini, imagine she stays there as you move back to the center.

Leaving the Karma Dakini in the north, come back to the center, keeping your eyes closed, and sit facing east in the place where you began.

* Take a moment to become again the Buddha Dakini—the white dakini of spaciousness, feeling the wisdom flames of the union of awareness and emptiness.
* In front of you is the blue Vajra Dakini, emanating wisdom flames of mirror-like wisdom and clarity.
* To your right is the Ratna Dakini, emanating wisdom flames of equanimity and enriching presence.
* Behind you is the Padma Dakini, emanating wisdom flames, embodying the red energy, the wisdom of discernment.
* To your left is the Karma Dakini, emanating the wisdom of the all-accomplishing action, and the release of striving.

Feel yourself complete in this mandala—all the emanations of wisdom are your own true nature. Your whole being is present here. Your whole being has been transformed into the Mandala of the Five Dakinis. *You are the Mandala of the Five Dakinis.* In this moment of completion, take time to rest here. This is the time of healing the disjointed fragmented energies in your life. Notice how it feels. Rest here. Just rest in the luminosity of the mandala, feel yourself embodying the buddha dakini with her retinue of the other four dakinis surrounding you. Rest your awareness in all-encompassing space, feel yourself embodying wisdom. Rest as long as you like here. If your mind wanders, sound the five seed syllables again, activating the five dakinis: BAM HA RI NI SA. When you are ready, move on to the dissolution.

DISSOLUTION

Now the Mandala of the Five Dakinis begins to dissolve. The four dakinis in the four directions dissolve into the central Buddha Dakini, one at a time: starting with the Vajra Dakini, then the Ratna Dakini, the Padma Dakini, and finally the Karma Dakini.

Gradually the Buddha Dakini dissolves up from her feet and down from the top of her head into a luminous sphere of white light at her heart, which then also dissolves. Rest in whatever is present after the dissolution.

DEDICATION OF MERIT

Having rested in emptiness for as long as you feel suitable, dedicate the merit, the accumulation of positive energy that you've generated through this transformation, to the benefit of all beings everywhere.

14

JOURNEY WITH THE DAKINI

Despite the infinite variety of mandalas, whether produced by tantric meditators, or in the dreams and active imagination of Jung's patients, or individuals anywhere in the world, we find a fundamental conformity of pattern, for they originate in the collective unconscious of mankind. They are symbols of unity, reconciling opposites on a higher level of consciousness. At the same time, they are a means of expression of a universal reality, and by being contacted they produce profound effects inducing transformative experiences.

—RADMILA MOACANIN

The following meditation can be added in order to receive specific insight into a certain wisdom dakini. Once you have finished the practice of the Mandala of the Five Dakinis:

* Turn in the direction of the wisdom dakini with whom you felt most identified, or the dakini representing the transformation of the encumbered pattern that seems most active in your life at the moment.

* Sit facing in that direction (or stay in in the center if it is the Buddha Dakini).
* Close your eyes and keep them closed as much as possible until the end of the process. Do the Nine Relaxation Breaths. (See page 155.)
* Then do the generate the motivation to practice for the benefit of yourself and all beings; this is called raising bodhicitta.

JOURNEY WITH THE DAKINI MEDITATION

STEP 1: INVOKE THE PRESENCE OF THE DAKINI

* Call on the dakini with whom you would like to have further communication. Sounding her seed syllable once, see the dakini in front of you, carrying the hooked knife ornamented with the symbol for her respective family in her raised right hand, holding the skull cup at her heart with her left hand, luminous, and emanating the wisdom of that family. The seed syllables are BAM for Buddha Dakini, HA for Vajra Dakini, RI for Ratna Dakini, NI for Padma Dakini, and SA for Karma Dakini. As the dakini appears before you, notice the details of the dakini: her size, color, character, and the look in her eyes. Notice something about the dakini you did not see before.
* Now notice the environment around the dakini. What kind of place is she in? What is the feeling in the environment? Is she in a place you've been? Can you see the time period? Can you see the country she is in? Do you notice any smells or sounds? Is she on this earth or in another dimension? If it is another dimension, notice the details of that place.

STEP 2: THE DAKINI TAKES YOU ON A JOURNEY

* Now imagine that the dakini takes you on a journey to a special place.
* You follow, walking behind the dakini. Notice what the path is like and how it changes as you proceed. (Pause.) Do you notice any smells or sounds? What is the feeling in the environment?
* When you arrive at the special place the dakini is taking you; notice where it is.
* What are the qualities of the place that surrounds you? What time of day is it? What is the temperature? Are there any particular smells? What era is it? How do you feel in this place? Does it remind you of anywhere you've been before?
* Your dakini then explains why she has brought you here and why this place is important to you.

STEP 3: ASK THE DAKINI YOUR QUESTIONS

* Now in this place, ask the dakini any questions you have. You can ask one or several questions.

STEP 4: TAKE THE SEAT OF THE DAKINI AND ANSWER THE QUESTION

* Once you have asked the question(s), switch places and take the seat of the dakini. Take a moment to settle into the dakini's body. Notice how it feels to be in the dakini's body. How does your normal self look from the dakini's point of view? After settling into the dakini's body, answer the question(s), speaking as the dakini.

STEP 5: RETURN TO YOUR ORIGINAL SEAT

* You can continue to dialogue with the dakini in this way, asking as many questions as you like.
* When you are finished, return to your original position. Take a moment to feel the help and protection that the dakini has offered you. (Pause.)
* Now the dakini turns away, and when she turns back she is holding a gift for you.
* The dakini gives you the gift. You hold it and notice the details of the gift. The dakini explains its meaning.
* Then the gift with all its potency dissolves into your heart. Notice the feeling of the gift inside you. (Pause.)
* Now see the dakini in front of you, look into her eyes, and feel her energy pouring into your body. As you feel the energy of the dakini entering you, it spreads all the way down to the soles of your feet, to your fingertips, and throughout your whole body. (Pause.)
* Now imagine that the dakini dissolves into light. Notice the color of this light. Feel the light dissolving into you, integrating this luminosity into every cell of your body. Take note of the feeling of the integrated energy of the dakini in your body.
* Now you, with the integrated energy of the dakini, also dissolve.

STEP 6: REST IN AWARENESS

* Rest in the state that is present after the dissolution, just rest. (Pause.)
* Pause until discursive thoughts begin again. Now gradually come back to your body, recalling the feeling of the energy of the dakini in your body. (Pause.)

* Now as you open your eyes, maintain the feeling of the energy of the dakini in your body, and see the world through the eyes of the dakini.

DEDICATION OF MERIT

Dedicate the merit, the accumulation of positive energy that you've generated through this transformation, to the benefit of all beings everywhere.

POST-MEDITATION

As you go about the rest of your day, imagine that you are the dakini and that everyone you meet is a manifestation of your mandala. As you eat, you are feeding the dakini; as you dress, you are dressing her. Imagine that the world is transformed into a luminous dimension; this is called pure perception.

15

CREATING A DAKINI
MANDALA ALTAR

Without my piece of earth, my life's work would not have come into being.

—C. G. JUNG

I was teaching in Switzerland at the Jung Institute, a large beige stucco house with green shutters on the bank of the lake, in the town of Küsnacht, a suburb of Zurich. The rooms are beautifully carved oak paneling and parquet hardwood floors. It has a boathouse on the lake and a small mandala garden next to it.

Martin and Sabine Kalff were hosting me in their fifteenth-century house with floorboards a foot and a half wide in Zollikon, a little town above the lake, which Martin and his brother Peter had inherited from their mother, Dora Kalff. She was a student of Dr. Jung's who trained with him as a Jungian analyst and also studied Tibetan Buddhism. She developed the now world-famous Sandplay Therapy, which to some extent was inspired by what happened to Dr. Jung at this beach. (See Sandplay Dakini Mandala practice on page 286.) When he was trying to recover from his disorienting split with Dr. Sigmund Freud, Jung decided to allow himself to play as he had as a child with sand and stones on the beach of the lake.

The beach is not wide, maybe fifteen or twenty feet; it is near a walking path that passes behind the first row of houses in front of the lake. Now there is a park there. It has gray gravel, sand, and small stones.

Dr. Jung had found himself in a state of disequilibrium after parting ways with Freud, and so he decided to do whatever his unconscious first suggested to him. He did this because he had a memory of when he was about ten years old and played passionately with building blocks, creating little houses and castles. This memory was accompanied by strong emotions that made him realize that in his childhood he'd had a creative life, which he had since lost.

Jung took this as a hint from his unconscious and began to play on this beach near his home. He created houses and castles, building a whole village. But when he came to the moment of creating the altar for the church in his village, he felt hesitant and unsure how to proceed. So in his usual way, he wandered down the beach to see what appeared. He came upon a red stone formed into a perfect pyramid about an inch and a half high that had been naturally polished by the water from the lake. He realized it was the perfect altar, and as he placed it under the dome of the church he had created. This triggered a memory of the first important dream he'd had as a child, of an underground phallus, which he came to understand as the beginning of his intellectual life. This recollection gave him a feeling of satisfaction, so he continued to play at the lake's edge every day the weather permitted:

> Naturally, I thought about the significance of what I was doing, and asked myself, "Now really, what are you about? You are building a small town, and doing it as if it were a rite!" I had no answer to my question, only the inner certainty that I was on the way to discovering my own myth.

For the building game was only a beginning. It released
a stream of fantasies which later I carefully wrote down.

This sort of thing became consistent with me, and at
any time in my later life when I came up against a blank
wall, I painted a picture or hewed a stone. Each such experience proved to be a *rite d'entrée* for the ideas and works
that followed hard upon it.[67]

Creativity stemming from the spontaneous discovery of the
stone altar for his church became the beginning of the healing of unfinished business from his childhood. This combination—allowing
himself to play and to see what would spontaneously manifest in the
environment, and finding significance in what manifested spontaneously and in dreams—became a seed for his life's work, informing
his psychotherapy practice and the development of Jungian therapy.

Dr. Jung's inspiration and intuitive insight from the creation of
an altar reminds me of the importance of creating altars. A home
without an altar is like a person with no soul. A home without an altar
has no spiritual center, no place for the inner life of the occupants to
dwell. If you have an altar or several altars in your home, they become the outer message of your inner process.

An altar can be important and should really be personal, to have
personal significance. Throughout my life I have shifted between
very traditional Tibetan Buddhist altars and those that I have created
myself, or a combination of both. In the time after I had disrobed
when I began my family, I realized it was important to make my altar
my own, so I began to put things on it other than the traditional seven
offering bowls. I added perhaps a stone I had found that had personal
significance, or a feather, or a drawing.

My altars were living spaces, which changed over the years, but I
have always had an altar. I even carry a portable altar when I travel.
Usually I have a small statue of Tara or the Buddha or Machig Labdrön, and sometimes small offering bowls, but always a candle and

incense. Without my traveling altar, I feel I somehow can't find a centered space where I am staying. As soon as my altar is up, I feel happy and at home.

ALTAR FOR THE
MANDALA OF THE FIVE DAKINIS

An altar for the Mandala of the Five Dakinis can be made simply by placing scarves of the five colors of the families over a square cardboard box turned upside down as a base. It's good if whatever base you use is actually square because the mandala's center is square; a square or round table is even better. However, it is important not to get too hung up on details, and just make an altar; let it be your personal altar.

It's best to use new scarves of solid colors, but here you can also be creative and find things among fabrics that you already have, or that you find or purchase.

Then to the east, drape the blue scarf over that side of the box, to the south place the yellow scarf, to the west the red scarf, and to the north the green scarf. Then in the center, arrange the white scarf covering the top and the intersection of the other four scarves. You can then simply place one white candle, protected in a container, in the center. This can be your dakini altar; then add things that are meaningful to you around the candle.

If you wish to make it more elaborate, you can get candles in the five colors, or containers of the five colors with white candles inside, and place them in the appropriate directions with the white one in the center. You can also find other objects in the five colors for your altar. And you may come upon items that symbolize the families, and gradually build your altar with found objects or things of symbolic significance for your work with the five families. Some people have made an entire room—their bedroom or another room—into an

altar by painting the four walls in the four colors and the floor and
ceiling white. Others have simply placed colored paper in the shapes
of the families on the walls: a blue circle for vajra, a yellow square
for ratna, a red upward-pointing triangle for padma, and a green
semicircle with the flat side up for karma. Some have also chosen to
wear different colors according to which Buddha family they want
to invoke. During Dakini Retreats everyone in the group wears the
color of the family we are focusing on. It makes a strong impact to
look around and see everyone wearing all blue, all red, all yellow,
and so on.

If you have an image of the five-dakini mandala, you can place it
on the wall behind your candles. The altar can change and grow over
time. Every once in a while it's good to strip it down to its simplest
form, and then rebuild it. It should be something that's pleasing for
you to look at, and becomes your own mandala in your home.

When you are working with a certain family, you can also focus
your altar on that. For example, if you have issues with depression
and procrastination, you might create a buddha family altar, covering the whole altar with white fabric and using white candles and
objects like the eight-spoked wheel that symbolize buddha family. If
you want to focus on anger concerns, you can choose blue fabric and
objects such as a vajra, a blue bowl of water, and a mirror to represent
vajra family. If you have problems with prosperity or pride, yellow
fabric, a yellow candle, and objects of gold or things representing the
earth create a ratna altar.

If you have relationship issues and are working intensely with
the padma family, turn your altar into a padma altar with a red candle, red fabric, and other things representing this family. And when
struggling with the karma family emotions of envy, jealousy, and
workaholic tendencies, create a green altar with a green candle,
green fabric, and add whatever else comes to you that represents the
karma family to you. When you see your buddha family altar, you

will be reminded of the transformation of that family's encumbered pattern into the wisdom.

For me, an example of ratna altar magic occurred when we moved back to the United States from Italy in 1986. I didn't have enough money for my three quickly growing children. I was a single parent and bought a house that was really over my head. I literally was feeding the kids rice and beans, and I didn't know how I was going to get them new shoes. I bought a station wagon from the Hasidic community near where I lived called New Square. Typically the Hasidic families have a lot of children, so commonly they have big station wagons to fit the whole family. I bought a large used station wagon with three seats from a family in New Square, but the car had seen better days, and it was a diesel engine.

After about two weeks, the station wagon started spewing forth clouds of black smoke as only diesels can. I had already put a bumper sticker on it with a picture of the blue planet earth and the words *Love Your Mother.* Whenever I stopped at a light, the car would spew toxic clouds of black smoke, which surrounded this bumper sticker. People would pass me after the traffic light and make "what the ... !" gestures.

It was pretty embarrassing, but I had to drive my kids to school, birthday parties, lessons, stores, and just get around. I had no choice. Then I was coming home after a family gathering in Massachusetts that winter. It was after dark, and I had my three kids with me. Suddenly the station wagon started making a weird clunking sound, and then just stopped on the six-lane highway. I managed to get the car over to the side into the breakdown lane. New England winter is very cold and damp, and I was feeling desolate on the icy highway in the wind with cars zooming by.

I managed to get the wagon towed and then restarted, so I could drive home, but the mechanic said the transmission was going, and I realized I needed a new car. I was doing a lot of the dakini mandala practice at the time, so I thought: *Okay, I'm going to focus on the Ratna Dakini. I need to try to do something. I can't go on like this.*

I put the Ratna Dakini image in the middle of the mandala and set up a ratna altar. I spread a golden-colored cloth on the shrine, and added a golden bowl full of gold-foil-wrapped chocolate coins. I got some yellow roses and a yellow pillar candle and placed them there too. I turned my seat to face south with the altar in front of me and started doing the practice every day. I even started wearing some yellow scarves and shirts I had. I wasn't sure anything would change or if it would work, but I visualized myself as the Ratna Dakini. I felt my body as if it were made of golden light and emanating intense wisdom flames. I felt myself embodying the wisdom of equanimity and enriching presence. I opened my energy field to receive the blessings of the dakinis and felt the stability of the earth supporting me.

About ten days later, I was at a party in New York City, and I saw my old friend Jim. I'd known him in Italy, but he was American. As I was leaving, he said, "I put something in your bag. Don't look now, it's a gift for you."

I was really curious about what he'd given me. As soon as I was out on the street, I started fumbling around in my bag to see. It turned out he had put $500 into my bag.

So that's how it started. The next thing that happened was that my parents came to visit. At the end of their stay, my father said, "We'd like to talk to you about something."

Whenever my father said that, I knew it was something serious. I was afraid he was going to tell me he was seriously ill or something like that. After we got settled in my living room, me in a white armchair and my parents on the couch, he said, "We've been thinking about you and have decided to give you some money. It's some of the money that you would have eventually gotten as inheritance, but it seems like you need it now." So within a matter of weeks, my ratna situation had changed, and my parents decided to pay for the children's school, which was a Waldorf school and not cheap. The Ratna Dakini had manifested really fast; but you need to really enter the practice deeply, it's not automatic that these kinds of manifestations will occur.

CREATING ALTARS WITH CHILDREN

Creating an altar can be both a fun and a meaningful thing for a child. It can be as simple as clearing a shelf for them in their room. You can either offer some structure, ideas of what they might want to put on it, or let them decide. For example, I recently gave my granddaughter a statue of Tara for her altar. She treasures it, and sits with it with her best friend, who she told me is "really into Tara," and they do Tara mantras together. And since the family retreat at Tara Mandala, during which she had the part of Green Tara in the retreat's play and was painted all green, this became more meaningful for her.

You could create a five-dakini mandala altar with your child or children and teach them about the five families at the same time. I know a family who every Sunday morning lit the five candles together as a family practice. They did a short practice of the mandala, and gradually the children came to understand the meaning of the five families. Even just taking turns lighting the candles and saying the meaning begins to introduce them to the mandala.

However, a child's shrine need not have any particular representations of deities or buddhas, and might have representations of other religions, or might simply consist of things that are precious and special to the inner life of that child. Creating an altar is a fun game to play in nature and also at the beach, where you can create altars instead of sand castles. (The practices below in drawing a mandala or creating one in nature can also be done with children.)

Altars can be magical places, quite literally. My daughter Sherab created very elaborate altars as a child, both in nature and in her room, which she shared with her sister. I remember her altar in our ground-floor apartment in Rome. It sat on a table about three feet square, and on it she had the Buddha statue, a postcard of Saint Francis, a postcard of Krishna playing the flute, and various other things. In *Women of Wisdom*, I shared this story of the magical importance of an altar even for a child:

> When my oldest daughter Sherab was six, she asked for a Buddha statue. She made it clear she wanted a real one, not a toy Buddha from Chinatown. So her father sent a beautiful small Buddha statue from America, made by a friend of his who had learned traditional Tibetan metal-casting methods.
>
> The Buddha was hollow with a little metal plate sealing the bottom in the traditional Tibetan fashion. According to the Tibetan customs, Buddha statues are filled with sacred substances, and a cedar spine is placed in the center with relics tied at the level of the chakras, and then they are consecrated. But we had not filled nor consecrated her Buddha.
>
> Sherab loved her Buddha more than any of her toys and set up an elaborate shrine with all her stuffed animals around it "listening to teachings." Whenever she was given candy or other gifts she would offer some to the Buddha.
>
> In November 1982, nine-year-old Sherab and I went to Nepal together. She felt a profound connection with Buddhist culture. The stupas—everything Buddhist—evoked a deep response in her. Her days were full of making elaborate offerings at the stupas and her nights were

full of dreams of traveling to luminous realms and receiving teachings from light beings.

When we left, on the plane she cried all the way to Delhi, saying, "How can you take me away from my home?" I felt terrible.

One day, a few days after we got back to Rome, Sherab and Aloka came to me and said, "There's something in Sherab's Buddha." At the time I was busy and I didn't think much about it.

Then a few days later they told me again. This time I decided to investigate. We went to her shrine and shook the Buddha. Sure enough there was something rolling around inside. So I pried off the metal base, and we peered inside. We found a pure white *ringsel* the size of a large pea. Ringsels are relics that may appear in sacred places or come out of the ashes of cremated lamas. It was whiter than anything I've ever seen. It glowed. The consistency was hard—like crystallized sugar, but much denser. You could see some white on the sides of the Buddha inside where this beautiful sphere "grew." . . . Faith makes room for magic.[68]

16

MANDALA WORK WITH
YOUR HANDS™ AND MORE

Often the hands will solve a mystery that the intellect has struggled with in vain.

—C. G. JUNG

Mandala Work with Your Hands™ allows you to create your own mandala, and as Dr. Jung says, "Handwork allows things to come forth from us that we might not consciously be able to access, and takes us beyond the intellect allowing our innermost being to express itself." It also can be healing and creative.

Here I've given you a few ideas to get you started on how to handwork your own mandala, but you can also create your own handwork—perhaps make a quilt or knit something, or you could make a mandala sculpture, or even write a script for a mandala play.

DRAWING A DAKINI MANDALA

Have all your art materials ready. It is useful to use black or beige paper so you can use white for the buddha family. Oil pastels are nice because you can smudge them, but you can also use colored pencils, markers, or paint. The mandala can be any size. When Jung began to draw mandalas, he did one every day in a small notebook.

STEP 1:

* Sit quietly for a moment and notice how you feel.
* Connect with the mandala within yourself as the central dakini surrounded by the four retinue dakinis. Feel that the center of the mandala is the seed syllable in your heart chakra as the main dakini. Sound the five seed syllables, creating the energy of the mandala around you and inviting the five dakinis to be present: BAM, HA, RI, NI, SA.
* Imagine light coming from your heart through your hands into the materials you have gathered; bless your drawing materials with your hands.
* When you feel ready, draw a circle, and then at the center of that circle another smaller circle representing the buddha family; then make four quadrants for the vajra, ratna, padma, and karma families. This can be loosely drawn or carefully measured (using a plate, a compass, etc.).
* Then draw whatever comes to you using the colors of each direction and with variations of the colors if you have them (different shades of white, blue, yellow, red, green). You can draw the traditional geometric forms associated with the element of that quadrant, such as circles for water and vajra, squares for earth and ratna, triangles for fire and padma, half circles for air and karma, and points or small circles for bindu and buddha. You can also make random forms, symbolic forms, or descriptive personal drawings of animals, people, or whatever comes to you. Let yourself be free within the basic structure.

STEP 2:

Once you feel you have finished drawing your mandala, look at it and directly ask the mandala some questions, either silently or out loud. Record the answers to all the questions in your journal.

First ask: "What is the main message of this mandala?"

Continue by asking questions about specific things you see or feel in the mandala drawing. Then let the part of the mandala you have asked answer.

For example, you could ask a question such as: "What is that circle in buddha family?"

Then have that part of the mandala answer. For example, it might say: "That circle is the experience of wholeness that you feel when you meditate outside on space while looking at the sky. This is an important meditation you should do frequently."

Of course, the mandala isn't literally speaking to you—it's a part of yourself that is answering—but the vehicle of the mandala allows you to tap intuitive insights that you might not get just doing the meditations.

Another question you might ask is: "Why is there a young girl in the karma family?" Then have the figure answer for herself, for example: "I am here because I represent the child who was always forced to hurry and do more work. I want freedom."

Or perhaps you might ask: "Why is there a feeling of agitation from the ratna family?"

Then let the mandala respond, perhaps: "I am reflecting your state of agitation, which is connected to not feeling good enough."

And so on . . .

You can ask as many questions as you like, especially those pertaining to the particular family you are working with. Imagine that the mandala is answering, and write down the answers in your journal or record them on your smartphone to listen to later.

If you don't ask any questions and just look at the mandala, you won't get direct insights.

STEP 3:

At the end, ask the mandala:

* "What can I learn from this mandala?"
* "Do you have anything more to tell me?"

CREATING THE DAKINI MANDALA IN NATURE

Gather together materials you are drawn to for your mandala, such as rocks, sand, feathers, wood, metal, shells, water, and flowers. Have all your materials ready.

STEP 1:

* Sit quietly for a moment and notice how you feel.
* Connect with the mandala within yourself as the central dakini surrounded by the four retinue dakinis. Feel that the center of the mandala is the seed syllable in your heart chakra as the Buddha Dakini. Sound the five seed syllables, creating the energy of the mandala around you and inviting the five dakinis to be present: BAM, HA, RI, NI, SA.
* Imagine light coming from your heart through your hands into the materials you have gathered, and bless the materials with your hands.
* When you feel ready, draw a circle in the ground or sand with a stick. Within the circle make four quadrants for the vajra, ratna, padma, and karma families, leaving space in the center for buddha family. Then place whatever objects feel right according to the five families into the mandala.

STEP 2:

Ask questions as described previously in Drawing a Dakini Mandala. You can ask any questions that come up, and especially those about the particular family you are working with. Let the mandala answer, and write down the answers in your journal.

STEP 3:

At the end, ask:

* "What can I take with me from this mandala?"
* "Do you have anything more to tell me?"

SANDPLAY DAKINI MANDALA

Sandplay Therapy was originated by Dora Kalff, a student of Dr. C. G. Jung, as a therapeutic way to work with the unconscious and dreams through play. This technique uses a tray of sand and numerous small figures to facilitate creative play. In this case, we are not doing the therapy, but rather using the tray and figures for mandala work. Sandplay Therapy is based on the idea that the psyche possesses a natural tendency to heal itself, which was Dr. Jung's belief in using the mandala work. Similar to how our physical injuries heal under supportive conditions, the psyche also has a natural wisdom that emerges when it is left free to operate naturally in a safe situation.

The aim of Sandplay is to activate healing energies at the deepest level of the psyche through the use of miniatures and the sand tray to reflect the person's inner world. Through creative play, unconscious processes are made visible in this three-dimensional form. If you have access to a sand tray with the plethora of miniatures from the real and imaginary worlds that carry symbolic meaning (used by Sandplay psychotherapists, and available to order on the Internet), you can do mandala work in the sand tray.

STEP 1:

* Sit quietly for a moment and notice how you feel.
* Connect with the mandala within yourself as the central dakini surrounded by the four retinue dakinis. Feel that the center of the mandala is the seed syllable in your heart chakra as the Buddha Dakini. Sound the five seed syllables, creating the energy of the mandala around you and inviting the five dakinis to be present: BAM, HA, RI, NI, SA.
* Imagine light coming from your heart through your hands into the materials you have gathered, and bless the materials with your hands.
* When you feel ready, draw a large circle in the sand with a smaller circle in the middle. Within the large circle make four quadrants for the vajra, ratna, padma, and karma families, leaving space in the center for buddha family. Then place whatever objects feel right in the five family quadrants according to the meaning of each one and your intuitive sense of where they should go.

STEP 2:

Ask questions as described previously in Drawing a Dakini Mandala. You can ask any questions that come up, and especially those about the particular family you are working with. Let the mandala answer, and write down the answers in your journal. Let the sandplay mandala answer, and you can also have specific figures in the sandplay speak for themselves.

For example, if you placed a miniature white horse there in the buddha family space, you could ask the horse: "Why are you there in my mandala?"

The white horse might answer: "I am in the center because I am the spirit of freedom and the wildness of space. I want to take you into spacious freedom." This is just one possibility; ask and answer your own questions according to the miniatures you put in the mandala.

STEP 3:

At the end ask:

* "What can I take with me from this mandala?"
* "Do you have anything more to tell me?"

WEARING THE WISDOM DAKINI COLOR

Another way to work with the wisdom dakinis is by wearing a particular dakini's color. Color is very powerful. Many of us wear black a lot, which is the combination of all the colors. But black isn't one of the five colors and lacks luminosity. If you know you're working with a certain family, try experimenting and wearing at least some articles of clothing in that color. It can be very transformative, because when you look down you'll see that color and it impacts your mind. Some people have found it powerful to try wearing all the colors, while others have discovered that they really enjoy wearing certain colors they normally would never have chosen. In the Dakini Retreats I teach, when we move from one family to the next, we all wear the clothes of that color, and so when you look out at the retreat, the participants reflect back the color of that particular family. In Brazil, at New Year's time, they wear underwear and bikinis that are the color of the energy they want to evoke for the new year; for example, white for peace, red for passion, and so on. If you want to wear the dakini colors in a more secret way, you could follow the Brazilian custom but use the colors of the five families!

REGRESSION PRACTICE
WITH THE FIVE FAMILIES

You can do this process in order to gain access to more information about your history and patterns with each of the buddha families. In my longer retreats, I take participants through each of the five families with this regression process, and then participants journal about their experience afterward and work with what is uncovered. Here you will be guiding yourself. If you have a history of trauma, I would not suggest you do this by yourself; instead, get guidance from or do it with a psychotherapist before you do it. If you have no fears of what will be uncovered by doing a regression, then it's fine to do this on your own.

STEP 1:

* Lie down and make yourself comfortable, with a pillow or whatever you need to be able to relax. Have writing materials ready—this can be some blank paper, a journal dedicated to your work with the buddha families, or perhaps a large sketchbook where you can also do your mandala drawings.
* Working from this present moment back through time, we will look at the pattern of the family you are working with. This is the encumbered pattern or the poison of that family. We will look at how this pattern has played out in your life. We do this because it gives you an experience you can relate to within yourself.
* After you lie down, close your eyes and get comfortable. Take a moment to settle, to really land where you are; connect with the earth under you, and feel an invisible cord running into the center of the earth.
* Set the intention to see only what would be helpful to see on your journey, and generate the motivation that it benefit all beings.

STEP 2:

* Begin with reviewing the last few days, noticing any instances of the encumbered pattern of the family you are working with (for example, ignorance for buddha family, anger for vajra family, pride for ratna family, craving for padma family, and envy for karma family). Choose one family to work with for each regression. Simply notice what is happening. (Pause.)

* Now take a deep breath, and with the exhalation review the last few months. Notice any tendencies to go into this poison. Just looking at yourself, notice what is happening and what is triggering this. (Pause.)

* Take another deep breath, and with the exhalation go back into the last year, seeing the pattern of this particular family very clearly. Allow your breath to carry you back to see the encumbered pattern. See specific instances from the past year. Notice when you do this how it feels. (Pause.)

* Take another deep breath and release gradually, then with the exhalation scan back through your adult life. Notice times when perhaps this family pattern was stronger than others. Notice what is going on, how it feels in your body, seeing how you can get caught in this poison. (Pause.)

* Seeing clearly as you breathe deeply, observe how the pattern takes over. See if there were specific periods in your life when this pattern was really strong. Just see what is useful to see . . . and what you are ready to look at. (Pause.)

* Take a deep breath and, exhaling, go into your teenage years, scanning from late teens backward to early adolescence. Look at high school, junior high school. What are you doing at this time? What is this family pattern doing at this time? Notice what is happening. Look at specific incidences. (Pause.)

* Take another deep breath . . . way down into your abdomen; releasing it, allow it to carry you into childhood. Notice what is going on with your parents or siblings . . . things at school or with friends . . . see just what is helpful at this time. (Pause.)
* Take another deep breath, and as you breathe out let it carry you into being a toddler . . . a young child. Four, three, two years old, a year. Learning to walk. See perhaps instances of this family pattern in your family. What patterns are you noticing? (Pause.)
* Another deep breath, and as you exhale let it carry you into being a baby. Look for the roots of this poison. (Pause.)
* Another deep breath, and as you release it let it carry you into your birth and back into the time in your mother's womb. Feel what is going on with your parents. How does it feel to be in your mother's womb? (Pause.)
* And another breath; as you release it, let it carry you into the time of conception. What is happening with your parents? What are you being drawn toward—what is magnetizing you? Is there anything to do with this particular buddha family here at this time? (Pause.)

STEP 3:

* Now, like a bird flying over your life starting from conception, review the encumbered family pattern that you have seen. Precisely and clearly see the development of your patterns from conception through birth, early childhood, childhood, teen years, adult years, the past year, and into the present, scanning over the time, seeing patterns.
* Now when you are ready, sit up and open your eyes. Take your journal and write down what you remember from your journey. This should be done for each family and

will provide you with a great deal of information to help
you understand your emotional patterns connected to each
family. You can also use this information to work through
the patterns of the families with Feeding Your Demons®,
the guided meeting with the dakini, mandala drawing, or
other processes suggested in this book.

MANDALA WORK FOR LIFE PASSAGES

One of the things that I always did with my children as they were
growing up was to mark life passages with ceremonies and to create
rituals around holidays, and we still do this. For instance, at Christmas we write aspirations and wishes on small squares of colorful
paper, and either say them aloud or keep them to ourselves; then we
roll up the papers and tie them with ribbon onto the Christmas tree,
so it becomes a "wish-fulfilling tree." For Thanksgiving, we hold
a gratitude circle, where each person speaks out loud what they are
grateful for; this gives the holidays more meaning.

For birthdays, we light three candles: one for the past year, one for
the present moment, and one for the future. For each one, the birthday
person speaks about that particular time before lighting the candle. I
find that this ceremony creates a meaningful moment of being witnessed by friends and family during your birthday, which normally can
be a fairly meaningless event. For my seventieth birthday, I decided to
do more than the three candles and to make a birthday mandala.

We were celebrating my birthday as a family on the north shore
of the Hawaiian island of Kauai, and I found a special place at Tun-
nels Beach. It was a circle of trees just back from the ocean. The trees
were a kind of Hawaiian evergreen with long, wispy tendrils hanging
down. First, my friend Gaela and I took sticks and defined a circle of

about twelve feet. As soon as we made the circle, the place felt different. Then we made a cross in the circle, creating four quadrants. In the center, I drew another circle to create the space for buddha family. Then I began to look around for natural objects in the five colors. I found red leaves for padma, yellow leaves for ratna, and green sprigs for karma, as well as white coral and shells for buddha. I placed a candle in the middle. I couldn't find anything blue—and then suddenly my granddaughter Luna Violet appeared with a cup of water, the element and shape of vajra!

As I placed each object in the mandala, I made an aspiration connected to my birthday. During the day, I circumambulated the mandala several times, adding things to make more aspirations: for buddha, aspirations to do with my meditation practice development and retreats; for vajra, increasing clarity; for ratna, prosperity and enriching presence; for padma, love and relationship; and lastly, for karma, accomplishment of my spiritual activities.

Sometimes I just sat and looked at the mandala, feeling the transference of a state of wholeness and the imprint of these aspirations. I also sat in the center, feeling the mandala around me. For most of the day, I lay on my back in the circle of trees next to the mandala, looking up at the circle made above me by the tree branches and feeling the effect of the natural mandalas around me. Once in a while I went swimming or snorkeling, and was blessed by an amazing encounter with a large sea turtle, called *honu* by the Hawaiians, that took me on a journey through the underwater landscape.

At the end of the day, the whole family gathered, and each person offered a found flower or leaf or something from the beach to add to the mandala's section of the appropriate family, making a prayer with their offering. By the end it looked so beautiful, laden with flowers and leaves. Then we all circumambulated around it clockwise as you would a Buddhist mandala. It was simple, but made the day at the beach a meaningful birthday ritual.

This is the mandala created at the time of Lama Tsultrim's seventieth birthday, celebrated with family on Kauai, Hawaii.

Bodhi Allione making an offering into the Buddha family section of Lama Tsultrim's birthday mandala.

Mandalas can be created for any occasion you wish. For a wedding, the couple could create a mandala together; for a memorial, friends and loved ones could bring mementos for the deceased and speak about why they brought what they did. You can do a mandala for a life passage on paper or with a painting. Once you know the five families and wisdom dakinis and their meanings, you can create rituals for any kind of life passage. Afterward you can write about what each object or family section means to you or tells you.

Conclusion

First and foremost, a mandala delineates a consecrated superficies and protects it from invasion by disintegrating forces. . . . But a mandala is much more than just a consecrated area that must be kept pure. . . . It is, above all, a map of the cosmos. It is the whole universe in its essential plan, in the process of emanation and of reabsorption.

—GIUSEPPE TUCCI

I began this book with the question many women ask: how to integrate spirituality into their daily lives? In our journey through the five families and our meditations on the elements and the mandala, we have seen how to work with the circumstances that present themselves to us be they emotional upheavals or encounters with the elements. I also talked about the split from the ground of being and the strategies the ego creates as a result of the fear that arises from that rupture. When we can tap into that root cause of all emotional upheaval and learn to return to the ground of being, all our suffering dissolves. We have seen that spirituality is in us, our bodies are sacred and being in a female body is a blessing, our experience of the sacred is in the body. It is not in an abstract male figure requiring transcendence and for us to get up and out of this world to be spiritual. It is in the experience of the union of nature and spirit, matter and spirit that we can heal ourselves and our world. We have also seen how to honor the earth by giving back whenever we take from her, and the importance of meaningful rituals and altars in our homes.

There is a story of the great teacher Padma Sambhava being initiated by his female teacher Kungamo, who turns him into the seed syllable HUM and swallows him. As he passes through her body he receives the empowerments of Maha Yoga and then he comes out through her vulva.

In a way, we have also passed through the body of the dakinis in the journey through this book, going through the dimensions of the Buddha Dakini, the Vajra Dakini, the Ratna Dakini, the Padma Dakini, and finally the Karma Dakini. You have been initiated into their worlds, one by one, and have been reborn from their sacred vulvas.

Still, the nature of the dakini is mysterious, and finding the way to her will be a personal journey for each of you. May you know her intimately, as if you had passed through her body and been born from her. Each of you will come into your own felt experience of the dakini. Should you choose to go deeper into her mysterious home, with the guidance of a teacher and authentic transmission, knowing her may become the gateway to the deepest wisdom. This book helps open that gate to her mandala, her world, her mysterious home, the mirror of the mind.

Although I have studied the dakini for many years and done extensive years of practice with the dakini mandala in several different forms, still when I try to explain what the dakini is, my mind can go blank. The dakini is in that very state of blankness; her gift is non-conceptuality that opens into compassion. She is a felt presence of fierce compassion that defies definition. The sacred feminine is like that: by its very nature it defies logic. When the monk Saraha approached the Arrow Smith Dakini, she said, "The Buddha's meaning can be known through symbols and actions, not through words and books." So it is paradoxical to write a book about the dakinis, whose very nature is beyond words.

These are challenging times, and we are met with chaos and change at every turn. To find the powerful dakinis now, and to be able to dive deeply into their mandala and to hold it as a centering template from which you live, creates a stabilizing and empowering source to draw from in whatever activity you find yourself. The dakini represents the secret mystical quality of absolute insight. She is an ally and a wise companion. And my aspiration is that by communicating with her and honoring the dakini, we will begin to heal our inner and outer world. My journey to and with the dakini has been going on for half a century and has paralleled the rapid changes on earth, changes that have become more devastating daily. I have become convinced that it is her wisdom that we need now.

At the time the Buddha taught the path of renunciation and celibacy, the monastic life was the ideal for those pursuing awakening. Some nine hundred years later, the Tantric movement in India brought us an integration of Tantra and Buddhism, creating Vajrayana Buddhism, where the ideal model was the siddha, a layperson who reaches enlightenment by integrating their life with practice, which includes relationship and sexuality as part of the path. Monks like Naropa left

"My journey to and with the dakini has been going on for half a century and has paralleled the rapid changes on earth, changes that have become more devastating daily. I have become convinced that it is her wisdom that we need now."

their monastic lives because of encounters with women, taking these women as teachers. Women and stories from this era have parallels in our world today, in the sense that we are coming out of a patriarchal, logos-dominated culture, like that of the monks, and the wisdom of women is being introduced, affecting the whole society. Women who are in touch with the dakini principle and the wise feminine need to work alongside men, and in leadership positions. This should not be an optional feature of our society, but a requirement.

"Women who are in touch with the dakini principle and the wise feminine need to work alongside men, and in leadership positions. This should not be an optional feature, but a requirement."

It must be emphasized in everything that I have said that the dakini mandala is based in Mahayana Buddhism, and therefore has at its foundation a dedication to compassion and emptiness and an emphasis on caring for others in every thought and action. The mandala grows out of a profound recognition of the interdependence of all life. Simultaneously, in the mandala we have a recognition that all phenomena have as their true nature emptiness, and that appearances are a radiant expression of the ground of being. As we remember the importance of the enlightened feminine in this book, as in the story of Tara that I shared in the Introduction, we must bear in mind that ultimately in the absolute state, gender is an illusion, just another one of those illusions that we attach to and fixate on so firmly.

At the same time, as Tara also said, in the relative world, empowerment has been the domain of one gender. And therefore she vows:

"Those who wish to attain supreme enlightenment in a man's body are many, but those who wish to serve the aims of beings in a woman's body are few indeed; therefore may I, until this world is emptied out, work for the benefit of sentient beings in a woman's body."[69] She makes the commitment not only for enlightenment, but to have all our voices heard: our human rights respected, violence and rape cease, sexual harassment end, and women's issues represented at the table where decisions that affect us all are being made.

One of the beautiful things about the 2017 Women's March was how much fun and partnership the women and men experienced together. There was a spirit of joy and nonaggression in their firmness and their fierceness, wearing their pink "pussy power" hats with little cat ears while simultaneously protesting things that are deadly serious. Never before has a protest simultaneously occurred over seven continents with many millions involved, with no violence and so much joy and humor. This tells us something about how our world would be with women in leadership.

In your journey through the Mandala of the Five Dakinis, you have had the opportunity to access your own innate wisdom within the context of the traditional mandala and hopefully had profound insights doing it. From time immemorial, the circle with its four directions and unifying center has been a cosmic allegory. We have moved through this allegorical journey through the five families, from the space of buddha family, to the watery clarity of vajra family, to the enriching presence of ratna family, and on to the heat and creativity of padma family, all finding expression in enlightened activity in the karma family. This journey is a construct in which you can develop your wisdom and compassion, and with the dakinis you also develop that ineffable power of the wild and wise, the instinctive and sexual, the fierce power of the divine feminine. We create a lot of suffering in our lives and in the lives of others, despite good intentions, by not having an awareness of our emotional patterns, and by not having a method to transform them. The mandala offers a universal template of wholeness and healing, and within it we embody the five wisdom dakinis.

Imagine if all the women (and all genders, for that matter) of the world were to access this aspect of themselves, and they stood up for peace, freedom, and compassion supported by this deep centering meditation. Imagine if those millions of women in the Women's March had all gone home with the Mandala of the Five Dakinis and practiced it, each connecting her mandala with all the other mandalas of the women practicing on seven continents. We would have a different world. Let's hold that vision and make it a reality by sharing the Mandala of the Five Dakinis with friends and practicing together.

As long as we define ourselves by who we should be, how powerful we can be, what we should look like, through the definitions of others, we can never know our true power and what effect we can have on our world. To do this, we need to have the inner strength necessary to break our conditioning, and the work with the dakini mandala can give us this. Through transforming the emotions into wisdom and our own body into the luminous presence of the dakini, stabilizing that through meditative concentration, we change inside, and then this creates an outer transformation.

"Through transforming the emotions into wisdom and our own body into the luminous presence of the dakini, stabilizing that through meditative concentration, we change inside, and then this creates an outer transformation."

This is a moment in history when we have been called upon to manifest the wisdom of the empowered feminine, which as we have seen is historically respectful of the natural world, understanding the interdependence of humans and the world that surrounds us. Since the destiny of women and the destiny of nature have always been parallel, and since women are major proponents of ecological awareness, by women taking their power back and manifesting it in the world, our ecological situations will be subsequently transformed, bringing balance, generating healing, and producing a culture of peace.

Acknowledgments

I would like to begin by thanking my Tibetan teachers and all those who seek to preserve their precious teachings, which are unique and powerful. May the Buddhist teachings benefit the whole world through boundless generosity. Particularly I would like to thank my teacher Chögyam Trungpa Rinpoche, who opened the teachings of the mandala and the five buddha families to the West in the 1970s as one of the first things he taught. He was the seminal influence who set me on the path of meeting and entering the mandala so many years ago, both in his teachings on the five families and through the Vajra Yogini practice he transmitted. I'd also like to acknowledge my teacher Chögyal Namkhai Norbu Rinpoche, who opened the gate of Dzogchen teachings to me and has been an exemplary embodiment of those teachings since I met him in 1978. Also I want to thank Go-chen Tulku Sang-ngag Rinpoche, on whom I have relied since the beginning of Tara Mandala in 1994; he has guided every step of our development and helped me personally in innumerable ways, including consulting about this book.

Thanks to Patti Watcher, who, in her dakini style, connected me to my publisher Zhena Muzyka, who founded the Enliven imprint of Atria within Simon & Schuster. She immediately understood and supported this book. Thanks to Emily Han, my creative and flex-ible editor. Also I'd like to thank Ulli Jaklin, my excellent and dedi-cated assistant, who sustained me during the writing of the book and worked intensively on the image permissions and lots of other re-search assistance, meanwhile handling my teaching schedule, feeding the horses, and everything else that keeps my life going. And many thanks to Bodhi Stroupe for doing all the five buddha families diagrams and Matthew Cannella for help with the images. I'd also like to thank Jenny Terbell for editing early versions of the manuscript, and John Cunningham for book development ideas and references. And, most important, my ever-encouraging editor, Resa Alboher, who while undergoing challenging health issues worked intensively on the manuscript, bringing it to the point of fruition.

Thanks to Amy Chender for brainstorming, understanding the importance of the book, and support in getting the book to the world. I would also like to express appreciation to Paulette Cole, Ellen Booth Church, Jeff Tipp, Adriano Clemente, Don Milani, Ken Green, Martin Kalff, Cynthia Rubenstein, Laura May (PJ) Pavicevic-Johnston, Sandy Gougis, Lore Zeller, Naomi Levine, Lama Gyurme, Acharya Malcolm Smith, and Jacqueline Gens for help and advice along the way.

Gratitude to those connected to Tara Mandala—Lopön Chandra Easton, Lopön Charlotte Rotterdam, Reid Meador, Kimberly Rettenwander, Clinton Spence, Aly O'Desky, Laura Vitale, Ingrid Li, Ani Thubten Palmo, Natalie Baker, and all the residents for helping in various significant ways during the time I was writing the book. And especially thanks to Susan Szpakowski, Bridget Bailey, Carol Bailey, Sarah Jacoby, and Michelle Stransky for reading and commenting on the manuscript. Thanks to my late husband, David Petit, for doing the mandala work with me and always having faith in the importance of my writing.

Deepest thanks to my children, Sherab, Aloka, and Costanzo; sons-in-law Eric Adolphi and Trevor Sands; and my daughter-in-law Cady Allione for their ceaseless love and support. And thanks to my grandchildren: Luna Violet Sands (who drew mandalas with me and gave me ideas about how to do the mandala work with children; see page 16 of the photo insert), Truman James Sands, Otto Ziji Adolphi, Enzo Tashi Adolphi, Bodhi Archer Allione, and Jalu James Allione, for enriching my life in immeasurable ways.

Lama Tsultrim and her three children: (left) Sherab Kloppenburg, (behind) Costanzo Allione, (right) Aloka Sands. *Photograph by Deborah Howe*

Lama Tsultrim's family, Kauai, Hawaii, 2017. From left (back row): Aloka Sands holding Truman James Sands; Eric Adolphi, husband of Sherab Kloppenburg; Sherab Kloppenburg holding Enzo Tashi Adolphi; Costanzo Allione holding baby Jalu James Allione; Cady Allione holding Bodhi Archer Allione; Lama Tsultrim with Otto Ziji Adolphi and Luna Violet Sands.

Now that we have journeyed through the Mandala of the Five Daki-nis, and you have been introduced to the mandala principle and the five buddha families, I thought it would be good to explore some of the commonly asked questions that arise when people engage in the mandala work.

What should I do if it's really difficult to connect with one of the families, or I feel that I don't really have any relationship to that family?

Interestingly enough, what I've found again and again is that when people feel they don't have any relationship to a family, there's usually something hidden, something the person has been avoiding looking at, or something buried so deeply in the psyche that the person isn't consciously aware that the issue exists. Often, too, the obvious patterns and emotions that we are aware of are masking something else. And when we really uncover all the parts of our psyche and see our own mandala, we find that we do indeed have energy and issues in each of the five families, just as we also come to know and are able to experience the wisdom of each family. So I would encourage you, if you are not feeling a connection to a particular buddha family, to just keep exploring and be open to finding a connection and then notice what happens. It also would be good to ask yourself: What might I be in denial about that is represented in this family?

Can I be more than one family?

The simple answer is yes, definitely, you can be more than one family—and in fact most people are, and you can be all five. Sometimes you find that someone is just a very clear ratna or padma or vajra or whatever, but usually people are a little more mixed than that, and someone might appear to be a different family in different contexts. For example, in relationships, padma might have dominance; but in the person's professional life, karma might rule their emotions and behavior. So you can definitely be more than one family, in the same way that we are different people in different situations— one way with our children, for example, and another with our boss and yet another with our friends. Also, in regards to this question of being more than one buddha family, there is the idea of the exit family that Trungpa Rinpoche talked about, which I discussed in Chapter 7.

It's good to be aware of all the family patterns and to remember that our energy is just energy, and that every form of energy has the potential to be transformed into wisdom. One of the wonderful things about Vajrayana is that the stronger our afflictions are, the stronger the encumbered patterns, the stronger the wisdom will be. So it's actually considered to be really good for a Vajrayana practitioner to be very passionate, or very angry, or very lazy, or whatever the dominant obstructing emotion might be, because an equal intensity of that energy will be transformed into the wisdom.

What if I get stuck in the emotion? Say for instance that I'm doing these five family meditations and the energy doesn't transform, and I've intensified it, and then suddenly I'm kind of stuck with the emotion. I have activated something that I wasn't ready for.

This is something that can happen when we engage in deep work like this. If you find in your work with the buddha families that you do get stuck in an emotion, what I'd encourage you to do is to keep working with the sound and the light and the visualization connected to the transformed wisdom aspect of that family. For example if you get stuck in an anger pattern, work with the seed syllable of the vajra family and the color blue: sound the seed syllable slowly and in a deep voice so that your body resonates with the sound. Go to the Vajra Dakini meditation in the vajra family chapter. I have definitely found that if you do put your attention into these elements of the meditation, the energy does transform.

If for some reason you uncover something that is really difficult, perhaps a memory of something like abuse that you hadn't had before, and you notice that all kinds of strong feelings are suddenly bubbling up to the surface—if it becomes overwhelming, then I would encourage you to seek professional help. See a licensed psychotherapist to create a safe container for the emergence of these memories. On our taramandala.org website there is a list of licensed psychotherapists certified in Feeding Your Demons®. Many of them offer online counseling sessions and are trained in the mandala work. It's actually a good sign when more memories emerge. It means your unconscious knows you are ready for more information. Our unconscious will protect us by not letting us remember things that we can't handle, but do get the professional support you need.

Will mandala work improve my life?

Short answer: yes! I would say that anything that brings us to greater awareness of our patterns and gives us a meditation practice to work with those patterns does improve our lives and the lives of those around us. I have seen again and again that the mandala work does lead to great progress; and if you were to go more deeply into it in a mandala retreat such as the Dakini Retreat or through a traditional Tibetan Buddhist practice, you will also find that things do advance. When you're working with the mandala, things may change faster; you may sense accelerated change. What I've also discovered in my own experience is that, over time, change is always positive. It might seem like things are falling apart or happening too fast, but if you stick with the process, suddenly you find yourself in a very new and fresh experience of your life. Your life does change and in a positive way.

Can I do this on the spot? What if I get a phone call, for example, and something happens that really makes me angry and I can't stop what I'm doing to go and meditate—what can I do then?

Well, what I've found to be very effective is to simply sound the seed syllable right where you are—silently if necessary; imagine the sound and the light, work with the color of the family that is being triggered, and just be with the energy in your body. First take a moment and become present in yourself, noticing, for example, "I'm really angry," noticing where you feel that in your body—maybe your jaw is tight and your heart is beating fast, your shoulders are tense. Simply become mindful of whatever you feel in your body, and then transform it with the sound and the light and become the dakini connected to the emotion of that family being triggered. It's like being a quick-change artist. I think you will find it effective. You could be lying in bed at night, worrying and obsessing about something or someone, and then just do this practice right where you are and allow it to cut through the obsessive thinking, then rest in the wisdom energy.

Our work with the mandala doesn't necessarily have to be only within the context of a sitting meditation practice. But remember, doing this instant practice is not in any way a substitute for a meditation practice. It is important never to forget that anything of value that we do in life requires effort and diligence. You don't become a great runner by never running. You don't become a great skier by never skiing. We need to train: practice is all about that, and we can't expect to have results without doing the practice. This is true of any practice we undertake in our life.

I'd really like to encourage you to develop a daily practice at the same time every day, to follow through with that and then, if you'd like to go deeper with this work, enter Magyu, The Mother Lineage (see page 323.) Early morning is generally a good time, before your day begins. With this practice of the Mandala of the Five Dakinis, it's very good to do group Dakini Retreats; also you can do solo retreats for a day or a week or so. If you're feeling the need to do longer retreats than that, I'd truly encourage you to work with an authorized teacher from Tara Mandala (see taramandala.org).

Appendix A:
Abbreviated Mandala of the Five Dakinis

The following practice is a simpler version of the Mandala of the Five Dakinis meditation practice you learned in Chapter 13 that you can follow daily or as often as you like.

This is a traditional practice with refuge and the raising of bodhicitta, the intention to do the practice for all beings. Having this practice allows you to enter into the dakini mandala in a meditative way and takes you to the possibility of experiencing the ground of being within the context of the mandala. It is a powerful stand-alone practice. (If you come to a Wisdom Rising retreat, I will often give the transmission for this practice. And if you enter Magyu: The Mother Lineage, which I share in the Additional Resources, this will become a core practice for you.) All traditional Vajrayana practice requires in-person transmission, so if this interests you, seek out an authentic teacher. The following practice is an introduction and does not pretend to be something with the depth of a full Vajrayana sadhana. The parts in italics are recited and the other sections are instruction.

REFUGE

Visualize the Mandala of the Five Dakinis in front of you as the heart essence of all the refuges. In the center is the white Buddha Dakini, in front of her is the blue Vajra Dakini, to her right is the yellow Ratna Dakini, behind the Buddha Dakini is the red Padma Dakini, to her left is the green Karma Dakini.

Taking Refuge:

NAMO:
I take refuge in the Three Jewels:
Buddha, Dharma, and Sangha.

Repeat three times.

RAISING BODHICITTA:
Knowing the heart essence of my being, and that of all beings,
to be primordially awake and manifesting as ceaseless com-
passion; I cultivate the intention to practice in order to single-
handedly place all living beings, my parents, in the state of the
five primordial wisdoms.

Repeat three times.
Dissolve the refuge mandala and rest for some time in primordial purity.

MANIFESTING THE MANDALA
OF THE FIVE DAKINIS

Sit in the center; become the white Buddha Dakini.

Become the fierce, luminescent white Buddha Dakini. She
stands on a sun disk on a white lotus, with her right leg raised
and her left leg extended in the dancing posture, surrounded by
blazing wisdom flames.
She holds the wheel-ornamented trigug, the hooked knife,
in her raised right hand. The skull cup is held in her left hand
at her heart. The khatvanga staff—symbol of the hidden
consort, skillful means and compassion—rests in the crook

of her left arm. Her three eyes of wisdom gaze into fathomless space.

In her heart is the white seed syllable BAM on a sun disk on a white lotus. She is the embodiment of the transformation of confusion into all-encompassing wisdom.

Repeat the seed syllable three times. The first time, manifest yourself as the Buddha Dakini. The second time, as the Buddha Dakini, send light out to the wisdom beings. The third time, the primordial wisdom light returns from the wisdom beings, and the Buddha Dakini is fully activated and empowered:

BAM. Manifest yourself as Buddha Dakini.

BAM. Send light out to the wisdom beings.

BAM. The primordial wisdom light returns from the wisdom beings, and the Buddha Dakini is fully activated.

Move slightly forward into the east and become the blue Vajra Dakini.

Become the fierce, luminescent dark-blue Vajra Dakini. She stands on a sun disk on a blue lotus, with her right leg raised and her left leg extended in the dancing posture, surrounded by blazing wisdom flames.

She holds the vajra-ornamented trigug in her raised right hand. The skull cup is held in her left hand at her heart. The khatvanga staff—symbol of the hidden consort, skillful means and compassion—rests in the crook of her left arm. Her three eyes of wisdom gaze into fathomless space.

In her heart is the blue seed syllable HA on a sun disk on a blue lotus. She is the embodiment of the transformation of anger into mirror-like wisdom.

Repeat the seed syllable three times:

HA. Manifest yourself as Vajra Dakini.

HA. Send light out to the wisdom beings.

HA. The primordial wisdom light returns from the wisdom beings, and the Vajra Dakini is fully activated.

Move to the south, turning to your right, and become the yellow Ratna Dakini.

Become the fierce, luminescent golden-yellow Ratna Dakini. She stands on a sun disk on a yellow lotus, with her right leg raised and her left leg extended in the dancing posture, surrounded by blazing wisdom flames.

She holds the jewel-ornamented trigug in her raised right hand. The skull cup is held in her left hand at her heart. The khatvanga staff—symbol of the hidden consort, skillful means and compassion—rests in the crook of her left arm. Her three eyes of wisdom gaze into fathomless space.

In her heart is the yellow seed syllable RI on a sun disk on a yellow lotus. She is the embodiment of the transformation of pride into the wisdom of equanimity.

Repeat the seed syllable three times:

RI. Manifest yourself as Ratna Dakini.

RI. Send light out to the wisdom beings.

RI. The primordial wisdom light returns from the wisdom beings, and the Ratna Dakini is fully activated.

Move to the west, turning to your right, and become the red Padma Dakini.

> *Become the fierce, luminescent red Padma Dakini. She stands on a sun disk on a red lotus, with her right leg raised and her left leg extended in the dancing posture, surrounded by blazing wisdom flames.*
>
> *She holds the lotus-ornamented trigug in her raised right hand. The skull cup is held in her left hand at her heart. The khatvanga staff—symbol of the hidden consort, skillful means and compassion—rests in the crook of her left arm. Her three eyes of wisdom gaze into fathomless space.*
>
> *In her heart is the red seed syllable NI on a sun disk on a red lotus. She is the embodiment of the transformation of craving into discriminating-awareness wisdom.*

Repeat the seed syllable three times:

> *NI.* Manifest yourself as Padma Dakini.
> *NI.* Send light out to the wisdom beings.
> *NI.* The primordial wisdom light returns from the wisdom beings, and the Padma Dakini is fully activated.

Move to the north, turning to your right, and become the green Karma Dakini.

> *Become the fierce, luminescent green Karma Dakini. She stands on a sun disk on a green lotus, with her right leg raised and her left leg extended in the dancing posture, surrounded by blazing wisdom flames.*
>
> *She holds the sword-ornamented trigug in her raised right hand. The skull cup is held in her left hand at her heart. The*

khatvanga staff—symbol of the hidden consort, skillful means
and compassion—rests in the crook of her left arm. Her three
eyes of wisdom gaze into fathomless space.

In her heart is the green seed syllable SA on a sun disk on
a green lotus. She is the embodiment of the transformation of
envy into all-accomplishing wisdom.

Repeat the seed syllable three times:

SA. Manifest yourself as Karma Dakini.

SA. Send light out to the wisdom beings.

SA. The primordial wisdom light returns from the wisdom beings, and the Karma Dakini is fully activated.

Return to your original position in the center of the mandala and rest your mind in the vastness of uncontrived awareness, the ground of being, deeply experiencing the actual embodiment of the Mandala of the Five Dakinis, the luminous manifestation of the five primordial wisdoms. If your mind wanders, sound the seed syllables again without changing position.

DISSOLUTION

Dissolve each dakini of the retinue into the central Buddha Dakini, in order, starting with the blue Vajra Dakini. She dissolves into blue light and then dissolves into the heart of the central Buddha Dakini, then blue light spreads throughout your body, which is the Buddha Dakini. Feel the blue light moving inside yourself. In the same way, sound the seed syllables and dissolve Ratna Dakini, Padma Dakini, and Karma Dakini into the Buddha Dakini. Each time, feel the color swirling inside you. At the end, Buddha Dakini's body is full of swirling rainbow light. Then as you sound the seed syllable BAM, the Buddha Dakini dissolves into the BAM in her heart, and then the BAM dissolves into emptiness.

NI
ནི

RI   BAM   SA
རི   བཾ   ས

HA
ཧ

Rest in the ensuing empty, radiant, unfabricated presence.

Reemerge as the Mandala of the Five Dakinis for the dedication of merit.

DEDICATION OF MERIT

May any merit gained through this practice of the Mandala of the Five Dakinis swiftly bring all beings to the realization of the five wisdoms and the five lights, and through that blessing, may all beings without one exception be liberated.

Appendix B:
The Attributes of the Five Buddha Families

	BUDDHA	VAJRA
DAKINI SEED SYLLABLE	BAM	HA
DIRECTIONS	Center	East
SYMBOL	Wheel	Vajra
ELEMENT	Space	Water
COLOR	White	Blue
POISON / OBSTRUCTED PATTERN	Ignorance, Delusion, Depression, Spacing Out	Anger, cold and hot
WISDOM	All-Encompassing Wisdom	Mirror-like Wisdom
AGGREGATE	Consciousness	Form
TIME	No Time, Totality of Everything	Dawn
SEASON	Winter	Late Autumn
LANDSCAPE	Winterscape on the Plains, Desert, Big Sky	Rugged Mountains, Icy Rivers
SHAPE	Dot, Bindu	Circle
BODY TYPE	Relaxed, Round Body	Thin and hard, Angular, Sharp Features
SENSE PERCEPTION	Mind	Sight
VEHICLE	Lion	Elephant
MUDRA	Dharmachakra, Turning the Dharma Wheel	Bhumisparsa, Earth Touching

RATNA	PADMA	KARMA
RI	NI	SA
South	West	North
Jewel	Red Lotus	Double Vajra or Sword
Earth	Fire	Air
Yellow	Red	Green
Pride, Inadequacy	Craving, Compulsive Seduction, Lust, Longing, Desire	Envy, Ambition, Speediness
Wisdom of Equanimity	Wisdom of Discernment	All-Accomplishing Wisdom
Feeling	Perception	Volitional Action
High Noon	Sunset	Midnight
Early Autumn	Spring	Summer
Jungle, Fertile Valleys	Rolling Hills, Mossy Glens	Windy Place
Square	Upward-Pointing Triangle	Half Circle
Generous, Large, Statuesque	Shapely, Well Toned, Seductive	Thin, Wispy, Seen in Profile, Always Moving
Smell & Taste	Hearing	Touch
Horse	Peacock	Kinnara Bird (human-headed bird)
Varada, Bestowing, Giving	Dhyana, Meditation	Abhaya, Fearlessness

Additional Resources

TARA MANDALA® RETREAT CENTER

Vast view · Open heart
The Mandala of Tara is a symbolic template for the awakening
of the compassionate heart through the manifestation of Tara, the
female Buddha of compassion.

Tara Mandala was established by Lama Tsultrim Allione and her late husband, David Petit, in 1994, to foster the development of innate wisdom for the benefit of all beings. We are a vibrant international Buddhist community with groups around the world. The heart of the community is the seven-hundred-acre retreat center in Pagosa Springs, Colorado, sixty miles east of Durango, Colorado, and 150 miles north of Santa Fe, New Mexico.

We offer a complete path of meditation practice, study, and deep retreat in the tradition of Vajrayana Buddhism. We have established two complete practice paths focused on the teachings of Machig Labdrön, the eleventh-century Tibetan yogini who founded the tradition of Chöd—Magyu: The Mother Lineage, and Gateway, the lineage of Dzinpa Rangdrol.

MAGYU: THE MOTHER LINEAGE

The Magyu Program is an invaluable opportunity to enter this extremely fresh stream as taught by Lama Tsultrim and her authorized teachers. This path cultivates both the spiritual and the emotional

awakening of the practitioner by integrating ancient Tibetan Buddhist practices with psychological teachings that are appropriate
for our Western disposition. The psycho-spiritual integration work
in this path distinguishes it from other traditional Buddhist paths.
The Magyu Program works directly with each individual by helping to identify his or her encumbered emotional patterns and apply
relevant practices to transform those patterns, such as Feeding Your
Demons®, the Mandala of the Five Dakinis, the Mandala of the Five
Buddhas, and the Yab Yum Mandala as well as practices from the
historical lineage of Machig Labdrön. Each person in Magyu meets
monthly with a trained spiritual mentor and follows a path at their
own rate, as well as attends in-person retreats as is possible for the
student. It should be noted that Magyu is not only for women and
does have practices that relate to the sacred masculine, such as the
Mandala of the Five Buddhas and the Yab Yum Mandala practices.
There are also male teachers and mentors in the Magyu lineage. To
reiterate, ultimately we need divine partnership with all genders represented to come to wholeness.

GATEWAY PROGRAM

This ten-year program is for dedicated practitioners who cannot do
long-term retreat, but who wish to live a life imbued with intense
practice and complete the practices of the three-year retreat. The cur-
riculum consists of all the practices done in the traditional Vajrayana
three-year solitary retreat in the lineage of Dzinpa Rangdrol from
Do Khyentse Yeshe Dorje, but is adapted for the modern practitioner
living in the world who commits to some in-depth retreat and two
hours a day of meditation. This lineage is being established at Tara
Mandala through the kind guidance and blessings of Tulku Sang-
ngag Rinpoche, who received this cycle from his teacher, the great
Dilgo Khyentse Rinpoche.

To learn more about Lama Tsultrim's teachings, programs, and retreats, visit:

www.taramandala.org

Contact:

info@taramandala.org

Tara Mandala

PO Box 3040

Pagosa Springs, CO 81147

(970) 731-3711

We also have an online store:

dakinibookstore.mybigcommerce.com

store@taramandala.org

(970) 731-3711 ext. 2

Recommended Reading

The Chalice and the Blade: Our History, Our Future by Riane Eisler (New York: HarperCollins, 1987).

The Crystal and the Way of Light: Sutra, Tantra, and Dzogchen by Chögyal Namkhai Norbu (Ithaca, NY: Snow Lion, 2000).

Feeding Your Demons: Ancient Wisdom for Resolving Inner Conflict by Tsulrim Allione. (New York: Little, Brown, 2008).

The Five Wisdom Energies: A Buddhist Way of Understanding Personalities, Emotions, and Relationships by Irini Rockwell (Boston: Shambhala Publications, 2002).

Luminous Emptiness: Understanding the Tibetan Book of the Dead by Francesca Fremantle (Boston: Shambhala Publications, 2003).

The Mandala: Sacred Circle in Tibetan Buddhism by Martin Brauen (Boston: Shambhala Publications, 1998).

Mandala Symbolism and Techniques: Innovative Approaches for Professionals by Susan I. Buchalter (London: Jessica Kingsley Publishers, 2012).

Mandala: The Architecture of Enlightenment by Denise Patry Leidy and Robert A. F. Thurman (Asia Society Galleries, Tibet House, Shambhala Publications, 1998).

Orderly Chaos: The Mandala Principle by Chögyam Trungpa (Boston & London: Shambhala, 1991).

Passionate Enlightenment: Women in Tantric Buddhism by Miranda Shaw (Princeton, NJ: Princeton University Press, 1994).

Women of Wisdom by Tsultrim Allione (Boston & London: Snow Lion, 2000).

Glossary

AVALOKITEŚVARA MANTRA. Avalokiteśvara is the bodhisattva of compassion, and *Om Mani Padme Hum Hri* (Om Jewel in the Lotus Hum Hri), the mantra of great compassion.

BANDHUKA. A bright scarlet flower that is an erotic symbol in Sanskrit literature. Its scientific name is *Pentapetes phoenicea,* in English, a "noon flower."

BINDU. Sanskrit for "dot" and representing the tiny, still point in the center of a mandala from which the mandala's universe expands, a *bindu* is a shape representative of the buddha family, a tiny dot that expresses the totality of space.

BLACK CROWN CEREMONY. A ceremony in the Karma Kagyu lineage involving a crown symbolizing one made of the woven hair of one hundred thousand dakinis who wove their hair into a crown for him. This could be seen only by those with special spiritual powers. This crown was given to the Karmapa's fifth reincarnation, Deshin Shekpa, by the Chinese Yongle emperor (1402–1424), who had a vision of the Black Crown hovering over the head of Karmapa Deshin Shekpa. With the Karmapa's permission he had a visible copy of the crown made in black brocade and jewels and presented it to Karmapa. In this ceremony, once the crown is on the head of the Karmapa, he transforms himself into Avalokiteśvara, the Buddha of compassion, and enters a state of deep meditation and chants the mantra *Om Mani Padme Hum Hri* 108 times, sending compassion to all beings.

BODHICITTA. Sanskrit for "awakening the buddha mind" and thus at the relative level raising the intention to altruistically help others, and at the absolute level is the experience of our true condition.

BODHISATTVA. Sanskrit for a person who has awakened bodhicitta and generated the intention to live and practice solely for the benefit of all beings.

BUDDHA. Buddha means "enlightened" in Sanskrit, and the Buddha refers to the historical Siddhartha Gautama, who lived sometime during the sixth to fifth centuries BCE and who, after his own spiritual search and enlightenment experience under the Bodhi tree, spent the rest of his life teaching others, and founded the religion known as Buddhism. The term Buddha may be used for other forms of enlightened beings, such as the five Buddhas in the Buddhist Tantras. The five Buddhas were not historical figures like the Shakyamuni Buddha, but are representations of enlightened qualities and connected to the directions in the mandala.

BUDDHISM. A religion with various historical developments all beginning in India with the Gautama Buddha, born in approximately 563 BCE, and including Theravada (way of the elders), which developed at the time of the Buddha and spread to Thailand, Laos, Sri Lanka, Cambodia, and Myanmar; Mahayana (the great vehicle), which developed around the turn of the millennium and spread to Japan, Tibet, Korea, Vietnam, and China; and Vajrayana (Esoteric Buddhism), which developed in the medieval period and spread to Nepal, China, Tibet, Japan, Korea, and Malaysia. He passed into parinirvana in approximately 483 BCE.

CHAKRA. Sanskrit meaning "wheel." In Indian philosophy, it is believed that there are seven chakras, spiritual energy centers, in the human body.

CHENREZIG. The Tibetan name for Avalokiteśvara, Buddha of compassion. His mantra is *Om Mani Padme Hum Hri*.

CHÖD. A Tibetan meditation practice founded by the eleventh-century spiritual teacher and dakini Machig Labdrön that involves cutting through the demons (of ego grasping in a variety of forms) through the body offering.

DAKINI. An embodiment of the sacred feminine, a dakini is an enlightened female wisdom being who could appear as a human being or a meditational deity, an embodiment of wisdom, or as a protector of the lineage. In Tibetan the word for Dakini is *Khandro*, literally meaning "sky dancer," "she who moves through space." The wisdom dakinis are fully enlightened buddhas in Tibetan Buddhism. There are also other kinds of worldly dakinis, with fourteen kinds of dakinis altogether. There are also dakinis in Hinduism, but they are not enlightened beings in that tradition. Khandro Rinpoche is one of the very rare female reincarnations in Tibetan Buddhism, and her name literally means "precious dakini." She points out: "Traditionally, the term *dakini* has been used for outstanding female practitioners, consorts of great masters, and to denote the enlightened female principle of nonduality which transcends gender." Khandro Rinpoche defines the authentic dakini principle as "a very sharp, brilliant wisdom mind that is uncompromising, honest, with a little bit of wrath."[70]

DAKINI PRINCIPLE. Tenzin Palmo is quoted in Michaela Haas's book *Dakini Power* as saying that "the dakini principle stands for the intuitive force. Women get it in a flash—they're not interested in intellectual discussion which they normally find dry and cold with minimum appeal."[71]

DHARMACHAKRA. A symbol of the buddha family, this is an eight-spoked wheel representing the Eightfold Path to enlightenment according to the Buddha: right view, right intention, right speech, right action, right livelihood, right effort, right mindfulness, and right concentration.

DOHA. A form of poetry in rhyming couplets found in both Hinduism and Vajrayana Buddhism, doha are often recited as spontaneous poetry at Vajrayana feasts as a way to show insights into the nature of reality, and are often masked in metaphor or sometimes language with hidden meaning called "the twilight language" or "the language of the dakinis."

DORJE. The Tibetan word for the Sanskrit *vajra*, meaning both "diamond" or "king of stones" and also "thunderbolt." As an adjective, it means "indestructible, invincible, firm, stable"; the Sanskrit word is often translated as "adamantine." The thunderbolt references the divine weapon that is impervious and can victoriously cut through any situation. Its adamantine aspect evokes a laser's unbelievable focus and precision in cutting through matter. The *vajra* is a hand-held scepter that is held in the right hand and represents skillful means and the sacred masculine.

ENCUMBERED PATTERN. Each of the five buddha families has associated with it an encumbered pattern or poison. These are emotions that cause obstruction to our innate wisdom. Each of the encumbered patterns has a wisdom counterpart. The word for these encumbered patterns in Tibetan is *nyomong*, which literally means "drowsy" or "obscured."

EXIT FAMILY. Trungpa Rinpoche talked about the idea of the "exit family," which describes how one gets out of a situation. For example, a buddha family exit could be to space out or go into denial of what is happening, while a vajra family exit would be to get angry, and so on. The exit may be the same as your primary family or may be a different one, as if you entered a house (situation) through the grand front entrance, but exited through a very different back door.

FIERCENESS. In the Tibetan tradition, fierceness or wrathfulness represents a powerful energy. Wrath is the fastest-moving energy we manifest as human beings, and the fierce or wrathful deities you see in Tibetan art represent the energy that burns away limitations and ignorance. Fierce energy can be thought of as the way a mother animal defends her young, a laser beam of pure energy that when harnessed and directed is powerful and unstoppable. It is fierceness without aggression, anger, or hatred. Sometimes a wrathful manifestation is more effective than a peaceful approach.

FIVE BUDDHA FAMILIES. The foundational structures of the mandala principle. The five buddha families are buddha, vajra, ratna, padma, and karma. Each family has a unique personality and characteristics, as well as a specific encumbered emotional pattern and an enlightened wisdom counterpart.

FIVE WISDOM ENERGIES. The encumbered patterns or emotional poisons, when freed and transformed from ego's control, become the five wisdom energies: all-encompassing wisdom, mirror-like wisdom, wisdom of equanimity, wisdom of discernment, and all-accomplishing wisdom. Seeing the world as a mandala means recognizing the symbolic perfection of these energies.

INDIVIDUATION. Dr. Carl Jung's theory of a conscious discovery, or a recovery, of the psychic nucleus of oneself. The journey to individuation often begins with a wounding of the personality, requiring a reconnection with the greater Self to heal.

JALING. A Tibetan oboe, the translation is literally "Indian trumpet." These woodwind instruments have a lilting, melodious sound and are played in Tibetan ceremonies including the Black Crown Ceremony.

JNANA DHARMADHATU. One of the five transcendent wisdoms, *jnana dharmadhatu* is the wisdom of the buddha family, the wisdom of all-encompassing space. It's described as a "beginning-less wisdom," a knowing beyond the confines of conditioned reasoning mind—what we knew before the basic split, before our rupture from the ground of being. It is not wisdom from accumulated experience or study, but the recovered, or *re-cognized* wisdom that we achieve through meditation when we recognize our true condition.

JNANASATTVAS. Sanskrit for "wisdom beings." These are "wisdom deities" that you call upon to bless and merge with the deities of the mandala that you are visualizing.

KARMA. Sanskrit for "action" and also meaning "cause and effect." Also in its meaning as action karma is one of the five buddha families and emphasizes transforming envy and jealousy into all-accomplishing wisdom.

KARTARI. Probably the symbol most commonly associated with the dakini is what's called the *trigug* in Tibetan or the *kartari* in Sanskrit, usually referred to in English as "the hooked knife." This is a crescent-shaped knife with a hook on the end of the blade, modeled from the Indian butcher's knife and sometimes called a chopper. The handle of the knife can be ornamented with a variety of symbols—in the case of the five dakinis, each dakini has her family's symbol on the handle of her knife.

KHAITA. Tibetan for "harmonizing in space," a *khaita* is a joyful Tibetan dance done in groups.

KHANDRO. The Tibetan word for *dakini*, which means "sky-dancer," literally "she who moves through space." The dakini is the most important manifestation of the feminine in Tibetan Buddhist teaching. She can appear as a human being or as a deity, in which form she is portrayed as fierce, surrounded by flames, naked, dancing, and wearing bone ornaments. She holds a staff in the crook of her left elbow, representing her inner consort, her internal male partner, and in her raised right hand a hooked knife, representing her relentless cutting away of dualistic fixation. She is compassionate and, at the same time, relentlessly tears away the ego. She holds a skull cup of blood in her left hand at her heart, representing impermanence and the transformation of desire. She is an intense and fierce image to behold.

KHATVANGA. A staff that the dakini holds in the crook of her left arm. Its essential meaning is that of "hidden consort" or "inner consort"; at its top is a vajra (thunderbolt) symbolizing the masculine. With this staff the dakini has the power to stand alone, she has internalized the masculine. Two scarves adorn the khatvanga, representing the union of Mahayana and Vajrayana: the Mahayana path of compassion and the Vajrayana path of transformation. So essentially the function of this staff is a support, a spear that protects, and a stake. This is the dakini's impersonal yang energy, her masculine, which makes firm, which nails down; this is the strength of skillful means and compassion, which she has integrated into herself.

KYIL KHOR. The Tibetan word for *mandala*, *kyil* meaning "center" and *khor* meaning "that which surrounds the center" or "the swirl surrounding the center." The Tibetan mandala describes a circular pure dimension divided into four quadrants, and surrounded by a protective fire circle that prevents invasive energies from entering. There are hundreds of different Tibetan Buddhist mandalas, and each one contains a center, usually a square separated into four sections or directions, from which the rest of the mandala radiates and to which that radiation returns. The Tibetan mandalas symbolize three-dimensional palaces with deities inside and they contain deities that symbolize qualities of enlightenment.

LUNG. Tibetan for "wind" or "breath," *lung* is the air element in our body. Lung disturbances are seen within the karma family and can cause the mind to keep moving. Experienced doctors of Tibetan medicine are able to identify and calm the disturbed winds of the more gross types of wind disorders, using the tools of diet, behavior, medicines, and external therapies, but deeper lung disturbance is hard to cure.

MADHU. Meaning "honey" or "sweet" in Sanskrit and other Indo-Aryan languages, in Tantric practice *madhu* refers to the female sexual fluid.

MALA. Buddhist prayer beads, often used to count recitations of mantras.

MANDALA. The word *mandala* in Sanskrit means "the circle," and can also be interpreted as *manda*, meaning "the supreme or the best," plus *la*, meaning "the marker or completion," combining to denote "the place that holds or contains the ultimate essence." The earliest form of the Buddhist mandala appeared in the third century CE, but it was more widely diffused during the Tantric Buddhist period between 500 and 1200 CE in India, and its usage followed the spread of Vajrayana Buddhism to China, Korea, Japan, and Malaysia. In earliest Vedic literature, *mandala* already had the meaning of a sacred enclosure or a place for a spiritual practice or ritual. The circle with a seminal nucleus in the center and four quadrants is the basic form of the mandala, and reflects the structure of the universe from the smallest microcosm to the vast macrocosm.

MANTRA. Sanskrit sacred sounds chanted aloud or repeated silently and believed to have spiritual power.

MA RIGPA. The encumbered buddha family pattern, but also a term used for the general state that ensues after the rupture from the ground of being. Usually translated as "ignorance," *ma rigpa* in Tibetan literally means "nonawareness."

MUDRA. Meaning "sign" or "token" in Sanskrit, a symbolic hand gesture. Different mudras are associated with different buddhas. For example, some mudras include a gesture of touching the earth, a gesture to signify meditation, a gesture to show fearlessness, or a gesture of generosity.

NAGINI. From *naga* in Sanskrit and Pali, meaning "cobra" or "snake." In Tibetan Buddhism, *nagas* and the female *naginis* are water spirits that live in lakes and guard treasures. A Mahayana legend says that nagas were asked by the Buddha to guard the treasures of the *prajna-paramita* literature until Nagarjuna was ready to discover them and spread their message.

NYOMONG. Tibetan for "encumbered patterns," *klesa* (or "poison") in Sanskrit, with the literal meaning of "drowsy" or "obscured."

ONE GROUND, TWO PATHS, TWO RESULTS. A Tibetan teaching in the *Prayer of Samantabhadra*. The phrase "one ground, two paths, two results" describes the one ground is all-pervasive, but there has been a split from the ground, creating the experience of self and other, which is the root of our suffering. One ground is often referred to as the "ground of being," or the Great Mother, meaning literally, "the ground out of which all beings and all things arise."

PADMA. Meaning "lotus" in Sanskrit, padma buddha family's encumbered pattern is craving and seduction and whose wisdom is the wisdom of discernment. Padma's symbol is a red lotus. In Vajrayana Buddhism the lotus represents our enlightened nature, because while the lotus grows in the muck, it emerges from the mud completely unscathed and fragrant. It would seem these two realities could not coexist, yet the lotus is ultra-pure and unaffected by the polluted water that provides the fertile matrix from which it emerges.

PRATYAVEKSHANA. Sanskrit for "discerning wisdom," which is the wisdom of the padma family. The wisdom of discernment carries with it a quality of empathetic concern and caring for others and profound insight into the nature of reality. It also has an investigative curiosity, an ability to see deeply into the nature of things. There is a deep knowing, beyond ordinary ego-centered knowing, that penetrates into the core of reality. We see the Buddha Amitabha with both hands in meditative equipoise, deep in contemplation. All the other buddhas have their hands in gestures indicating some kind of activity; only Amitabha tells us he is in deep meditation with no other activity.

RAGA. The Sanskrit word for "passion," which can also mean color, specifically red, or a musical piece in Indian music. Each musical raga evokes certain emotions, so the color red is tied to emotions. Brilliant magnetizing red is the padma family's color, a blazing red that reflects the element of fire—a fire that helps us to digest, helps the blood to circulate, and warms the body; the energy of the sun, the energy of life.

RANG NGO SHE. A Tibetan expression meaning "to know one's own face." An important expression because, paradoxically, our own face is continually with us, like primordial wisdom itself, yet we don't see it unless we look in a mirror. And though our face is continually with us, in a world without mirrors or reflections we would have no way to know our own face except to feel it. It is through meditation, which is a kind of reflection in that we turn the mind back on the outward-moving energy, that we begin to know our own true condition, our own true face.

RATNA. The Sanskrit word *ratna* means "jewel," and the wish-fulfilling golden jewel is the ratna family's symbol. The ratna family was known in ancient times to be ideal for rulers and kings, because it was their duty to provide stability and prosperity for their subjects. The encumbered pattern associated with ratna is arrogance, a pride that includes insecurity, the need to inflate oneself through bragging or name dropping, creating the need to consume, to shop, to eat, to save, and to hoard, and the enlightened wisdom of ratna is the wisdom of equanimity or equality.

RINGSEL. A Tibetan word for relics that may appear in sacred places or come out of the ashes of cremated lamas; they may be white or of the five colors. Generally they are white and reproduce spontaneously.

SADHANA. A daily spiritual practice in Vajrayana; in Sanskrit, it literally means "a means for accomplishing something."

SAMSARA AND NIRVANA. *Samsara*—Sanskrit for "world" or "wandering"—is the condition of suffering in cyclical rebirth. *Nirvana* means "a quenching" or "cessation" and is the cessation of suffering and release from cyclic existence.

SEED SYLLABLES. Sacred sounds in Sanskrit coming down from a tradition more than a thousand years old. They are not randomly made up. Because Sanskrit is a sacred language, mantras and seed syllables were not translated into Tibetan but were left in the original Sanskrit. Each of the five wisdom dakinis has a seed syllable associated with her family: Buddha Dakini—BAM; Vajra Dakini—HA; Ratna Dakini—RI; Padma Dakini—NI; Karma Dakini—SA.

SELF. Used by Dr. Carl Jung not in the egocentric sense of the word as it is used in Buddhism, but rather signifying the Self as the fully individuated person.

SIDDHA. Sanskrit for "the perfected one" or "one who is accomplished." In Buddhism it has come to mean a spiritual master, implying spiritual powers called *siddhis*. There is also the meaning in Tibetan practice of a layperson who reaches enlightenment by integrating their life with practice.

SKULL CUP. A symbol associated with the dakini, holding the nectar of nondual knowledge. It's a symbol of emptiness, and the cauldron of transformation, and above all impermanence. In centuries past, yogis and yoginis lived in the charnel grounds, where corpses were brought and cremated or fed to the jackals. These were places outside the confines of conventional society, places between life and death with a continual confrontation with death and impermanence. They would make huts out of skulls and musical instruments and ornaments out of bones. They would eat and drink out of human skulls as cups, which became a very primal image of impermanence.

STUPA. Literally "heap" in Sanskrit, a stupa is a Buddhist shrine representing the mandala, which is the basic structure of the cosmos in the Tantric Buddhist tradition—the circular architecture of the centered enlightened experience, a cosmological representation of the universe. Its main function is that of a reliquary, which contains the relics of the Buddha and other great masters of meditation.

SUKRA. In sexual Tantra, a term used for both male and female sexual fluids.

TADREL. Tibetan for "jealousy" and the encumbered pattern of the karma family. Tadrel also has within it the process of comparing oneself to others and the feeling of envy and the need to hurry to "keep up with the Joneses." Thus, embodied within the word is a combination of envy and ambition. It is connected to karma buddha family.

TANTRA. Around nine hundred years after the life of the Buddha, the Tantric movement in India brought us an integration of Tantra and Buddhism, where the ideal model was the siddha, a layperson who reaches enlightenment by integrating their life with practice, which includes relationship and sexuality as part of the path. Buddhist Tantra, also known as Vajrayana (indestructible vehicle) or Esoteric Buddhism, or Mantrayana, is a complex practice system embedded in meditation, deity yoga, and mandalas, with an emphasis on the necessity of a spiritual teacher and transmission. Tantra uses the creative act of visualization, sound, and mudras (hand gestures) to engage our whole being in the process of meditation. It is a practice of complete engagement and embodiment of our whole being. It should be distinguished from Neo-Tantra, which is a variety of sexual practices taught in the West.

THREE KAYAS. The Sanskrit word *kaya* means "body," and the three kayas are the three spiritual dimensions: *dharmakaya*, the formless body of enlightenment; *sambhogakaya,* the body of enjoyment, which is the dimension of luminosity; and *nirmanakaya*, the embodied enlightenment that we find in this dimension, in our world, such as the Buddha or the Dalai Lama.

VAJRA. Sanskrit for "diamond" or "thunderbolt." Vajra refers both to the vajra family and to its symbol, which looks like a small scepter, a central hub with prongs radiating out from it in opposite directions that come to a point; the prongs are the energetic power emitting from the hub. The vajra has no use other than as a ritual implement, a symbol of power in Buddhism, Jainism, and Hinduism. Vajra is also the name of one of the buddha families. The encumbered pattern of the vajra family is a hot anger or a cold passive aggression, and the enlightened wisdom is mirror-like wisdom that reflects everything with great clarity, and yet is unaffected by what reflects in it.

VAJRAYANA. Also known as Tantric Buddhism or Esoteric Buddhism (see *Tantra* and *Buddhism*), it arose in the Buddhist context in Medieval India and was embraced by the Pala kings and thereby spread widely, eventually making its way to Tibet and other countries. The mandala practices come from the Vajrayana period.

YAB YUM. The joining of male and female buddhas in sexual union. The Tibetan term *yab yum* literally means "father-mother."

Notes

1. Cynthia Eller, *Living in the Lap of the Goddess: The Feminist Spirituality Movement in America* (Boston: Beacon Press, 1995), 136.
2. Maria Mies and Vadana Shiva, *Ecofeminism (Critique. Influence. Change.)* (London & New York: Zed Books, 2014); Rosemary Radford Reuther, *Sexism and God-Talk: Toward a Feminist Theology* (Boston: Beacon Press, 1983); Karen J. Warren, *Ecofeminist Philosophy: A Western Perspective on What It Is and Why It Matters* (Lanham, MD: Rowman & Littlefield, 2000); Mary Daly, *Beyond God the Father: Toward a Philosophy of Women's Liberation* (Boston: Beacon Press, revised edition 2015); Joanna Macy, *Coming Back to Life: The Updated Guide to the Work that Reconnects* (Gabriola Island, BC: New Society, revised edition 2014); Joanna Macy, *Active Hope: How to Face the Mess We're In without Going Crazy* (Novato, CA: New World Library, 2012); Sherry Ruth Anderson and Patricia Hopkins, *The Feminine Face of God: The Unfolding of the Sacred in Women* (New York: Bantam Books, 1991).
3. Dana Nuccitelli, "2017 Is So Far the Second-Hottest Year on Record Thanks to Global Warming," *The Guardian* (July 13, 2017), https://www.theguardian.com/environment/climate-consensus-97-per-cent/2017/jul/31/2017-is-so-far-the-second-hottest-year-on-record-thanks-to-global-warming.
4. Ibid.
5. UNHCR, "Frequently Asked Questions on Climate Change and Disaster Replacement," The UN Refugee Agency (November 6, 2016), http://www.unhcr.org/uk/news/latest/2016/11/581f52dc4/frequently-asked-questions-climate-change-disaster-displacement.html.
6. Liat Clark, "Great Barrier Reef," *Wired* (April 10, 2007), http://www.wired.co.uk/article/great-barrier-reef-coral-bleaching-damage-2017.
7. Naomi Klein, *This Changes Everything: Capitalism vs. the Climate* (New York: Simon & Schuster, 2015), 6.
8. World Health Organization (WHO), "Violence Against Women," ac-

cessed October 7, 2017, http://www.who.int/mediacentre/factsheets/fs239/en.

9. Caitlin Gibson and Emily Guskin, "A Majority of Americans Now Say That Sexual Harassment Is a 'Serious Problem,'" *The Washington Post* (October 17, 2017), https://www.washingtonpost.com/lifestyle/style/a-majority-of-americans-now-say-that-sexual-harassment-is-a-serious-problem/2017/10/16/707e6b74-b290-11e7-9e58-e6288544af98_story.html?utm_term=.2dda5484db9d.

10. Chögyam Trungpa, *The Collected Works of Chögyam Trungpa, Volume 6* (Boston & London: Shambhala, 2004), 289.

11. "Justin Trudeau promotes feminist movement of men sticking up for women," *The Independent*, video: 1:00, from Justin Trudeau speaking at an inaugural WE Day UN event at Madison Square Garden on Sept. 20, 2017, posted by Harriet Agerholm, Sept. 21, 2017, http://www.independent.co.uk/news/world/americas/justin-trudeau-men-feminist-movement-stick-up-women-sexism-canada-prime-minister-a7960196.html.

12. Erica Chenoweth and Jeremy Pressman, "This Is What We Learned by Counting the Women's Marches," *The Washington Post* (February 7, 2017), https://www.washingtonpost.com/news/monkey-cage/wp/2017/02/07/this-is-what-we-learned-by-counting-the-womens-marches/?utm_term=.e9c314a6bade.

13. Women's March, "Sister Marches," accessed October 7, 2017, https://www.womensmarch.com/sisters.

14. Tsultrim Allione, *Women of Wisdom* (Boston & London: Snow Lion, 2000), 15.

15. Chögyam Trungpa, *The Sadhana of the Embodiment of All the Siddhas* (unpublished, 1969).

16. Robert L. Fantz and Simón B. Miranda, "Newborn Infant Attention to Form of Contour," *Child Development* 46, no. 1 (975), 224–28, http://www.jstor.org/stable/1128853.

17. Don Slater, *Consumer Culture and Modernity* (Cambridge, UK: Polity Press, 1997).

18. Gretel Ehrlich, *The Future of Ice: A Journey into Cold* (New York: Vintage Books, 2004), 7.

19. C. G. Jung, *Mandala Symbolism* (Princeton, NJ: Princeton University Press, 1972), v.

20. C. G. Jung, *Civilization in Transition: The Collected Works, Volume 10* (London & New York: Routledge, 2014), paragraph 843.

21. C. G. Jung, *The Archetypes and the Collective Unconscious, The Col-

lected Works, Volume 9, Part I (London & New York: Routledge, 1968), 388.

22. Lori S. Wiener and Haven B. Battles, "Mandalas as a Therapeutic Technique for HIV-Infected Children and Adolescents: What Do They Reveal?" *Journal for HIV/AIDS and Social Services* 1, no. 3 (2002): 27–39.

23. Deborah Elkis-Abuhoff et al., "Mandala Drawings as an Assessment Tool for Women with Breast Cancer," *The Arts in Psychotherapy* 36, no. 4 (2009): 231–38.

24. Patti Henderson, David Rosen, and Nathan Mascaro, "Empirical Study on the Healing Nature of Mandalas," *Psychology of Aesthetics, Creativity, and the Arts* 1, no. 3 (2007): 148–54.

25. Nancy A. Curry and Tim Kasser, "Can Coloring Mandalas Reduce Anxiety?" *Art Therapy: Journal of the American Art Therapy Association* 22, no. 2 (2005): 81–85.

26. Chögyam Trungpa, *The Tantric Path of Indestructible Wakefulness: The Profound Treasury of the Ocean of Dharma, Volume 3* (Boston & London: Shambhala, 2013), 295.

27. David F. Germano, *Poetic Thought, the Intelligent Universe, and the Mystery of Self: The Tantric Synthesis of rDzogs Chen in Fourteenth Century Tibet, Volume 2* (Ann Arbor, MI: University Microfilms International Dissertation Information Service, 1992), 925.

28. Chögyam Trungpa, *The Collected Works of Chögyam Trungpa, Volume 7* (Boston & London: Shambhala, 2004), 89–90.

29. Ibid., 87.

30. Tsultrim Allione, *Women of Wisdom*, 23.

31. Ibid., 106.

32. Miranda Shaw, *Passionate Enlightenment: Women in Tantric Buddhism* (Princeton, NJ: Princeton University Press, 1994), 42.

33. Ibid., 74.

34. Ibid.,155–56.

35. Ibid.,157.

36. Ibid., 38–39.

37. The chapter about the relationship with the local protector dakinis: "Chapter 30: Guiding Instructions on the Bardo" from C. C. Chang (translator), *The Hundred Thousand Songs of Milarepa, Volume 1* (New York: University Books, 1962), 333–54.

38. Ibid., 336.

39. Tsultrim Allione, *Women of Wisdom*, 106–107.

40. Miranda Shaw, *Passionate Enlightenment*, 90.

41. Tsultrim Allione, *Women of Wisdom*, 121.
42. Ibid., 175.
43. Vicki Mackenzie, *Cave in the Snow: Tenzin Palmo's Quest for Enlightenment* (New York: Bloomsbury, 1998), 75–76.
44. Ibid., 133.
45. Michaela Haas, *Dakini Power: Twelve Extraordinary Women Shaping the Transmission of Tibetan Buddhism in the West* (Boston & London: Snow Lion, 2013), 3–4.
46. Herbert Guenther, trans., *The Life and Teaching of Nāropa* (London: Oxford University Press, 1963), 54.
47. Terry Clifford, *Tibetan Buddhist Medicine and Psychiatry: The Diamond Healing* (Delhi: Motilal Banarsidass, 1994).
48. Miranda Shaw, Personal letter to Tsultrim Allione, 1988.
49. Miranda Shaw, *Passionate Enlightenment*.
50. Tsultrim Allione, *Feeding Your Demons: Ancient Wisdom for Resolving Inner Conflict* (New York: Little, Brown, 1988).
51. Chögyam Trungpa, *The Tantric Path of Indestructible Wakefulness: The Profound Treasury of the Ocean of Dharma, Volume Three* (Boston & London: Shambhala, 2013), 296.
52. Chögyam Trungpa, *Transcript 5 Buddha Seminar Talk 2* (unpublished).
53. John Daido Loori, ed., *The Art of Just Sitting: Essential Writings on the Zen Practice of Shikantaza* (Boston: Wisdom Publications, 2004), 21.
54. William Shakespeare, *The Tempest* (Hyderabad: Orient Longman, 2001), 81.
55. Chögyam Trungpa, *The Tantric Path of Indestructible Wakefulness*, 301.
56. Norma Levine, *The Miraculous 16th Karmapa: Incredible Encounters with the Black Crown Buddha* (Arcidosso: Shang Shung Publications, 2013).
57. Stan Tatkin, *Wired for Love: How Understanding Your Partner's Brain and Attachment Style Can Help You Defuse Conflict and Build a Secure Relationship* (Oakland: New Harbinger Publications, 2011).
58. Sue Johnson, *Hold Me Tight* (New York: Little, Brown, 2008), 46.
59. Francesca Fremantle, *Luminous Emptiness: Understanding the Tibetan Book of the Dead* (Boston & London: Shambhala, 2003), 129.
60. Tsoknyi Rinpoche, "Tsoknyi Rinpoche on Lung," Tibet and Buddhism (March 28, 2012), https://tsoknyirinpoche.org/8877/tsoknyi-rinpoche-interview-lung.
61. Science Daily, "New Report Finds 43 Percent Increase in ADHD Diagnosis for US Schoolchildren," *Science Daily* (December 8, 2015), https://www.sciencedaily.com/releases/2015/12/151208150630.htm.

62. Richard Saul, *ADHD Does Not Exist: The Truth About Attention Deficit and Hyperactivity Disorder* (New York: HarperCollins, 2014).

63. C. G. Jung, *Synchronicity: An Acausal Connecting Principle* (Bollingen, Switzerland: Bollingen Foundation, (1993) [1952]).

64. C. G. Jung, *Synchronicity: An Acausal Connecting Principle* (Princeton, NJ: Princeton University Press, 1969), 109–110.

65. The Eightfold Path is the fourth of the Four Noble Truths—the Buddha's first teaching: it includes right view, right aspiration, right speech, right action, right livelihood, right effort, right mindfulness, right concentration.

66. Complete set of eight bone ornaments: crown, earrings, choker necklace, long necklace, belt, apron (girdle), bracelets and armlets, anklets.

67. C. G. Jung, *Memories, Dreams, Reflections*, recorded and edited by Aniela Jaffe (New York: Vintage Books, 1989), 174.

68. Tsultrim Allione, *Women of Wisdom*, 43.

69. Jo Nang Tāranātha, *Origin of the Tara Tantra* (Dharamsala: Library of Tibetan Works and Archives, 2009).

70. Ibid.

71. Michaela Haas, *Dakini Power*, 1–2.

Bibliography

Allione, Tsultrim. *Feeding Your Demons: Ancient Wisdom for Resolving Inner Conflict*. New York, Boston & London: Little, Brown and Company, 2008.
———. *Women of Wisdom*. Boston & London: Snow Lion Publications, 2000.

Anderson, Sherry Ruth, and Patricia Hopkins. *The Feminine Face of God: The Unfolding of the Sacred in Women*. New York: Bantam Books, 1991.

Argüelles, José and Miriam. *Mandala*. Boston & London: Shambhala, 1995.

Beer, Robert. *The Encyclopedia of Tibetan Symbols and Motifs*. Boston: Shambhala, 1999.

Berliner, Helen. *Enlightened by Design: Using Contemplative Wisdom to Bring Peace, Wealth, Warmth & Energy into Your Home*. Boston & London: Shambhala, 1999.

Blofeld, John. *The Tantric Mysticism of Tibet: A Practical Guide to the Theory, Purpose, and Techniques of Tantric Meditation*. New York: Causeway Books, 1974.

Brauen, Martin. *The Mandala: Sacred Circle in Tibetan Buddhism*. Boston: Shambhala, 1998.

Buchalter, Susan I. *Mandala Symbolism and Techniques: Innovative Approaches for Professionals*. London & Philadelphia: Jessica Kingsley Publishers, 2013.

Byrne, Rhonda. *The Secret*. New York: Atria Books, 1996.

Chandra, Lokesh, Musashi Tachikawa, and Sumie Watanabe. *A Ngor Mandala Collection*. Kathmandu & Nagoya: Vajra Publications & Mandala Institute, 2006.

Chang, Garma C. C., trans. *The Hundred Thousand Songs of Milarepa, Volume 1*. New Hyde Park, NY: University Books, 1962.

Chenoweth, Erica, and Jeremy Pressman. "This Is What We Learned by Counting the Women's Marches." *The Washington Post*. February 7, 2017. https://www.washingtonpost.com/news/monkey-cage/wp/2017/02/07/this-is-what-we-learned-by-counting-the-womens-marches/?utm_term=.e9c314a6bade.

Clark, Liat. "Great Barrier Reef." *Wired*. April 10, 2007. http://www.wired
.co.uk/article/great-barrier-reef-coral-bleaching-damage-2017.

Clifford, Terry Joan. *Tibetan Buddhist Medicine and Psychiatry: The Diamond Healing*. Delhi: Motilal Banarsidass, 1994.

Cornell, Judith. *Mandala: Luminous Symbols for Healing*. Wheaton, IL:
Quest Books, 2006.

Curry, Nancy A., and Tim Kasser. "Can Coloring Mandalas Reduce Anxiety?" *Art Therapy: Journal of the American Art Therapy Association* 22,
no. 2 (2005): 81–85.

Daly, Mary. *Beyond God the Father: Toward a Philosophy of Women's Liberation*. Boston: Beacon Press, 2015.

Ehrlich, Gretel. *The Future of Ice: A Journey into Cold*. New York: Vintage
Books, 2004.

Eisler, Riane. *The Chalice and the Blade: Our History, Our Future*. New York:
HarperCollins, 1987.

————. *Sacred Pleasure: Sex, Myth, and the Politics of the Body—New Paths
to Power and Love*. San Francisco: HarperCollins, 1996.

Eller, Cynthia. *Living in the Lap of the Goddess: The Feminist Spirituality
Movement in America*. Boston: Beacon Press, 1995.

Elkis-Abuhoff, Deborah, Morgan Gaydos, Robert Goldblatt, Marie Chen,
and Sage Rose. "Mandala Drawings as an Assessment Tool for Women
with Breast Cancer." *The Arts in Psychotherapy* 36, no. 4 (2009): 231–38.

Fantz, Robert L., and Simón B. Miranda. "Newborn Infant Attention to
Form of Contour." *Child Development* 46, no. 1 (1975): 224–28, http://
www.jstor.org/stable/1128853.

Fields, Rick, ed. *Loka 2: A Journal from the Naropa Institute*. Garden City,
NY: Anchor Press, 1976.

Fincher, Susanne F. *Creating Mandalas: For Insight, Healing, and Self-Expression*.
Boston & London: Shambhala, 2010.

————. *The Mandala Workbook: A Creative Guide for Self-Exploration, Balance, and Well-Being*. Boston & London: Shambhala, 2009.

Fisher, Robert E. *Buddhist Art and Architecture*. New York: Thames and
Hudson, 1995.

Fremantle, Francesca. *Luminous Emptiness: Understanding the Tibetan Book
of the Dead*. Boston & London: Shambhala Publications, 2003.

Fulkerson, Mary McClintock, and Sheila Briggs, eds. *The Oxford Handbook
of Feminist Theology*. Oxford: Oxford University Press, 2012.

Garling, Wendy. *Stars at Dawn: Forgotten Stories of Women in the Buddha's
Life*. Boulder, CO: Shambhala, 2016.

Germano, David F. *Poetic Thought, the Intelligent Universe, and the Mystery of Self: The Tantric Synthesis of rDzogs Chen in Fourteenth Century Tibet, Volume 1.* Ann Arbor, MI: University Microfilms International Dissertation Information Service, 1992.

———. *Poetic Thought, the Intelligent Universe, and the Mystery of Self: The Tantric Synthesis of rDzogs Chen in Fourteenth Century Tibet, Volume 2.* Ann Arbor, MI: University Microfilms International Dissertation Information Service, 1992.

Gibson, Caitlin, and Emily Guskin. "A Majority of Americans Now Say That Sexual Harassment Is a 'Serious Problem.'" *The Washington Post.* October 17, 2017. https://www.washingtonpost.com/lifestyle/style/a-majority-of-americans-now-say-that-sexual-harassment-is-a-serious-problem/2017/10/16/707e6b74-b290-11e7-9e58-e6288544af98_story.html?utm_term=.2dda5484db9d.

Govinda, Anagarika. *Foundations of Tibetan Mysticism.* Boston & York Beach, ME: Weiser Books, 1969.

Guarisco, Elio, Adriano Clemente, and Jim Valby, trans. *The Marvelous Primordial State: The Mejung Tantra, A Fundamental Scripture of Dzogchen Semde.* Arcidosso: Shang Shung Publications, 2013.

Guenther, Herbert V., trans. *The Life and Teaching of Nāropa.* London: Oxford University Press, 1963.

———, trans. *The Life and Teaching of Nāropa.* Boston & London: Shambhala, 1986.

———, trans. *The Royal Song of Saraha: A Study in the History of Buddhist Thought.* Seattle: University of Washington Press, 1969.

Guenther, Herbert V., and Chögyam Trungpa. *The Dawn of Tantra.* Berkeley & London: Shambhala, 1975.

Haas, Michaela. *Dakini Power: Twelve Extraordinary Women Shaping the Transmission of Tibetan Buddhism in the West.* Boston & London: Snow Lion Publications, 2013.

Hall, Nor. *The Moon and the Virgin: Reflections on the Archetypal Feminine.* New York: Harper & Row Publishers, 1980.

Harding, Sarah, trans. *Machik's Complete Explanation: Clarifying the Meaning of Chöd.* Boston & London: Snow Lion, 2013.

Henderson, Patti, David Rosen, and Nathan Mascaro. "Empirical Study on the Healing Nature of Mandalas." *Psychology of Aesthetics, Creativity, and the Arts* 1, no. 3 (2007): 148–54.

Hillman, James. *Insearch: Psychology and Religion.* Woodstock, CT: Spring Publications, 1996.

Hunt, Swanee. *Rwandan Women Rising*. Durham & London: Duke University Press, 2017.

Johnson, Sue. *Hold Me Tight: Seven Conversations for a Lifetime of Love*. New York, Boston & London: Little, Brown and Company, 2008.

Jung, C. G. *Aspects of the Masculine*. Princeton, NJ: Princeton University Press, 1989.

———. *The Archetypes and the Collective Unconscious, The Collected Works of C. G. Jung, Part 1, Volume 9*. Princeton, NJ: Princeton University Press, 1990.

———. *Civilization in Transition. The Collected Works, Volume 10*. London & New York: Routledge, 2014.

———. *Man and His Symbols*. Garden City, NY: Doubleday & Company, 1969.

———. *Mandala Symbolism*. Princeton, NJ: Princeton University Press, 1972.

———. *The Red Book: Liber Novus. A Reader's Edition*. New York & London: W.W. Norton, 2009.

———. Recorded and edited by Aniela Jaffe. *Memories, Dreams, Reflections*. New York: Vintage Books, 1989.

———. *Synchronicity: An Acausal Connecting Principle*. Princeton, NJ: Princeton University Press, 1969.

"Justin Trudeau promotes feminist movement of men sticking up for women." *The Independent*. Video: 1:00. From Justin Trudeau speaking at an inaugural WE Day UN event at Madison Square Garden on Sept. 20, 2017. Posted by Harriet Agerholm, Sept. 21, 2017. http://www.independent.co.uk/news/world/americas/justin-trudeau-men-feminist-movement-stick-up-women-sexism-canada-prime-minister-a7960196.html.

Leidy, Denise Patry, and Robert A. F. Thurman. *Mandala: The Architecture of Enlightenment*. New York: Asia Society Galleries, 1998.

Levine, Norma. *The Miraculous 16th Karmapa: Incredible Encounters with the Black Crown Buddha*. Arcidosso: Shang Shung Publications, 2013.

Loori, John Daido. *The Art of Just Sitting: Essential Writings on the Zen Practice of Shikantaza*. Boston: Wisdom Publications, 2004.

Luke, Helen M. *Woman, Earth and Spirit: The Feminine in Symbol and Myth*. New York: Crossroad, 1989.

Klein, Naomi. *This Changes Everything: Capitalism vs. the Climate*. New York: Simon & Schuster, 2014.

Mackenzie, Vicki. *Cave in the Snow: Tenzin Palmo's Quest for Enlightenment*. New York: Bloomsbury, 1998.

Macy, Joanna. *Coming Back to Life: The Updated Guide to the Work That Reconnects*. Gabriola Island, BC: New Society, 2014.

Macy, Joanna, and Chris Johnstone. *Active Hope: How to Face the Mess We're in without Going Crazy.* Novato, CA: New World Library, 2012.

Magee, Matthew. *Peruvian Shamanism: The Pachakúti Mesa.* Chelmsford, MA: Middle Field Publications, 2002.

Mies, Maria, and Vandana Shiva. *Ecofeminism (Critique. Influence. Change.).* London & New York: Zed Books, 2014.

Moacanin, Radmila. *The Essence of Jung's Psychology and Tibetan Buddhism: Western and Eastern Paths to the Heart.* London: Wisdom Publications, 1986.

Norbu, Chögyal Namkhai, and Adriano Clemente. *The Supreme Source: The Fundamental Tantra of Dzogchen Semde Kunjed Gyalpo.* Ithaca, NY: Snow Lion Publications, 1999.

Nuccitelli, Dana. "2017 Is So Far the Second-Hottest Year on Record Thanks to Global Warming." *The Guardian.* July 31, 2017. https://www.theguardian.com/environment/climate-consensus-97-per-cent/2017/jul/31/2017-is-so-far-the-second-hottest-year-on-record-thanks-to-global-warming.

Padmasambhava and Jamgon Kongtrul. *The Light of Wisdom, Volume IV.* Boudhanath, Hong Kong & Esby: Rangjung Yeshe Publications, 2001.

Rathbun, Catherine. *Developing the World Mind: A Study of the Elements Mandala of Tibetan Buddhism.* Toronto: Friends of the Heart, 2002.

Reps, Paul. *Zen Telegrams.* Rutland, VT & Tokyo: Charles E. Tuttle Company, 1959.

Richardson, Diane. *Slow Sex: The Path to Fulfilling and Sustainable Sexuality.* Rochester, VT: Bear & Company Publishing, 2012.

Ruether, Rosemary R. *Sexism and God-Talk: Toward a Feminist Theology.* Boston: Beacon Press, 1983.

Rockefeller, Steven C., and John C. Elder, eds. *Spirit and Nature: Why the Environment Is a Religious Issue.* Boston: Beacon Press, 1992.

Saul, Richard. *ADHD Does Not Exist: The Truth About Attention Deficit and Hyperactivity Disorder.* New York: HarperCollins, 2014.

Science Daily. "New Report Finds 43 Percent Increase in ADHD Diagnosis for US Schoolchildren." *Science Daily.* December 8, 2015. https://www.sciencedaily.com/releases/2015/12/151208150630.htm.

Shakespeare, William. *The Tempest.* Hyderabad: Orient Longman, 2001.

Simmer-Brown, Judith. *Dakini's Warm Breath: The Feminine Principle in Tibetan Buddhism.* Boston & London: Shambhala, 2001.

Shaw, Miranda. *Passionate Enlightenment: Women in Tantric Buddhism.* Princeton, NJ: Princeton University Press, 1994.

Slater, Don. *Consumer Culture and Modernity.* Cambridge, UK: Polity Press, 1997.

Tāranātha, Jo Nang. *Origin of the Tara Tantra*. Dharamsala: Library of Tibetan Works and Archives, 2009.

Tatkin, Stan. *Wired for Love: How Understanding Your Partner's Brain and Attachment Style Can Help You Defuse Conflict and Build a Secure Relationship*. Oakland, CA: New Harbinger Publications, 2011.

Trungpa, Chögyam. *The Collected Works of Chögyam Trungpa, Volume 7*. Boston & London: Shambhala Publications, 2004.

——. *Orderly Chaos: The Mandala Principle*. Boston & London: Shambhala, 1991.

——. *The Path of Individual Liberation*. Boston & London: Shambhala, 2013.

——. *The Sadhana of the Embodiment of All the Siddhas*. Unpublished copy, 1969.

——. *The Tantric Path of Indestructible Wakefulness: The Profound Treasury of the Ocean of Dharma, Volume 3*. Boston & London: Shambhala Publications, 2013.

——. *Transcript 5 Buddha Seminar Talk 2*. Unpublished.

Tsoknyi Rinpoche. "Tsoknyi Rinpoche on Lung." *Tibet and Buddhism*. March 28, 2012. https://tsoknyirinpoche.org/8877/tsoknyi-rinpoche -interview-lung.

Tucci, Giuseppe. *The Theory and Practice of the Mandala: With Special Reference to the Modern Psychology of the Subconscious*. New York: Samuel Weiser, 1973.

UNHCR. "Frequently Asked Questions on Climate Change and Disaster Replacement." The UN Refugee Agency. November 6, 2016. http://www .unhcr.org/uk/news/latest/2016/11/581f52dc4/frequently-asked-ques tions-climate-change-disaster-displacement.html.

Von Franz, Marie-Louise. *C. G. Jung: His Myth in Our Time*. Toronto: Inner City Books, 1998.

Warren, Karen J. *Ecofeminist Philosophy: A Western Perspective on What It Is and Why It Matters*. Lanham, MA: Rowman & Littlefield, 2000.

Whitmont, Edward C. *Return of the Goddess*. New York: Crossroad, 1984.

Wiener, Lori S., and Haven B. Battles. "Mandalas as a Therapeutic Technique for HIV-Infected Children and Adolescents: What Do They Reveal?" *Journal for HIV/AIDS and Social Services* 1, no. 3 (2002): 27–39.

Women's March. "Sister Marches." Accessed October 7, 2017. https://www .womensmarch.com/sisters.

Woodman, Marion, and Elinor Dickson. *Dancing in the Flames: The Dark Goddess in the Transformation of Consciousness*. Boston: Shambhala, 1997.

World Health Organization (WHO). "Violence Against Women." Accessed October 7, 2017. http://www.who.int/mediacentre/factsheets/fs239/en.

Permissions

The author and the publisher gratefully acknowledge and thank the following for the permission to use previously published photographs.

Page 30: "Pilgrims circumambulating the stupa clockwise whilst spinning its prayer wheels—Swayambhunath." Photograph by Jorge Lascár. Source: https://www.flickr.com/photos/jlascar/172282370 94/sizes/o/. Licensed under Creative Commons 2.0.

Pages 38 and 40: "The 16th Karmapa Rangjung Rigpe Dorje." Courtesy of Diamond Way Buddhism.

Page 47: "Red cabbage." Photograph by Biush. Source: https://commons.wikimedia.org/wiki/File:Red_cabbage.tiff. Licensed under Creative Commons 3.0.

Page 75: "Chögyam Trungpa Rinpoche." Courtesy of the Shambhala Archives. VTR Photo Collection #2005.1.103.

Page 142: "Shadow Patterns, Gold Dunes." Photograph by Great Sand Dunes National Park and Preserve. Source: https://www.flickr.com/photos/greatsanddunesnpp/21092019348/sizes/o/. Licensed under Creative Commons 2.0

Pages 160, 185, 205, and 228: Details from "Vajra Varahi." Kham Province, Eastern Tibet; 18th century; ground mineral pigment on cotton. Rubin Museum of Art. Gift of the Shelley and Donald Rubin Foundation, C2006.66.396 (HAR 839).